Advance Praise

"If you're sure you need to incorporate AI into your company's strategy but don't quite know how to proceed, this book is for you. The authors integrate rigorous strategy frameworks with up-to-date technological insights to deliver a supremely valuable guide for today's business leaders. The many practical examples and handy worksheets add to the welcome usefulness of the book."

Donald C. Hambrick, PhD – *Evan Pugh University Professor and Professor of Management at The Pennsylvania State University*

"In a crowded field of AI strategy books, this one rises above the noise thanks to the deep academic rigor and real-world consulting experience of the authors. Drawing on firsthand work with leading firms across industries, Hutzschenreuter and Lämmermann offer a practical, research-based framework that business leaders can trust and act on."

Dr. Mary C. Lacity – *David D. Glass Chair and Distinguished Professor of Information Systems at the University of Arkansas*

"The book 'AI Business Strategy' is a must-read for executives navigating AI-driven markets. It clearly explains how to practically embed AI into your business strategy, from idea generation to implementation. Importantly, it also shows how AI tools can support better decision-making, offering real-world examples and easy-to-follow frameworks. Concise, clear, and impactful!"

Dr. Florian Gröne – *Partner & Global Telecommunications Sector Leader with PwC's Strategy& in New York*

"AI Business Strategy offers a rigorously researched yet eminently practical framework for integrating machine learning into every facet of corporate strategy, filling a crucial gap in the existing literature on AI adoption and value creation. The highlights of this book are the AI Business Strategy Frame with its step-by-step guidance and the hands-on worksheets. Together, they translate economic theory into concrete managerial actions that will drive productivity and competitive advantage. This book is an indispensable companion for executives, consultants, and scholars aiming to navigate the fast-evolving AI ecosystem with clarity, discipline, and confidence."

Ajay Agrawal, PhD – *Professor at the University of Toronto and Founder of the Creative Destruction Lab*

"AI is reshaping business – this book shows how to respond with purpose and clarity. A must-have guide for leaders and practitioners navigating AI-driven change, rich in examples and grounded in rigorous research. Thomas Hutzschenreuter and Tim Lämmermann do a splendid job demystifying AI's strategic impact."

Dr. Sebastian Raisch – *Professor of Strategy at the University of Geneva*

"The book *AI Business Strategy* offers a rare and welcome blend of conceptual rigor and practical relevance. By systematically integrating the distinctive technical capabilities of emerging AI (particularly its self-learning nature) with the fundamentals of business strategy, the authors present an actionable framework that stands out as a valuable contribution. This is a timely and insightful guide for practitioners, educators, students, and strategists alike."

Mohammad Hossein Jarrahi, PhD – *Professor at the University of North Carolina*

AI BUSINESS STRATEGY

A Managerial Guide to Success

Thomas Hutzschenreuter and Tim Lämmermann

Routledge
Taylor & Francis Group
LONDON AND NEW YORK

Designed cover image: Thomas Hutzschenreuter and Tim Lämmermann

First published 2026
by Routledge
4 Park Square, Milton Park, Abingdon, Oxon OX14 4RN

and by Routledge
605 Third Avenue, New York, NY 10158

Routledge is an imprint of the Taylor & Francis Group, an informa business

British Library Cataloguing-in-Publication Data
A catalogue record for this book is available from the British Library

ISBN: 978-1-041-14165-5 (hbk)
ISBN: 978-1-041-14162-4 (pbk)
ISBN: 978-1-003-67317-0 (ebk)

DOI: 10.4324/9781003673170

Typeset in Garamond
by Apex CoVantage, LLC

Contents

Figures

Tables

Worksheets

Preface

WELCOME TO THE AGE OF AI IN BUSINESS!

As you may experience firsthand, contemporary technology systems based on artificial intelligence (AI) fundamentally reshape how companies across all industries create value and compete in markets. AI's power primarily comes from its probabilistic machine learning nature, enabling algorithms to learn relevant task knowledge autonomously. Firms can purposefully leverage this unique self-learning ability of today's AI systems to innovate digital products and services, boost productivity within internal value chain functions, or support organizational decision-making processes with business intelligence.

Given their transformative potential, machine learning-based AI must generally be considered a strategic rather than merely an operational instrument. To stay competitive and financially successful in the future, self-learning AI systems must increasingly become a vital part of a firm's business strategy. Those who fail to implement and use powerful AI systems will have significant disadvantages and, thus, risk falling behind their peers.

Therefore, while existing digital business strategy approaches do not account for machine learning's very specific characteristics, this book is an innovative, practical guide to help you initiate, formulate, and implement your own AI-oriented business strategy. It is grounded in research and practical experience generated over the last years, culminating in the *AI business strategy frame*© that equips you with essential knowledge to deal strategically with machine learning-based AI systems.

More specifically, we conducted numerous research-based, case-study-oriented collaborations and consulting projects on AI strategy topics with globally leading companies across various industries, including semiconductors, consulting, IT, automotive, pharmaceuticals, real estate, industrial manufacturing, and finance. We incorporated learnings and insights from projects with, among others, Siemens, AWS, Airbus, BCG, BSH, Infineon, Microsoft, and BMW. These organizations and many others we work with are embedded as illustrative examples of how to deal with today's AI systems strategically in this book. Drawing on our experience, we also designed 15 practical, hands-on worksheets to help you immediately apply your newly gained insights.

Since our book avoids overly technical discussions, it can be used by managers, executives, consultants, entrepreneurs, or anyone interested in this timely topic. The book can also serve as a valuable teaching resource for graduate and executive education programs with direct practice material. On top of that, it can deliver novel impulses for applied management scholars or institutions exploring AI's strategic impact on business and society.

We want to thank all reviewers of this book who provided valuable ideas on further improving this manuscript. We extraordinarily thank Isabel Voice and Grace Collier from Routledge for their supportive and expert guidance throughout the publication process.

We hope you enjoy the read and have fun putting the insights from this book into direct practice!

Thomas Hutzschenreuter and Tim Lämmermann

Part I

INTRODUCTION

1

WHY YOU NEED AN AI BUSINESS STRATEGY

"The age of AI has started . . . a new computing era that will impact every industry and every field of science."[1]

—Jensen Huang, CEO of Nvidia

Today's powerful AI systems are predominantly based on probabilistic machine learning techniques that enable an algorithm to learn relevant task knowledge autonomously. This unique self-learning ability can fundamentally transform how companies across all industries conduct their business. It offers opportunities to innovate products and services, improve operational efficiencies, or facilitate organizational decision-making. Accordingly, one must see machine learning-based AI as a powerful strategic instrument that can help achieve competitive and financial advantages in novel ways. In this chapter, we demonstrate the increasing business relevance of AI, indicating the need for firms to systematically integrate the technology into their overall business strategies. Furthermore, we explain how this book purposefully guides you to create an impactful AI business strategy for your own business context.

1.1 STRATEGICALLY NAVIGATING IN THE AGE OF AI

The last years have impressively demonstrated that we are about to enter a new business era, the era of artificial intelligence (AI). The rapid and dynamic advancements in the field of AI have shown extraordinary potential to revolutionize nearly every aspect of a firm's business operations.[2] Many firms are

DOI: 10.4324/9781003673170-2

well aware of this trend. According to a recent McKinsey survey, 78% of global firms use modern AI systems for at least one central business activity, and most plan to significantly increase their adoption efforts in the future.[3]

It is crucial to understand that not only big tech companies like Amazon, Google, Microsoft, Tencent, and others can perceivably leverage today's AI. Substantial business opportunities exist for every type of firm in every kind of industry.[4] Let us highlight some prominent industry use case examples.

In retail, for instance, AI-powered chatbots manage customer inquiries, while personalized product recommendations boost online sales. The financial sector leverages AI for fraud detection, risk assessment, and algorithmic trading on capital markets. Healthcare providers, in turn, use intelligent machines for medical image analyses, robotic surgery, the creation of treatment plans, and as virtual health assistants or agents. In manufacturing, AI-based machines can automate entire assembly lines, arrange just-in-time deliveries, and help prevent consequential production shutdowns with predictive maintenance functions. Autonomous vehicles, including cars, trucks, trains, ships, planes, and even drones, provide novel freight opportunities for the logistics sector.

All these use case examples indicate that today's AI systems can significantly reshape existing business practices. Company departments such as R&D, logistics, production, marketing, sales, recruiting, and many more can apply AI systems to improve the performance of their daily work tasks or fully rearrange them.[5] Similarly, executives may use the technology to facilitate decision-making with data-driven business analytics.[6] In addition, market products and services can be equipped with virtual or physical AI functions, strongly increasing customer value.[7] Because of all these promising opportunities, global AI investments are growing exponentially and are expected to surpass 800 billion USD by 2030 (Figure 1.1).

1.1.1 *Firms must learn how to systematically deal with today's AI*

Due to its transformative potential, AI has become a central topic in most boardrooms, including larger and smaller firms. Over the last few years, the percentage of CEOs identifying AI as the most transformative technology for their business has nearly tripled, and almost 60% say that the strategic adoption and scaling of AI systems will be of outstanding importance for them to achieve financial and non-financial firm goals.[8]

Whereas the strategic priority of AI places significant pressure on executives, AI adoption is generally not a simple undertaking. As you may have experienced firsthand, today's AI comes with many technology management

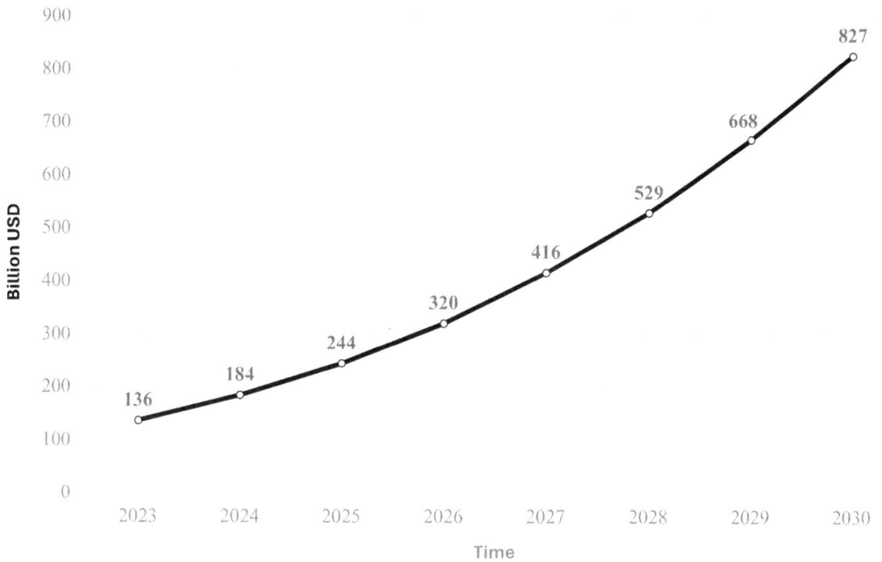

Figure 1.1 Global Market Size for AI Technologies[9]

challenges requiring adequate and sophisticated handling approaches.[10] Typical problems concern the strategic planning, identification of use cases, development and validation of AI systems, implementation, and company-wide scaling. The result is that the vast majority of adoption projects fail to make a perceivable business impact (scholars and practitioners estimate a range between 70% and almost 90%),[11] causing technology frustration and transformation delays. Those companies that fail to harness intelligent machines systematically will miss unique market opportunities, experience competitive disadvantages, and risk falling behind others that are more successful with their adoption endeavors.[12]

A major reason for the many adoption problems is that firms have difficulties dealing with the unique inherent working mechanisms of today's AI, which differ significantly from earlier AI or traditional information technology approaches.[13] Specifically, today's AI predominantly relies on probabilistic machine learning techniques, enabling algorithms to learn task knowledge autonomously by analyzing fitting training data.[14] Algorithms can self-learn powerful task knowledge by finding correlations with sophisticated statistical methods in training data. This self-learning ability is remarkable because it largely decouples IT systems from manual coding (you will learn much more about AI's powerful self-learning ability in Chapter 3).

If a technology system can effectively unfold such a self-learning ability, it can even cognitively outperform human beings for a particular task. It could autonomously identify task patterns that human experts are unaware of. In contrast, the performance of manually coded information systems heavily depends on human-inserted task knowledge represented in pre-defined algorithmic coding rules. Hence, while machine learning algorithms form their task knowledge by acquiring probability-based insights from new data, traditional information systems cannot learn independently, that is, without reprogramming. Their performance is only as good as the manually written code, which usually originates from the knowledge of human task experts.

1.1.2 *Machine learning-based AI must be seen as a strategic instrument*

When the unique self-learning ability of today's AI systems is purposefully applied to internal business processes (including decision-making) and market-oriented customer offerings, the technology can be used to gain competitive and financial advantages in novel ways.[15] Based on that, firms must perceive machine learning-based AI as a powerful strategic rather than an operational business instrument.[16] The more a company approaches AI strategically, the more it can use the technology to differentiate itself from competitors and increase its profit. However, using AI strategically does not mean implementing it anywhere. The goal must be to deploy it only where its technological self-learning ability provides substantial business impact through intelligent task automation and productive human-AI collaboration.[17]

A quickly growing number of powerful machine learning-enabled business opportunities logically indicate a higher and more urgent need to systematically integrate the technology into a firm's overall business strategy.

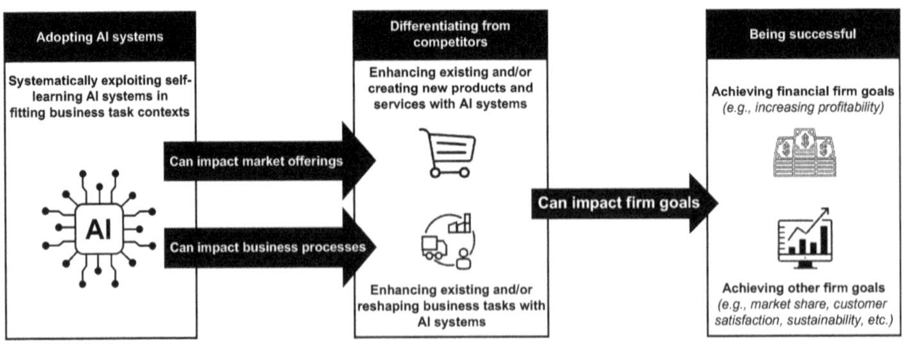

Figure 1.2 AI as a Strategic Instrument

In other words, the task of executives will be to create an AI-oriented business strategy that explicitly builds on the inherent working mechanisms of machine learning.[18] For this, a strategy continuum exists that ranges from minimal to full technology integration. Depending on individual preferences, organizational sizes, and industry or business contexts, firms can use machine learning to modify an existing strategy slightly, substantially recreate it, or design an entirely new AI-driven one. The larger the technology integration into a business strategy, the more a firm can transform itself to differentiate from competitors and positively impact its profitability.

While AI-oriented business strategies become increasingly relevant for firms, they must be distinguished from a more vague and general digital business strategy. An AI business strategy, as described in this book, explicitly builds on the unique characteristics of machine learning. A digital business strategy, in turn, usually treats an AI system like a regular IT application.[19] That is critical because the strategic adoption and utilization of powerful self-learning AI systems come with many new challenges compared to implementing other digital systems. As a result, this book opens up new opportunities and perspectives for technology strategists not covered by previous books.

Since only a few companies have taken decisive and strategic actions so far, now is the time to lay the foundation for becoming a future AI leader. History has repeatedly shown that companies failing to embrace technological transformation or waiting too long to do so risk not only the loss of their competitive edge but even their disappearance. Consider Nokia and BlackBerry, which both fell behind in the smartphone revolution.[20] Toys "R" Us is another example, as it, among other mistakes, did not sufficiently invest in e-commerce.[21] Therefore, as AI adoption accelerates globally, we urge practitioners to think about developing a fitting AI business strategy sooner rather than later. Using this book will effectively help you to do so.

1.2 WHO THIS BOOK IS WRITTEN FOR

Our book is a practical guide to initiate, formulate, and implement AI-oriented business strategies tailored to your specific needs. It provides a systematic framework, *the AI business strategy frame*©, designed for anyone who wants or needs to strategically engage with today's self-learning AI technologies, including managers, executives, consultants, entrepreneurs, and any other practitioner interested in this timely topic. The book also offers a strong foundation for teaching strategy and technology fundamentals to university and executive students, equipping them with the knowledge to better

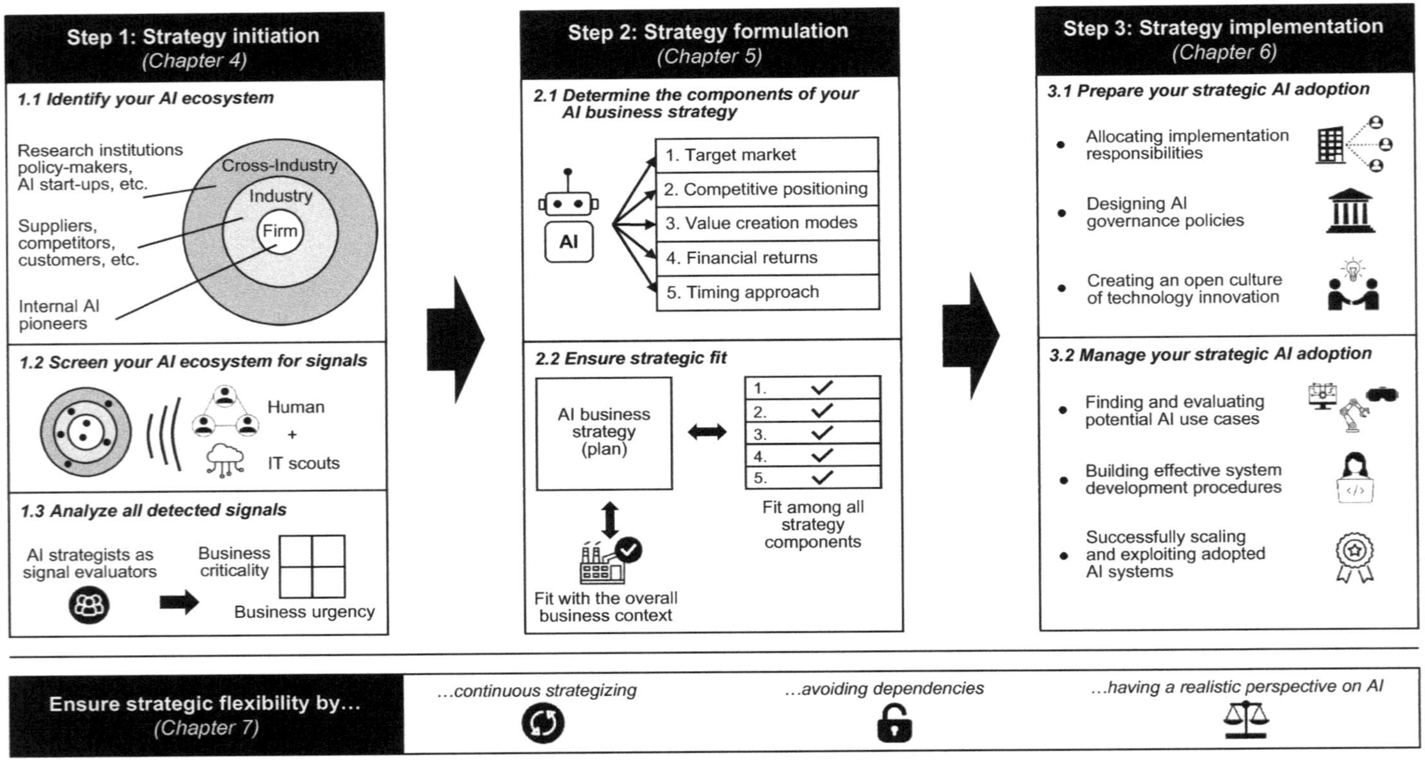

Figure 1.3 The AI Business Strategy Frame©

navigate within increasingly AI-driven business environments. Besides, this book aims to inspire scholars and applied researchers to explore new research avenues about the impact of AI on business and society.

Given the book's primary focus on practice, it is not written in a highly technical manner. Instead, it takes a business perspective on managing AI adoption and technology transformation. Our book is grounded in research and practical experience generated over the last years. More precisely, we conducted numerous research-based, case-study-oriented collaborations and consulting projects on AI strategy topics with globally leading companies across diverse industries, including semiconductors, consulting, IT, automotive, pharmaceuticals, real estate, industrial manufacturing, and finance. We incorporated learnings and insights from projects with, among others, Siemens, AWS, Airbus, BCG, BSH, Infineon, Microsoft, and BMW. These organizations and many others we work with are embedded as valuable real-world examples in this book of how to adopt and exploit today's AI systems strategically.

Drawing on our rich experience, we have also designed 15 hands-on worksheet templates for you, which are attached at the end of each chapter. These worksheets allow you to directly apply and practice your newly acquired knowledge from each chapter at your individual pace. By systematically going through these worksheets, you will initiate, formulate, and implement an AI business strategy for your own firm or any other selected case company. You can fill the worksheets out alone, with colleagues in your organization, with fellow students in your classroom, or with any other open-minded technology strategist available.

1.3 THE STRUCTURE OF THIS BOOK

Our book is structured into seven equally relevant chapters. Following the introduction, Chapters 2 and 3 provide fundamentals about business strategies and today's machine learning-based AI systems. We do not delve too deeply into technical details but provide a comprehensive overview of the most important aspects an AI strategist should be familiar with. Since understanding both areas will be crucial to unlock the full strategic potential of today's AI, this basic knowledge will substantially help you in all remaining chapters of this book.

The following four chapters sequentially introduce the core framework of this book, our *AI business strategy frame*© (see Figure 1.3). Since our framework is structured with a process perspective, we begin by demonstrating how firms should initiate their AI business strategy (Chapter 4). The chapter deals explicitly with gathering and evaluating potentially relevant AI-related information (signals) from internal and external firm environments.

Afterward, Chapter 5 shows how to formulate a well-structured AI business strategy based on the information gained from analyzing AI signals. We thoroughly discuss the shape and content of an AI business strategy, highlight various available decision options, and illustrate them with many different strategy examples. Moreover, we underline the relevance of creating fit among all strategy components as well as between the strategy and a firm's overall business context.

Chapter 6 focuses on the key aspects of successfully implementing an AI business strategy within organizations. Since strategy implementation drives transformational change, we elucidate how to proactively address relevant technology management challenges to adopt and leverage impactful machine learning-based AI systems effectively. In addition, we give many practical tips on identifying and evaluating use cases, adequately training machine learning algorithms, and successfully exploiting and scaling them for designated adoption tasks.

Lastly, in Chapter 7, we give final remarks on how to stay strategically flexible concerning further environmental change in the future, including technological progress in the field of AI. For instance, we show that AI business strategies must not be static but dynamically adjusted over time. On top of that, we note the need to avoid potentially critical dependencies and develop a realistic perspective on what AI can and cannot do today.

1.4 HOW TO GET THE MOST OUT OF THIS BOOK

This book is arranged in a way that guides you step by step through the process of creating individualized AI business strategies. After laying the necessary strategy and machine learning foundations, it dives into the most critical management themes to initiate, formulate, and implement a fitting AI business strategy. In the following, let us give you a few recommendations on how to get the most out of the book:

- Refer to the table of contents and the framework figures to navigate within the book. This practice will help you stay focused and understand how each chapter and its themes are connected.
- We encourage you to read Chapters 2 and 3 thoroughly, even though you are already familiar with these fundamentals. The two sections lay the logical foundation for our *AI business strategy frame*© and will help you better understand our approach in this book.

- Explore all the illustrations, tables, and real-world company examples we have included. They highlight key findings and provide you with inspiration for your own AI business strategy.
- Take your time filling out the 15 worksheets, but really do it. They will guide you in initiating, formulating, and implementing an AI business strategy for your selected company (this can be your own company or another firm that may interest you). The worksheet results, in turn, can spark valuable internal strategy discussions, serve as useful teaching cases, or generate ideas for novel research projects.
- The book includes numerous footnotes that offer complementary ideas, explanations, or references. Many footnotes refer to insightful academic literature or provide additional business case context. Access them if you want more information about a topic.
- You can use the index at the end of the book to search for specific terms or concepts. We organized the index alphabetically and referred to the pages where each topic is discussed within the book.
- A strategic AI transformation takes time. Hence, this book is meant to accompany you through your entire AI journey. Revisit it as a reference whenever needed.

NOTES

1 Pang, J., "Nvidia CEO Says Global Cooperation in Tech Will Continue under Trump Administration", *Reuters*, November 23, 2024, available at https://www.reuters.com/technology/artificial-intelligence/nvidia-ceo-huang-says-the-age-ai-has-started-2024-11-23/.

2 La Torre, D., Appio, F. P., Masri, H., Lazerri, F., and Schiavone, F., *Impact of Artificial Intelligence in Business and Society: Opportunities and Challenges* (New York: Routledge, 2024).

3 Singla, A., Sukharevsky, A., Yee, L., Chui, M., and Hall, B., "The State of AI: How Organizations Are Rewiring to Capture Value", *McKinsey*, March 12, 2025, available at https://www.mckinsey.com/capabilities/quantumblack/our-insights/the-state-of-ai.

4 McElheran, K., Li, J., Brynjolfsson, E., Kroff, Z., Dinlersoz, E., Foster, L., and Zolas, N., "AI Adoption in America: Who, What, and Where", *Journal of Economics & Management Strategy*, 33/2 (2024): pp. 375–415.

5 For more precise adoption stories, you can have a look at "The Adoption of Artificial Intelligence in Firms: New Evidence for Policymaking", *OECD*, May 2, 2025, available at https://www.oecd.org/en/publications/the-adoption-of-artificial-intelligence-in-firms_f9ef33c3-en.html.

6 Shrestha, Y. R., Ben-Menahem, S., and von Krogh, G., "Organizational Decision-Making Structures in the Age of Artificial Intelligence", *California Management Review*, 61/4 (2019): pp. 66–83.

7 Verganti, R., Vendraminelli, L., and Iansiti, M., "Innovation and Design in the Age of Artificial Intelligence", *Journal of Product Innovation Management*, 37/3 (2020): pp. 212–227.

8 For more information, refer to Furlonger, D., "How Your CEO Is Thinking About AI", *Gartner*, June 27, 2024, available at https://www.gartner.com/en/articles/how-your-ceo-is-thinking-about-ai; and also to Dewar, C., Keller, S., Malhotra, V., and Strovink, K., "Actions the Best CEOs Are Taking in 2023", *McKinsey*, March 15, 2023, available at https://www.mckinsey.com/capabilities/strategy-and-corporate-finance/our-insights/actions-the-best-ceos-are-taking-in–2023.

9 Further details are given by Thormundsson, B., "AI Market Size Worldwide", *Statista*, November 28, 2024, available at https://www.statista.com/forecasts/1474143/global-ai-market-size.

10 Specific technology management challenges are given in Hutzschenreuter, T., Lämmermann, T., Sake, A., and Ludwig, H., "Successfully Mitigating AI Management Risks to Scale Globally", *MIS Quarterly Executive*, forthcoming (2025).

11 Many firms are having problems to create perceivable business impact with today's AI systems. For instance, see the following references, including "AI Adoption in 2024: 74% of Companies Struggle to Achieve and Scale Value", *Boston Consulting Group*, October 24, 2024, available at https://www.bcg.com/press/24october2024-ai-adoption-in-2024-74-of-companies-struggle-to-achieve-and-scale-value; Ångström, R. C., Björn, M., Dahlander, L., Mähring, M., and Wallin, M., "Getting AI Implementation Right: Insights from a Global Survey", *California Management Review*, 66/1 (2023), pp. 5–22; "The Widespread Adoption of AI by Companies Will Take a While", *The Economist*, June 29, 2023, available at https://www.economist.com/leaders/2023/06/29/the-widespread-adoption-of-ai-by-companies-will-take-a-while; "Why Do 87% of Data Science Projects Never Make It into Production?", *VentureBeat*, July 19, 2019, available at https://venturebeat.com/ai/why-do-87-of-data-science-projects-never-make-it-into-production/.

12 Iansiti, M. and Lakhani, K. R., *Competing in the Age of AI: Strategy and Leadership when Algorithms and Networks Run the World* (Boston, MA: Harvard Business Review Press, 2020).

13 Important characteristics of machine learning-based AI are well described in Berente, N., Recker, J., Gu, B., and Santhanam, R., "Managing Artificial Intelligence", *MIS Quarterly*, 45/3 (2021): pp. 1433–1450; and Weber, M., Enger, M., Schaffer, N., Weking, J., and Krcmar, H., "Organizational Capabilities for AI Implementation – Coping with Inscrutability and Data Dependency in AI", *Information Systems Frontiers*, 25 (2022): pp. 1549–1569.

14 See McElheran et al. (2024), "AI Adoption in America: Who, What, and Where"; and Jordan, M. I. and Mitchell, T. M., "Machine Learning: Trends, Perspectives, and Prospects", *Science*, 349/6245 (2015): pp. 255–260.

15 Some interesting thoughts are given in Krakowski, S., Luger, J., and Raisch, S., "Artificial Intelligence and the Changing Sources of Competitive Advantage", *Strategic Management Journal*, 44/6 (2022): pp. 1425–1452; and in Reis, C., Ruivo, P., Oliveira, T., and Paulo, F., "Assessing the Drivers of Machine Learning Business Value", *Journal of Business Research*, 117 (2020): pp. 232–243.

16 See the following articles, including Borges, A., Laurindo, F., Spíonla, M., Gonçalves, R., and Mattos, C., "The Strategic Use of Artificial Intelligence in the Digital Era: Systematic Literature Review and Future Research Directions", *International Journal of Information Management*, 57 (2021): Article No. 102225; Davenport, T., *The AI Advantage: How to Put the Artificial Intelligence Revolution to Work* (Cambridge: MIT Press, 2018); and Shollo, A., Kopf, K., Thiess, T., and Müller, O., "Shifting ML Value Creation Mechanisms: A Process Model of ML Value Creation", *The Journal of Strategic Information Systems*, 31/3 (2022): Article No. 101734.

17 Raisch, S. and Fomina, K., "Combining Human and Artificial Intelligence: Hybrid Problem-Solving in Organizations", *Academy of Management Review*, 50/2 (2024): pp. 441–464.

18 We also recommend having a look at Hutzschenreuter, T. and Lämmermann, T., "What Is Your AI Strategy? Systematically Integrating Self-Learning Technologies into Your Business Strategy", *Academy of Management Perspectives*, forthcoming (2025).

19 A digital business strategy does usually not consider the unique technological characteristics of machine learning. Hence, the strategic adoption of today's AI requires firms to create a new type of strategy that explicitly builds on these specific characteristics.

20 An interesting article about the smartphone race is provided by Joshi, N., "Why Nokia and Blackberry Lost Their Edge", *Medium*, March 15, 2025, available at https://medium.com/@cast_shadow/why-nokia-and-blackberry-lost-their-edge-ab1c050d99e7.

21 More details are given in "Ten Things Toys 'R' Us Got Wrong (That You Can Get Right)", *Kearney*, May 8, 2018, available at https://www.de.kearney.com/cost-transformation/article/-/insights/10-lessons-retailers-can-learn-from-the-demise-of-toys-r-us.

Part II

FUNDAMENTALS FOR DEALING WITH AI BUSINESS STRATEGIES

2

UNDERSTANDING BUSINESS STRATEGIES

"The essence of strategy is in the activities – choosing to perform activities differently or to perform different activities than rivals."[1]

—Michael Porter, Strategy Professor at Harvard Business School

Business strategies are a powerful tool to effectively compete in markets and achieve pre-defined firm goals. However, the term strategy has become a very overused word in business language today. Many so-called strategies are neither industry-oriented, systematic, complete, nor implementable. So, what exactly is a business strategy, and how do firms create it? That is exactly what we will answer in this chapter. We discuss the history, purpose, and practicability of strategy in the light of competitive uncertainty (Section 2.1), describe the five essential components of every proper business strategy (Section 2.2), and underline the relevance of ensuring strategic fit (Section 2.3). Furthermore, we explain the three sequential phases of the strategizing process step by step (Section 2.4).

2.1 WHAT STRATEGY IS ABOUT

The concept of strategy originates from the ancient Greek word "strategía," which means generalship or troop leadership. In history, it was commonly used in military contexts. A strategy was developed to systematically lead one's own battle forces against those of the enemy to win battles and, thus, a war. Those who created such a war strategy were called strategists. Many

DOI: 10.4324/9781003673170-4

military strategists who had great success in the past, at least over a specific period, are still well known today, such as Sun Tzu, Alexander the Great, Julius Caesar, Genghis Khan, George Washington, and Napoléon.

Over time, the term strategy has not only been used in military contexts. Today, strategies occur in very different domains. Politicians, for example, can craft a strategy for getting elected in the next legislative period. Marathon athletes or basketball teams develop a strategy to win the gold medal during the next Olympic Games. Job applicants will think about how to impress recruiters during their interviews. Profit-oriented organizations require a sound business strategy to succeed in a market and reach pre-determined financial and non-financial goals.

2.1.1 *Strategies are needed for competition*

What do all these examples have in common? They clearly illustrate that strategy is essential in fields where competition exists.[2] In fact, strategies help us systematically deal with competitive environments to reach our pre-defined goals.[3] In other words, a strategy is necessary when the goals of an individual or group conflict with the goals of another individual or group. Success means enforcing my own will with the outcomes of my individual strategy and, thus, *ceteris paribus*, suppressing the will of my existing opponents.[4]

Let us revisit the previously given examples. The politician must secure more votes than other candidates to win an election. The marathon athlete must be the first one to cross the finish line. The basketball team must score more points than its opponents in a tournament. Job applicants have to show that they are more qualified than others. A firm wants to gain competitive and financial advantages over its rivals by winning customers in the market.

In contrast, when no competition exists, a strategy is typically not needed. In such a scenario, either one actor alone is involved, or the goals of different actors do not conflict. In short, nobody is incentivized to intentionally impede others from reaching their goals.[5] For instance, when a climber wants to reach the top of a mountain, she has it in her own hands to do so. By considering the physical conditions,[6] she is free to sufficiently train, identify the best route and timing, buy appropriate equipment, and so on. Notably, she still needs a systematic plan to climb a rugged mountain, but the plan would not be a strategy. This means that every strategy is a plan, but not every plan is a strategy.[7]

Another example is about problems that allow for a mathematically optimal solution. A production plan could be such a case. Under given constraints,[8] such as machine capacities, time intervals, or inventory availabilities, optimal schedules can be calculated, as usually no competition exists in production facilities. These schedules do not represent a strategy but a precise plan on when, where, and how to produce certain goods. Whether optimal schedules, however, can be exactly implemented as calculated in reality is another question.

Also, monopolies represent a business context in which competition does not exist. To optimize their profits, monopolists try to sell as many products or services as possible at the highest prices that customers accept. Theoretically, the company can determine its optimal profit scenarios with the help of mathematical models. In practice, other factors may also influence a monopolist's profitability, including governmental regulations.

2.1.2 Strategy as a tool to deal with competitive uncertainty

A business strategy evokes change through executing systematically preplanned market-oriented actions. The outcomes of a strategy determine success and failure. If the outcomes fulfill my pre-defined goals, I will be successful. If not, my strategy failed. Essentially, success and failure are always and everywhere subject to competitive uncertainty. Future environmental changes, including my own actions, can only be expected but never taken for granted. For example, if a firm plans to sell one million cars in a market this year, it is not possible to know in advance whether this target will actually be reached or not. Perhaps customers prefer the lower-priced vehicles of a competitor, technical defects are discovered, or a new player suddenly enters the market with more attractive transportation offerings. All these events can strongly reduce actual sales figures.

In competitive environments, uncertainty includes not only the actions of opponents but everybody and everything that could influence the ongoing competition. In the business world, this particularly concerns customers as they decide if and where they buy a particular product or service. In other words, they are the judges in a market competition. However, there are still many other factors shaping competitive uncertainty. For instance, unexpected economic or societal shocks might negatively impact strategy implementation. The European chemical, glass, and iron industries were unprepared for the extraordinarily high energy price shocks invoked by the Ukraine conflict.[9] Similarly, many firms were surprised by the speed of the various new business opportunities enabled by powerful AI assistants like ChatGPT and Microsoft Copilot.

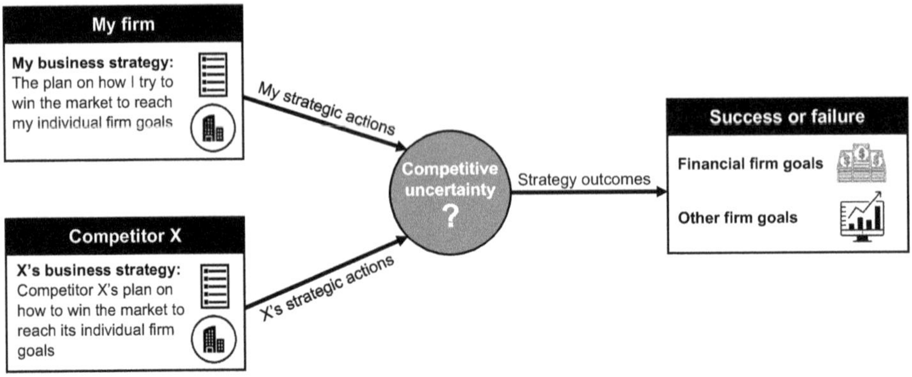

Figure 2.1 The Relationship of Strategy, Competition, and Uncertainty

It is important to emphasize that competitive uncertainty also relates to my actions. Even though I plan to go for a walk tomorrow, the plan cannot be implemented if I break a leg today. Similarly, even though firm strategists formulate a clear action plan, other employees might misunderstand their tasks, be resistant to change, or consciously deviate from the strategy, thus impeding its intended execution. That is a classic example of an intraorganizational strategy implementation problem.

In sum, uncertainty has enormous implications for a strategy. Since competitive environments are very dynamic, collected information is incomplete, and implementation obstacles can suddenly arise, it is impossible to know whether a specific strategy will ultimately lead to success. More drastically, we do not even know if a strategy exists at all that can lead to what we call success. However, a strategy crafted on a thorough information base that clearly communicates its logic for reaching specific goals is the best approach to practically deal with competitive uncertainty in a systematic way. Fortunately, competitors have to deal with uncertainty, too.

2.2 THE COMPONENTS OF A BUSINESS STRATEGY

Based on the relationship between strategy and competition, we define a business strategy as a systematic plan to achieve pre-defined firm goals in a competitive market environment.[10] However, a business strategy must consist of very different components resulting from the inherent nature of market competition. In sum, this includes five different but equally relevant strategy components, all shaped by many different decision options (see Figure 2.2).[11] In the following, we will briefly discuss each of them.

1. Target market:	Which products and services should be offered to which customers?
2. Competitive positioning:	How to differentiate from competitors (value-price ratio)?
3. Value creation modes:	How to realize well-functioning value creation processes?
4. Financial returns:	How to generate profit?
5. Timing approach:	What is the overall time horizon and sequence of executed actions?

Figure 2.2 The Five Components of a Business Strategy[12]

2.2.1 Component 1: target market

The first and probably most influential component of a business strategy is the target market. This decision is critical because it precisely defines the competitive environment a firm would have to deal with. A target market must clearly determine the products and services a company wants to offer, meaning its business scope.[13] For this, it is essential to reflect that consumer markets (B2C) are often very different from business markets (B2B), as potential customers in both areas usually have distinctive interests and needs.

Additionally, the geographical scope of a market should be taken into account. Customer preferences may vary significantly among countries or cultural areas. For instance, automotive manufacturer BMW focuses on selling large cars like SUVs in North America but more compact ones in European markets, reflecting regional customer preferences.

On top of that, it is advisable to think about the potential customer segments of a market. Typically, very different kinds of customers exist that have a distinct willingness to pay for a particular product or service. This implies that lower or upper customer segments could create distinguishable market conditions. For instance, while upper segments are often profitable niche markets, lower segments tend to represent mass markets as companies have to sell more to obtain good financial returns.

2.2.2 *Component 2: competitive positioning*

A second component of a business strategy is the competitive positioning, which focuses on how a firm plans to position its market offerings relative to those of competitors. A competitive positioning is closely related to the value-price ratio of a market offering in the eyes of an average target customer. One can position and differentiate oneself by offering better product or service quality, that is, increasing customer value, and/or by demanding lower prices than competitors.[14] If an interested customer perceives my value-price ratio as better than those of my rivals, she will predominantly buy my products or services if they are available to her.

Here are some examples of how firms position themselves. Regarding quality-oriented positionings, Mandarin Oriental hotels are known for their extraordinary luxury comfort. The hotel chain differentiates itself from less luxurious accommodations, but demands high prices simultaneously. Further, Amazon has quicker and more reliable delivery services than other e-commerce distributors that rely on external postal companies. On the price side, Ryanair has captured a significant market share in Europe by offering extremely low-cost flights to various popular destinations. The airline has deliberately eliminated all complimentary extras, focusing instead on providing the core flight as a standalone service. Similarly, the fashion brand H&M tries to offer mass-scale fashion products at relatively low prices.

If a firm can realize an outstanding position, it usually has a competitive advantage. That means it has the power to outperform its competitors by offering greater value to customers, offering better prices by operating more efficiently, or by a combination thereof. Importantly, competitive advantages must be protected from others. Unique positionings will inevitably be targeted for imitation or disruption by industry rivals or potential new market entrants. Hence, in the real world, competitive advantages are often only temporary.

Competitive advantages only occur if customers actively identify a firm's offerings and perceive their value-price ratio as relatively superior to alternatives from other companies. Advertisements and branding measures play a crucial role here because they can influence individuals' subjective product perceptions. For instance, they can increase customer awareness and product quality perceptions substantially.

2.2.3 *Component 3: value creation modes*

Third, a firm must determine how to create and ensure effective business processes to offer attractive products and services to the selected target market. In other words, it must orchestrate fitting value-creation modes that sufficiently address all required competencies for each value chain function. To create these competencies, companies can choose from very different value-creation modes that could also be combined.

For example, a company can focus on internal developments, meaning creating and applying business competencies in-house. Critical competencies do not always exist from the beginning, but firms can acquire them through internal experimentation or external imitation. This approach is often selected when firms have to deal with new strategic situations that they are inexperienced with, but do not want to become dependent on others. For instance, businesses expanding into foreign markets usually have to learn new regional market skills. Chinese low-cost product conglomerate Temu must learn more about the administrative and legal market peculiarities in European countries.[15]

However, internal developments can take a lot of time, and there is no guarantee that the required competencies will be really formable in-house. Hence, an alternative could be acquiring firms or subsidiaries with the necessary competencies. While acquisitions typically require a large amount of money,[16] they are instruments to transfer competencies like knowledge, technology, patents, and workforce from an existing organization (the target) into a different one (the acquirer). Further, acquisitions can create valuable synergy effects when firms fuse. Companies can accelerate innovation, gain access to new markets, and enhance a competitive edge by integrating or mutually sharing specialized capabilities. The merger of the German and US-based chemical manufacturers Linde and Praxair created approximately one billion USD in synergies by mutually integrating both firms into a novel stand-alone entity.[17]

To some extent, firms can also outsource their functional business activities. This is typically done when they face significant internal costs or knowledge disadvantages compared to external service providers. Overall, one can select from partial to full outsourcing modes. Today, firms can outsource various activities within value chain departments, such as logistics, production, sales, IT, recruiting, and finance. Nevertheless, outsourcing always creates dependencies for a firm on external competency providers.

An additional mode is about partnerships, like joint ventures. Such partnerships reduce the risk of a single company. They are beneficial if different parties can complement their strengths and compensate for each other's weaknesses. Starbucks, for example, entered the Indian coffee market through a 50–50 joint venture with Indian conglomerate Tata Consumer Products. This local company knew much more about local supply-chains, distribution networks, and customer preferences than Starbucks.[18]

2.2.4 Component 4: financial returns

It is essential to understand that a successful competitive positioning does not necessarily imply good financial returns, especially when value creation modes are relatively expensive. This is what we call unprofitable market share. Consequently, a fourth component of a business strategy must specify how a firm achieves a sufficient level of profitability. For this, one must consider the profit equation, consisting of revenue minus costs. While this sounds relatively easy, it requires much information search, estimation, calculation, and proper decision-making to succeed financially.

On the one hand, firms can establish very different types of revenue streams for the income side of the equation. The most classic examples are about the transfer of ownership, for example, when purchasing a refrigerator at the local electronics store, and the execution of agreed-upon services such as getting a haircut. Nevertheless, there exist many more revenue options. For instance, one can install subscription-based revenue streams to bind existing and future customers. This is done by the music streaming platform Spotify. Streaming customers would lose access to individually created playlists and a broad spectrum of downloadable songs if they terminate their subscriptions. An alternative option may include a pay-per-use revenue model, as seen with Taxi or car-sharing services like Uber and Lyft. There, you pay based on distance and time. Cross-selling is also a popular revenue mode. For instance, Nespresso generates more income from its coffee capsules than from its coffee machines. Other classic cross-selling examples are printers and ink, or razors and blades.

On the other side of the profit equation, there are also different ways of achieving cost advantages compared to other firms in a market. One prominent way for this is the realization of scaling or learning effects. Research estimates that doubling the production output of a firm approximately leads to a 10–30% unit cost decrease.[19] Other cost-cutting options might be related to outsourcing, offshoring, technology automation, interorganizational synergies, restructuring, and many more. We will talk about AI cost-cutting options in later chapters.

2.2.5 Component 5: timing approach

As competitive environments dynamically change, a business strategy's fifth and last component must deal with the time dimension. Indeed, strategies can consist of more short-term (often radical) or long-term-oriented (often incremental) actions. While shorter time horizons are typically more costly and less flexible, they can enable first-mover advantages or the chance to imitate successful leaders by being a fast second. In addition, they can also be used to surprise unprepared foreign competitors. Chinese car manufacturers like BYD or NIO have aggressively entered European markets with their new electric vehicle fleets since they could offer their cars at much lower prices.

Alternatively, long-term or incremental approaches are often less costly and leave more space for adjustments over time. The video streaming platform Netflix has increased its content production competencies over the last ten years, step by step.[20] The content spending ranged from 1.8 billion USD in 2012 to more than 18 billion USD in 2025.

However, the precise sequence of actions can be important for a strategy's time horizon, too.[21] Before increasing its global sales presence, Tesla had to build many new production facilities around the globe, so-called Gigafactories.[22] Amazon started to expand from its American core market to the British and German markets before entering other European countries. Some reasons for this have been the market size, available acquisition targets, or existing supply-chain structures.[23]

2.3 THE NEED FOR STRATEGIC FIT

While a business strategy consists of five different but equally important components, firms must make appropriate decisions for each of them. The goal is to achieve a so-called strategic fit, consisting of two layers.[24]

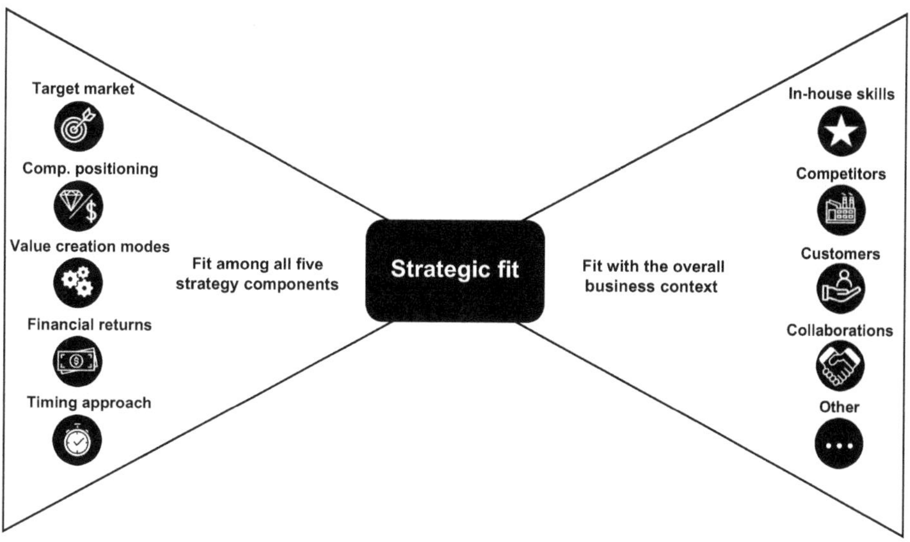

Figure 2.3 Two Dimensions of Strategic Fit

More specifically, to be effective, the decisions for each component must fit the decisions for all other components. Also, it has to realistically reflect the current environmental business context a firm is exposed to. Without considering these two dimensions of strategic fit, a business strategy will be less effective or even unable to achieve pre-defined firm goals.[25]

2.3.1 Fit among all five strategy components

First, a good business strategy is characterized by a sufficient fit among all five strategy components. That dimension of fit ensures that all individual decisions for strategy components are aligned and mutually reinforcing. In other words, a business strategy requires inherent, logical consistency. It must determine how a firm can successfully compete in a target market, establish effective business processes, enable sufficient financial returns, and execute its planned actions in a realistic timeframe.

A strategy with unaligned components, in turn, will most often block itself and lead to business failure. For instance, a radical market entry strategy through internal development and complex acquisitions, without a precise competitive positioning, but with relatively quick profit expectations, usually does not fit. Nonetheless, this is what Walmart did when it tried to expand its American retail store model to Europe and especially to Germany in 1997.[26] While Walmart focused on offering lower prices, it underestimated the intense competitive environment regarding local discount chain stores, as well as major retailers. A key problem was to match the highly efficient supply-chains of well-established incumbents. Even the acquisition of regional retail chains failed to provide the expected impact. Walmart exited the German market in 2006 after less than a decade.

2.3.2 Fit of a strategy with the overall business context

Second, executives must realize a fit between a strategy and their firm's overall business context. A business strategy should properly reflect the real-world conditions of both internal and external firm environments. Internally, this particularly involves understanding a firm's most important value chain functions for its ongoing business and critical bottlenecks.[27] Externally, firms must identify and analyze the actions of all types of key stakeholders within and outside their industry.

From an internal perspective, a firm must understand where it has outstanding competencies or resource advantages on which it can build its strategy. Extraordinary R&D competencies can be the catalyst for being the first to register a novel patent. Many pharmaceutical companies heavily invest in their R&D departments to earn monopoly rents for the duration of legal patent protections. Alternatively, some companies, like luxury product conglomerate LVMH, are betting on their strong marketing skills, which are the foundation for their international branding success in product categories such as champagne or fashion. Moreover, internal fit means that a strategy must ensure that different functional departments can effectively collaborate with each other. For example, logistics, production, and sales departments must be able to mutually align material flow and product transportation activities from initial suppliers to final customers.

From an external perspective, one has to differentiate between industry- and non-industry-specific stakeholders. Concerning an industry, a fitting strategy incorporates actual customer needs, the previous and expected actions of competitors, the availability of potential suppliers, and the trustworthiness of partners. Walmart did not sufficiently consider the habits of German customers, who were not really receptive to the American-style shopping experience. Moreover, a company with great supplier contracts might have more reliable resource access than other firms. During the COVID-19 pandemic, many companies struggled with semiconductor chip shortages. However, some firms like Apple tried to secure preferred or exclusive delivery contracts in advance, imposing a priority status over other firms in case of supply shocks.[28] Outside an industry, relevant players can be legal entities like governments, research institutions, and technology start-ups. Hence, a fitting strategy should obey legal regulations, the state of scientific research, potentially promising acquisition opportunities, and many more macro-environmental aspects.

2.3.3 A real-world example of a fitting business strategy

To better illustrate what a fitting business strategy can look like in reality, Figure 2.4 gives a quick and simplified extraction of Nike's business strategy. However, we would like to emphasize that business strategies, even within the same industry, often look very different. Further, they must be dynamically challenged since internal and external environments constantly change.

2.4 THE PROCESS OF STRATEGY-MAKING

Creating a fitting business strategy is a demanding and time-consuming process called strategizing. More precisely, strategizing consists of three sequential phases involving strategy initiation, formulation, and implementation

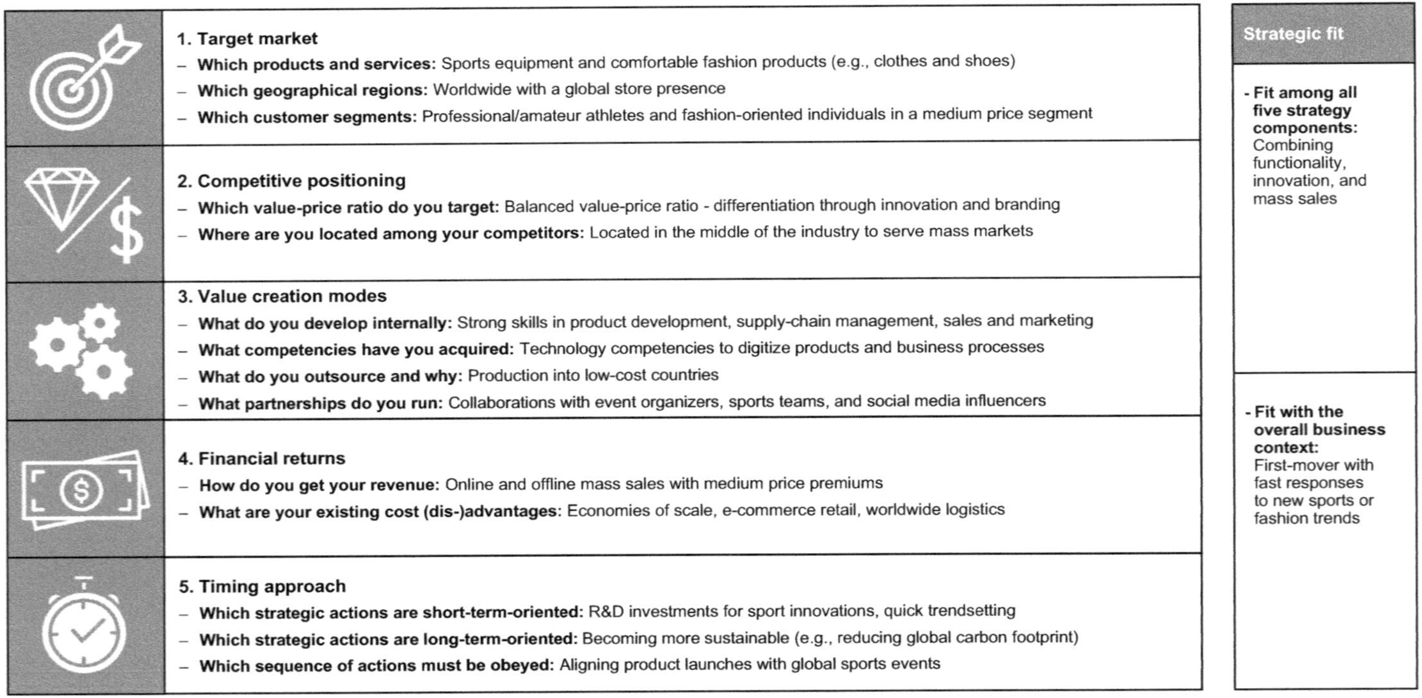

Figure 2.4 The Business Strategy of Nike in a Nutshell

(see Figure 2.5).[29] While going through all three phases is obligatory, strategizing should be seen as a continuous process. When business contexts substantially change or new insights are gained, it may be necessary to go through some process steps again. Furthermore, in reality, these three steps often overlap.

2.4.1 *Strategy initiation*

No matter whether firms want to adjust an existing business strategy or develop a new one, the strategizing process always gets initiated by some trigger signals resulting from environmental changes.[30] Signals are potentially relevant information from specific sources in a company's internal and external environment, such as institutions, organizations, departments, interest groups, or individuals. Internal signals could be about new product suggestions, ineffective business processes, decreasing sales, intraorganizational conflicts, or a new management board. External signals could be related to competitor actions, new market entrants, changing customer trends, enforced regulations, research innovations, public debates, etc. Since each signal can provide strategically relevant business information, firms should proactively detect and evaluate them.

Interestingly, firms do not detect and evaluate strategic signals equally. Due to limited resources, information asymmetry, or varying perspectives on the world, firms pay attention to very different environmental aspects. A signal perceived and interpreted as relevant by one firm is not necessarily perceived or similarly interpreted by another, perhaps not even by a competitor. In the light of uncertainty, this opens up the chance for strategic surprises, enabling operational, competitive, and financial advantages.

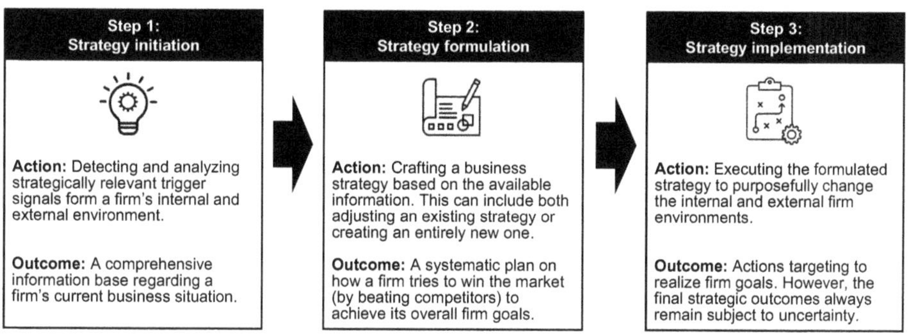

Figure 2.5 The Three Steps of Strategizing[31]

A prominent illustration is the Kodak case. In contrast to Sony and many other competitors, Kodak interpreted digital camera trend signals as less relevant in the 1980s. Therefore, Kodak stayed with analog cameras, which has led to its continuous market decline.[32] Another illustrative example is Apple and Microsoft. While Apple noticed the opportunity to introduce touch-display smartphones in the late 2000s, Microsoft did not believe in this innovation, as product prices have been relatively high compared to existing cell phones. Accordingly, Steve Ballmer, at that time CEO of Microsoft, publicly stated:

> "There's no chance that the iPhone is going to get any significant market share. No chance."[33]

However, we all know the very successful iPhone story.[34]

2.4.2 *Strategy formulation*

The second phase is the formulation of a fitting business strategy. To extract strategically relevant information for a business strategy, one must thoroughly analyze the implications of environmental signals for each of the five strategy components. What does the price decrease of my competitor mean for my positioning and profitability? Should I alter my value creation modes if my employees have not progressed in gaining the necessary competencies so far? Do my home country's new ecological or legal standards force me to slow down my preferred internationalization schedule?

Many different strategic analysis tools are used to analyze environmental signals.[35] Examples are the VRIN framework for identifying internal core competencies, Porter's five forces to assess an industry's attractiveness and allocated bargaining powers, or the PESTEL model to evaluate macro-environmental trends.[36]

When signals are analyzed, we can distinguish between two different formulation scenarios. First, one can create an entirely new business strategy. An example would be entering a new product market, which means a diversification, or a new geographic market area, which means internationalization. Formulating a new strategy for a new product or geographic market implies finding new and mutually fitting decisions for each strategy component, often from scratch. A second scenario is that an existing business strategy requires adjustments by reformulating one or more components. One could require updates for only one component but also for all five simultaneously. On top of that, the extent to which a strategy component should be modified can vary significantly, too.

A thorough strategy formulation phase usually takes time. Nonetheless, it is evident that competitive pressures often demand quick management decisions, leading to a quality-urgency trade-off. While a comprehensive and structured analysis of each strategic component helps a firm better navigate through its competitive environment, excessive delays can result in missed opportunities or hinder timely responses. It is the task of executives to handle such potential trade-offs.

2.4.3 *Strategy implementation*

The final step of strategizing is the strategy implementation phase, which is often underestimated. A well-formulated strategy is merely a systematic plan. Without its execution, nothing changes within the organization. Therefore, strategy implementation requires careful preparation and management effort to drive the actual organizational transformation.

For example, one has to allocate key roles and responsibilities to competent individuals so that the decisions for each strategy component are purposefully executed. In fact, it is essential to translate a business strategy into efficient operational plans for each value chain function. When entering a new business, the marketing department focuses on understanding and reaching new target customers, the procurement team may need to negotiate exclusive supplier contracts to secure critical resources, and the R&D units define the specific design and technical requirements of new products.

Ensuring that employees understand and support the business strategy is crucial as well. Since strategy implementation involves organizational change, resistance to new processes, working methods, technologies, or market scopes must be minimized. In addition, external stakeholders like suppliers, partners, and customers should not remain overly attached to outdated standards. By aligning individual motivations with strategic goals, firms can foster stakeholder engagement and drastically increase the likelihood of successful strategy implementation.

Notably, strategy implementation also requires steady and reliable control mechanisms. Frequent feedback loops are signals that help to understand if a firm is on the right track or whether it has to adjust strategy components again. Similarly, it must be ensured that all actions stick to existing compliance guidelines and are well-aligned with the firm's overall objectives.

2.5 CHAPTER SUMMARY

- Business strategies are a *practical tool* to deal with *competitive uncertainty*. They consist of *five* different but equally important *strategy components*:
  - The *target market* describes what types of products and services a firm offers at certain geographical locations to specific customer segments.
  - The *competitive positioning* highlights how a firm plans to win the market by differentiating from competitors via product/service quality and price.
  - The *value creation modes* determine how a firm installs effective business processes that allow it to operate in a selected market. This can involve internal developments, acquisitions, partnerships, or (partial) outsourcing.
  - The *financial returns* outline how a firm will become profitable, focusing on revenue generation and achieving cost advantages.
  - The *timing approach* states a strategy's time horizon and the sequence of planned core actions for its execution.
- Firms should strive for high levels of *strategic fit*. This includes fit among all five strategy components as well as fit of the strategy with the overall business context.
- The process of strategy-making is called *strategizing* and consists of three sequential phases:
  - First, in the *strategy initiation phase*, firms detect and interpret relevant trigger signals, potentially indicating the need to change an existing business strategy or develop a novel one.
  - Second, in the *strategy formulation phase*, firms analyze available information to determine how each component of a fitting business strategy should look.
  - Lastly, during the *strategy implementation phase*, firms operationally execute their developed strategy to proactively influence internal and external environments to reach their goals. This is where the actual transformation takes place.

2.6 HANDS-ON PRACTICE

Your first worksheet (Worksheet 1) helps you summarize the current business strategy of a selected company (choose wisely because it makes sense to work with this company in all other worksheets, too). Reflect on the five strategy components and the concept of strategic fit. If your selected firm is active in multiple businesses, we recommend choosing a core business or

1. My target market – Which products and services: – Which geographical regions: – Which customer segments:	**My strategic fit**
2. My competitive positioning – Which value-price ratio am I looking for: – Where am I located among my competitors:	- How do I ensure fit among all five strategy components:
3. My value creation modes – What do I develop internally: – What competencies have I acquired: – What do I outsource and why: – What partnerships do I run:	
4. My financial returns – How do I get my revenue: – What are my existing cost (dis-)advantages:	- How do I ensure fit with my overall business context:
5. My timing approach – Which strategic actions are short-term-oriented: – Which strategic actions are long-term-oriented: – Which sequence of actions must I obey:	

Worksheet 1 What Is Your Current Business Strategy?

conducting this exercise for different ones sequentially. This worksheet can also help you understand how much an existing strategy relies on certain technologies. Hence, it can be a good indicator of whether a firm is already strategically making use of today's AI or not.

After wrapping up the business strategy of your selected company, please think about who is responsible or involved in the strategizing process (Worksheet 2) of your chosen case company (consider initiation, formulation, and implementation phases). Responsible agents can be individuals, teams, departments, or a combination thereof. While this exercise helps you better understand a firm's strategy-making process, you will identify many experts who will be highly relevant for creating an AI business strategy. Identifying and connecting to them substantially facilitate your strategic AI transformation.

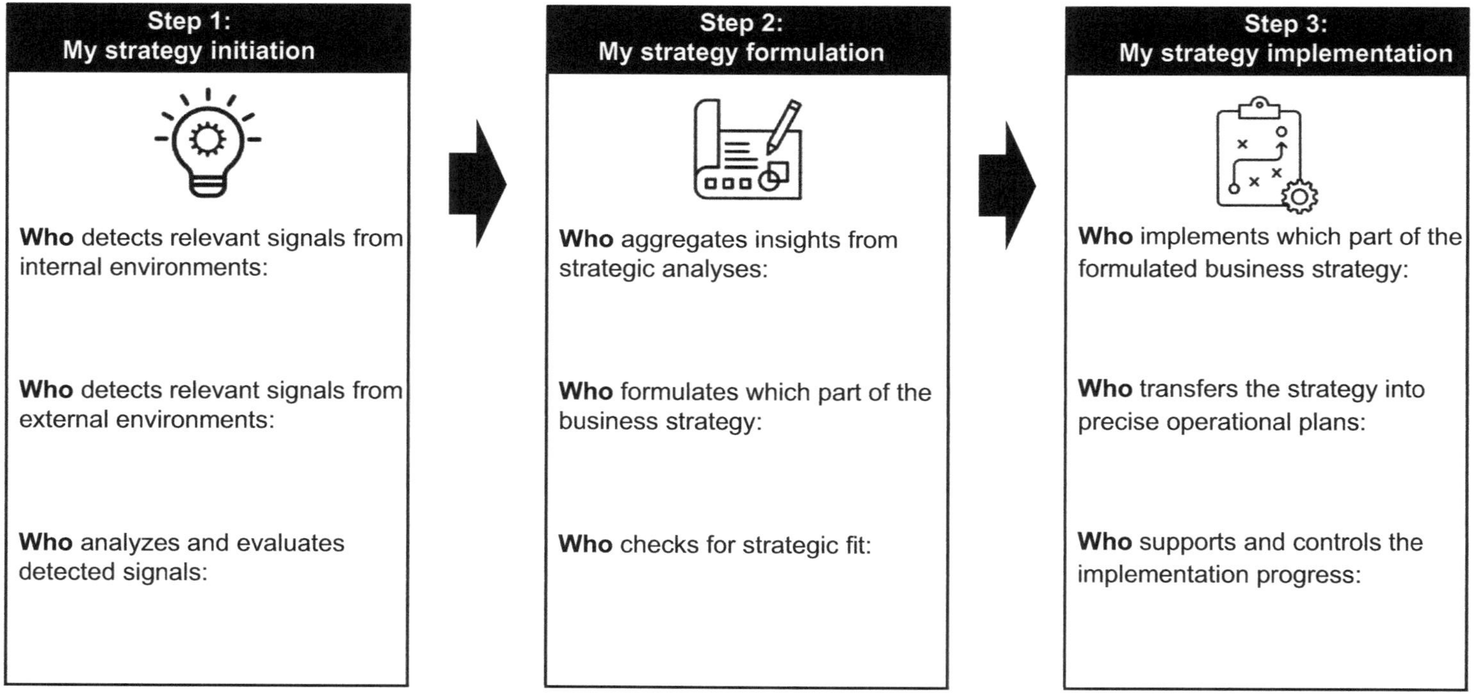

Worksheet 2 What Is Your Current Way of Strategizing?

NOTES

1 Porter, M. E., "What is Strategy?", *Harvard Business Review*, 74/6 (1996): p. 40.
2 For more details, we recommend reading the classic book by Porter, M. E., *On Competition*, 2nd edition (Boston, MA: Harvard Business Review Press, 2008).
3 Strategies are intended to reach pre-defined goals of individuals or groups. Without a vision and corresponding goals, no strategy can be formulated as it is not clear what you want to achieve.
4 Notably, a strategy is neither ethical nor unethical. Strategies should be viewed as a tool used by individuals or groups to achieve their goals. While these goals are often derived from personal values or norms, they can be either moral or immoral in the eyes of others.
5 Of course, this would assume that humans always act rationally, which is not the case. See, for example, Cohen, J. L., "Can Human Irrationality Be Experimentally Demonstrated?", *Behavioral and Brain Sciences*, 4/3 (1981): pp. 317–331.
6 In the case of the climber, this could mean to develop a realistic perspective on the current fitness level, different weather conditions, the difficultness of a certain mountain, etc.
7 A plan generally defines the intended future actions of an individual or group.
8 Constrains are often used to simplify real-world phenomena in a model description. However, the reality can still behave very differently than the model would indicate.
9 Crellin, F., Buli, N., and Chestney, N., "Gas Price Shock Set to Add to Europe's Industrial Pain", *Reuters*, December 6, 2024, available at https://www.reuters.com/business/energy/gas-price-shock-set-add-europes-industrial-pain-2024-12-06/.
10 At this point, we would like to briefly highlight the distinction between business strategies and corporate strategies to avoid confusion. While a business strategy focuses on how to compete in a selected market, a corporate strategy determines which markets a firm wants to compete in. When a firm is active in multiple businesses it has a so-called portfolio. Firms can create mutually aligned AI-oriented business strategies for their entire portfolio.
11 The five strategy components are a modified version from the classic articles by Hambrick, D. C. and Fredrickson, J. W., "Are You Sure You Have a Strategy?", *Academy of Management Perspectives*, 19/4 (2005): pp. 51–62; as well as Nag, R., Hambrick, D. C., and Chen, M.-J., "What is Strategic Management Really? Inductive Derivation of a Consensus Definition of the Field", *Strategic Management Journal*, 28/9 (2007): pp. 935–955.
12 See Hambrick & Fredrickson (2005), "Are You Sure You Have a Strategy?".
13 For a corporate strategy, each portfolio business represents a different target market.
14 A focus on comparatively low market prices is also called price or cost leadership strategy. A focus on customer value is known as a differentiation strategy. For more information about strategy archetypes, please see Porter, M. E., *Competitive Advantage: Creating and Sustaining Superior Performance* (London: Collier Macmillan, 1985).
15 For more details on the Temu case, please have a look at "Commission Opens Formal Proceedings against Temu under the Digital Services Act", *European Commission*, October 31, 2024, available at https://digital-strategy.ec.europa.eu/en/news/commission-opens-formal-proceedings-against-temu-under-digital-services-act.
16 The acquisition price is typically the overall company value of the targetplus a price premium. One would consider an acquisition if the overall price is below the combined value of acquirer and target created through synergies.
17 Refer to Burger, L., "Linde, Praxair Agree $65 billion Merger Outline, Ambitious Cost Savings", *Reuters*, December 20, 2016, available at https://www.reuters.com/article/world/europe/linde-praxair-agree-65-billion-merger-outline-ambitious-cost-savings-idUSKBN1491FV/.
18 Paramasivam, P., "India's Tata faces Pressure in Starbucks Joint Venture as Consumers Cut Back", *Reuters*, December 16, 2024, available at https://www.reuters.com/business/retail-consumer/indias-tata-faces-pressure-starbucks-joint-venture-consumers-cut-back-2024-12-16/.
19 Ghemawat, P., "Building Strategy on the Experience Curve", *Harvard Business Review*, 63/2 (1985).
20 Stoll, J., "Content Spending of Netflix Worldwide from 2012 to 2025", *Statista*, March 6, 2025, available at https://www.statista.com/statistics/964789/netflix-content-spend-worldwide/.

21 This is often called the principle of path dependency, expressing that your past decisions and those of others determine your current or future possible choices.
22 Sindreu, J., "From Ford to Musk, the Perils of Trying to Build a Global Auto Empire", *The Wall Street Journal*, March 21, 2025, available at https://www.wsj.com/business/autos/from-ford-to-musk-the-perils-of-trying-to-build-a-global-auto-empire-9974a0f4.
23 "Amazon.co.uk Launches in the UK with Huge Selection and Keen Pricing", *Amazon*, October 15, 1998, available at https://press.aboutamazon.com/uk/1998/10/amazon-co-uk-launches-in-the-uk-with-huge-selection-and-keen-pricing.
24 See, for example, Zajac, E. J., Kraatz, M. S., and Bresser, R. K. F., "Modeling the Dynamics of Strategic Fit: A Normative Approach to Strategic Change", *Strategic Management Journal*, 21/4 (2000): pp. 429–453.
25 The concept of strategic fit is also very well explained in Porter (1996), "What is Strategy?"; as well as Hambrick & Fredrickson (2005), "Are You Sure You Have a Strategy?".
26 Christopherson, S., "Barrier to 'US Style' Lean Retailing: The Case of Wal-Mart's Failure in Germany", *Journal of Economic Geography*, 7/4 (2007): pp. 451–469.
27 Value chain functions can be classified as primary and secondary functions. While primary functions are directly related to the products and services a firm offers on a market (e.g., logistics, production, marketing, and sales departments), secondary functions support with administrative activities necessary to enable and steer product-related activities (e.g., R&D, recruiting, finance, or IT departments).
28 Chao, C. and Shen, J., "TSMC to Give Top Priority to Car Chips, Apple Orders", *DigiTimes Asia*, June 22, 2021, available at https://www.digitimes.com/news/a20210621PD212.html.
29 For a thorough description of the strategy process, please refer to Hutzschenreuter T. and Kleindienst I., "Strategy-Process Research: What Have We Learned and What Is Still to Be Explored", *Journal of Management*, 32/5 (2006), pp. 673–720; as well as Mintzberg, H. and Lampel, J., "Reflecting on the Strategy Process", *MIT Sloan Management Review*, 40/3 (1999): pp. 21–30.
30 Gioia, D. A. and Chittipeddi, K., "Sensemaking and Sensegiving in Strategic Change Initiation", *Strategic Management Journal*, 12/6 (1991): pp. 433–448.
31 Hutzschenreuter & Kleindienst (2006), "Strategy-Process Research: What Have We Learned and What Is Still to Be Explored".
32 Mui, C., "How Kodak Failed", *Forbes*, January 18, 2012, available at https://www.forbes.com/sites/chunkamui/2012/01/18/how-kodak-failed/.
33 Sin, B., "These Are the People Who Thought the iPhone Would Fail", *Forbes*, January 9, 2017, available at https://www.forbes.com/sites/bensin/2017/01/09/these-are-the-people-who-thought-the-iphone-would-fail/.
34 Lovelace, B. Jr., "Steve Ballmer Explains His Biggest Mistake When It Came to the iPhone", *CNBC*, November 4, 2016, available at https://www.cnbc.com/2016/11/04/steve-ballmer-explains-his-biggest-mistake-when-it-came-to-the-iphone.html.
35 For more details about strategic analysis tools, we recommend Grant, R. M., *Contemporary Strategy Analysis* (Chichester: Wiley, 2013).
36 The VRIN framework helps to pinpoint business capabilities that are valuable, rare, inimitable, and non-substitutable. Further, Porter's five forces framework is used to determine the business attractiveness of an industry by evaluating the potential power of suppliers, customers, new entrants, substitutes, and existing competitors. The PESTEL model, in turn, provides insights into macroeconomic trends by examining political, economic, social, technological, ecological, and legal factors. For more details on strategy analyses tools, see Grant (2013), *Contemporary Strategy Analysis*.

3

UNDERSTANDING TODAY'S AI SYSTEMS

"AI is probably the most profound technology humanity has ever worked on."
—Sundar Pichai, CEO of Google[1]

The term AI has become omnipresent in both professional and everyday life. While no universally accepted definition exists of what AI truly entails today, some scholars and practitioners describe it as computer systems capable of performing tasks that traditionally require human-level intelligence. However, such a definition is quite vague and does not reflect that most of today's AI systems are shaped by their unique self-learning ability, as they are predominantly based on probabilistic machine learning techniques. Therefore, this chapter explains the most important technology basics to better understand contemporary AI. We will deal with the history of AI (Section 3.1), the inherent working mechanisms of machine learning (Section 3.2), the development of machine learning models (Section 3.3), the utilization of predictive and generative AI modules (Section 3.4), as well as task automation and human–AI collaboration (Section 3.5). On top of that, we will discuss different types of ethical concerns (Section 3.6) and algorithmic black box problems you should be familiar with (Section 3.7).

3.1 A BRIEF SUMMARY OF THE HISTORY OF AI

To better understand what today's AI is about, we need to look at the history of the field.[2] While AI originally is a subdomain of computer science

DOI: 10.4324/9781003673170-5

research, its history is much richer and longer than many might know. The roots of AI research could even be traced back to antiquity, exemplified by early developments in mathematical algorithms. Nevertheless, we will start in the first half of the 20th century, when foundational work in disciplines like machine computing, cognitive sciences, and formal logic began to take more shape.

For instance, a pivotal moment in the field's early development was the publication of Alan Turing's landmark article "Computing Machinery and Intelligence."[3] This article introduced the Turing Test, a method designed to assess when a machine can be considered intelligent. The test posits that if a human cannot distinguish between conversing with a machine or another human, the machine can be said to exhibit intelligent behavior.

3.1.1 *AI's birth as a research field*

Despite very important prework, many refer to the Dartmouth conference in New Hampshire when discussing AI's formal birth as a research field. The Dartmouth conference was a summer workshop in 1956 that brought together outstanding computer scientists, mathematicians, engineers, and many more experts from various related research disciplines. Some prominent names, among others, have been John McCarthy, Marvin Minsky, Claude Shannon, Herbert Simon, and Allen Newell. The central goal of the conference was to unify diverse research perspectives on intelligent machines, as articulated in the official conference proposal:

> "The study is to proceed on the basis of the conjecture that every aspect of learning or any other feature of intelligence can in principle be so precisely described that a machine can be made to simulate it."[4]

Although the conference did not produce immediate breakthroughs, it set the research agenda for the field in the following decades, marking the beginning of what would be known as the first AI summer.

In the following decades, many AI researchers were highly motivated and celebrated some early successes. For instance, new programming languages like LISP were developed, and computer programs started to solve relatively complex mathematical problems, such as the Tower of Hanoi game.[5] A team led by Joseph Weizenbaum programmed an information system named ELIZA, which was able to communicate with users in a natural human language. Due to the quick results, the field was very optimistic at that time. AI

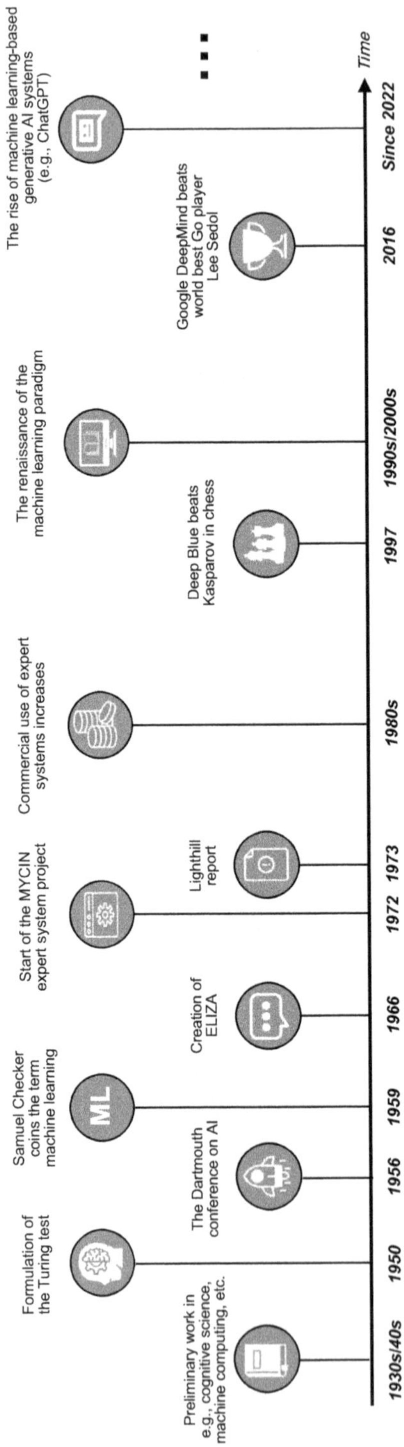

Figure 3.1 Essential Milestones in the History of AI

pioneer Marvin Minsky expressed his huge enthusiasm in an interview with Life Magazine in 1970, where he confidently predicted:

> "In from three to eight years, we will have a machine with the general intelligence of an average human being."[6]

However, things did not go as smoothly as anticipated, leading to the first AI winter. Indeed, early AI researchers' ambitious promises and expectations were not realized. The field was still far from achieving computer-based common-sense reasoning or human-level task intelligence, as proclaimed. While the limited technological infrastructure at that time played a pivotal role, another critical blow came from the so-called Lighthill Report in 1973, which summarized the numerous project failures and research dead ends in the preceding years.[7] As a result, public funding for AI research decreased perceivably at that time.

3.1.2 *The focus on symbolic expert systems*

In the meantime, an increasing number of researchers focused on so-called *expert systems,* which are computer programs that predominantly rely on domain knowledge extracted from human task experts.[8] More precisely, system developers gathered explicit knowledge[9] from various human task specialists and translated it into explicit machine code to guide algorithmic behavior.[10] Expert systems were typically coded with many logical rules expressed in symbolic representations. Through their manual coding, expert systems are usually fully deterministic.[11]

Some expert systems have been a great success in the past. For instance, the MYCIN expert system, developed at Stanford University, demonstrated impressive performance in diagnosing bacterial infections and creating appropriate treatment plans.[12] A boom of commercially applied expert systems occurred since the 1980s, leading to a second AI summer. An example was the XCON system used by American technology equipment manufacturer DEC.[13] Specifically, XCON automatically selected computer system components that fit customers' specific technological equipment needs.[14]

Another remarkable algorithm that used expert system approaches was Deep Blue, a chess-playing computer program developed by IBM.[15] In 1997, Deep Blue defeated the reigning world chess champion, Garry Kasparov, in a highly publicized six-game match. This victory marked the first time a computer, programmed with symbolic rules, had beaten a human world champion in a chess match under tournament conditions.

Despite some success, the expert system approach has lost attention over time. Researchers had to acknowledge that expert systems could not have been programmed for tasks with many complex dimensions or dynamically changing contexts.[16] In fact, many cognitive tasks typically require adaptation and self-improvement abilities. Therefore, static expert systems cannot be defined as truly intelligent machines. Further, human coding takes time, and resources are limited. Accordingly, the field has entered a second AI winter.

3.1.3 *The rise of the machine learning paradigm*

At the end of the last century, the field underwent an enormous paradigm shift. Instead of relying on manual programming, researchers increasingly focused on machine learning techniques.[17] These allow algorithms to learn task knowledge autonomously by detecting correlated task patterns represented in datasets with statistical methods.[18] Accordingly, such a self-learning ability implies significantly less manual coding effort.[19] Overall, we define machine learning as:

> "Computer systems being able to autonomously learn how to perform complex cognitive tasks."[20]

Importantly, today's machine learning-based AI systems are mostly probabilistic as they learn by detecting correlated data patterns. This strongly differentiates them from traditional IT systems and other manually programmed AI approaches, such as symbolic expert systems, that are usually more deterministic.[21] Whereas probabilistic machine learning systems come with very different technological characteristics than other digital applications, we will explicitly discuss them in the following sections.

Although the concept of machine learning was not new in the 1990s,[22] the paradigm gained more and more attention due to significant advances in computing power and the rising digital collectability of big datasets. Over the last decades, the increasing power of self-learning AI systems has evoked a third research summer, which we are still experiencing today.

A prominent milestone demonstrating the power of machine learning happened in 2016. Google DeepMind developed a machine learning system that has beaten the world's best human Go player, Lee Sedol. Go is an ancient board game that originated in China, in which two players take turns placing black and white stones on a grid. The objective is to surround the opponent's stones to control territory on the gameboard. Due to the large field and potential moves, Go is widely regarded as one of the most complex and strategically demanding games ever created.

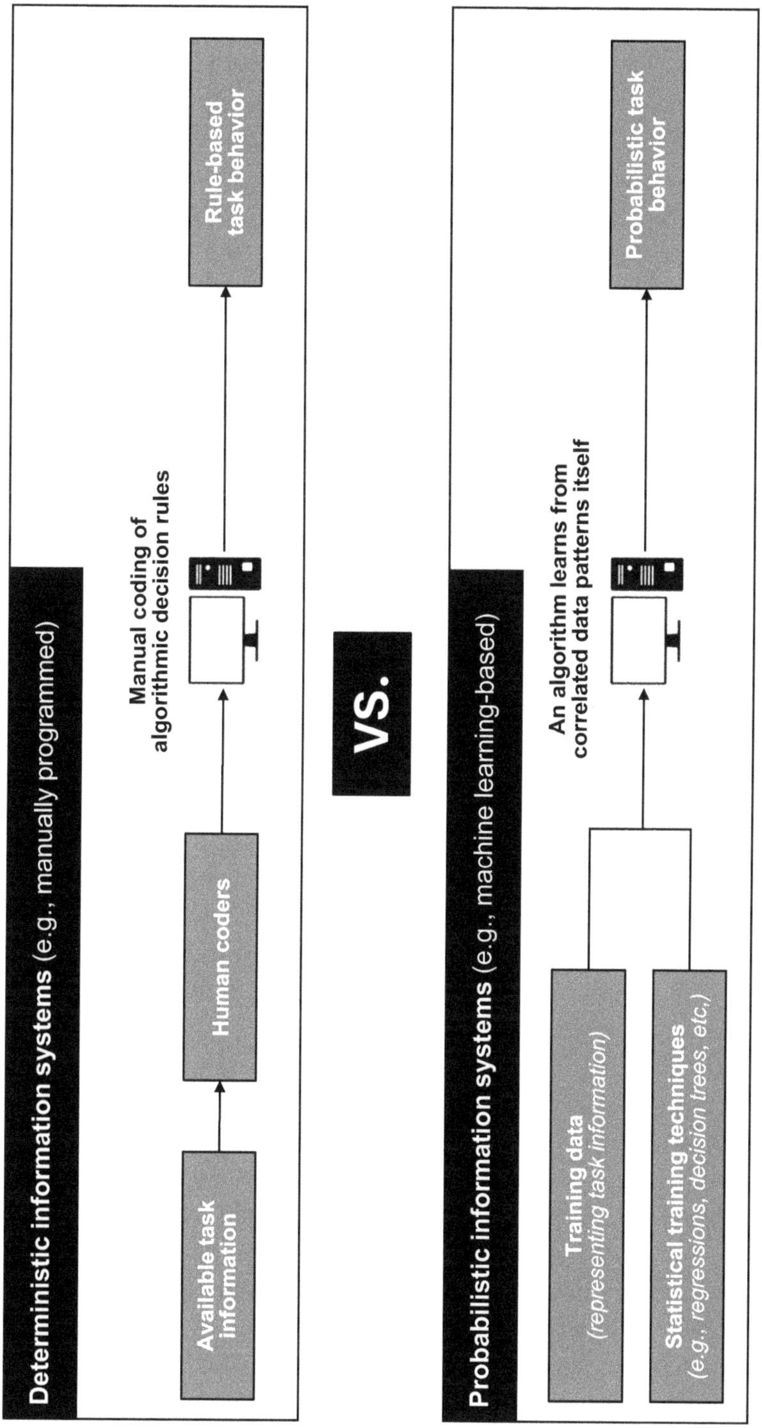

Figure 3.2 Comparing Deterministic and Probabilistic Information Systems

The machine learning paradigm fundamentally transformed the field, and most of today's AI systems predominantly rely on it.[23] Nevertheless, we want to note that since 2022, we have not entered a new paradigm but a new wave of machine learning applications, which builds on so-called generative AI.[24] In contrast to predictive AI that focuses on numerical forecasts and classifications, generative AI is about creating new types of content like texts, audio, or images (we will explore this in more detail within Section 3.4). While both output types can but do not necessarily have to be machine learning-based (expert systems, e.g., can also make estimations or produce content), predictive and generative machine learning systems are essential for today's business landscape.

However, one must acknowledge that we are still at the beginning of the AI era. Existing technological possibilities have apparent limitations, making clear that technology research still has much to explore.

3.2 THE POWER OF MACHINE LEARNING

Thanks to their unique self-learning ability, today's AI systems have the potential to cognitively surpass human beings in many different tasks.[25] When an algorithm can independently learn from large amounts of task data instead of human-inserted code, it might even acquire knowledge that experts are unaware of, thus potentially outcompeting them.[26] Nevertheless, the performance of a machine learning system strongly depends on the quality and quantity of its underlying training data. Besides the underlying IT infrastructure, which is necessary to obtain computing power or enforce cybersecurity standards, data is usually the biggest bottleneck. Data allows an algorithm to statistically create and update its task knowledge iteratively. The more accurately the training data represents real-world task contexts, the better the system can learn correlated patterns that drive its performance.[27]

Take Netflix's video recommendation system as an example. The more data it processes that explicitly reflects a customer's watching preferences regarding favorite genres, storylines, movie lengths, or actors, the more precise and personalized its recommendations become. All learned task knowledge together forms the so-called machine learning model, expressing an algorithm's view of the world. An effective algorithmic model strictly clarifies task goals, potential task actions, and critical task constraints.

Probabilistic machine learning techniques have driven significant advancements across several technology subfields. Let us briefly highlight some of today's most relevant playfields for machine learning.[28] Table 3.1 also provides a short summary.

Table 3.1 Some Important AI-Related Playfields

Natural language processing	Focuses on creating computer systems that understand, interpret, and generate human language
Computer vision	A branch of AI that enables computer systems to interpret visual data, such as images and videos
Robotics	Equips robots with intelligent abilities so that they can more quickly and precisely manipulate their physical environments
Business analytics	Transforms raw data into actionable insights to facilitate organizational decision-making

3.2.1 *Natural language processing*

First, natural language processing is related to the capability of speaking, listening, writing, and understanding human languages. It is a vital playfield for AI because it enables computers to reflect on, interpret, and generate human language, thus making interactions between individuals and machines easier.[29] Today, machine learning systems in this area are typically based on so-called large language models (LLMs). In a nutshell, LLMs are machine learning algorithms trained on vast amounts of text or audio data to probabilistically predict the next word in a sentence. Most LLMs harness different human languages simultaneously like English, French, Spanish, Mandarin, and Arabic.

Nowadays, natural language processing is used in many different business applications. Prominent examples are chatbot products like ChatGPT or DeepSeek, voicebots like Siri or Alexa,[30] and classic language translation or business report creation tools. It is also applied in text-based image generators such as Stable Diffusion or for sentiment analyses. The latter helps companies better understand customer opinions by analyzing text-based or verbal product reviews as well as social media posts. Due to the benefits of verbal human-machine communication and the explosive availability of corresponding software tools, firms are investing heavily in exploring innovative use cases applicable to modern LLMs.

3.2.2 *Computer vision*

Next, computer vision is a playfield directly related to human eyesight. It allows AI systems to analyze visual data, such as images and videos, to produce numerical or symbolic information. Hence, computer vision enables machines to identify objects, humans, environments, and even track movements. Use cases range from autonomous vehicles that navigate through traffic using camera sensors to medical imaging systems that diagnose different kinds of cancer with image abnormalities. Further, grocery retailers use computer vision technology to accurately detect which items customers take from the shelves for purchase (e.g., Amazon Go). Producing companies, in turn, implement AI-powered object detection to monitor production lines and better spot defective product materials during assembly.

3.2.3 *Robotics*

Another important playfield is AI-based robotics. This domain deals with creating machines that can learn how to purposefully manipulate their physical environments as accurately as humans can. In contrast to manually programmed robots, AI-powered ones can independently improve their performance by self-learning from past movements, either simulated or real ones. In manufacturing, this approach helps robotic arms grasp product components more quickly and precisely. In healthcare, self-learning robots execute or assist surgeons in delicate operations. Notably, autonomous vehicles like cars or drones are also a form of AI-based robotics capable of navigating through space.

3.2.4 *Business analytics*

A further relevant application domain is business analytics, helping organizations transform raw data into actionable insights to facilitate organizational decision-making. Due to the large number of managerial decisions, including operational, tactical, and strategic ones, machine learning techniques can be used for various types of analyses that provide, for example, critical information to the management. For instance, companies use AI-driven business intelligence tools to create and evaluate business reports, track market trends, or predict cost and sales figures. From an industry perspective, financial institutions apply business analytics for finding the best investment options or for fraud detection by identifying unusual transaction patterns. Wholesalers, in turn, often improve their inventory management and distribution network by predicting the expected product demand and by analyzing customer purchasing behavior.

3.2.5 *Other AI-related playfields*

We want to underline that many other playfields or research areas exist. Most of them could become highly relevant in the future.[31] In fact, the field of AI is very broad and dynamically advancing. An example of a relatively young but promising research avenue is federated learning which could enhance existing or lead to new playfields. In a nutshell, federated learning enables AI models to be trained across multiple decentralized devices without sharing raw data. Firms like Google started to increasingly investigate this technique for facilitating the statistical training of machine learning models.

3.3 TRAINING MACHINE-LEARNING SYSTEMS

Training machine learning-based AI systems involves several key steps. All of them are essential for ensuring a good performance of an algorithmic model within real-world adoption tasks.[32] To simplify things, we cut the system development process into three sequential steps that we will present in the following sections (see Figure 3.3). However, in reality, development approaches are usually much more complex, overlapping, and tailored to the underlying statistical training techniques. Furthermore, many firms only purchase pre-developed AI systems.

3.3.1 Data collection and preparation

Simplified, each development process begins with a data collection and preparation phase. First, one has to gather relevant task datasets from physical (e.g., sensors) and virtual information sources (e.g., existing databases). To some extent, data can be externally acquired, too. External sources could

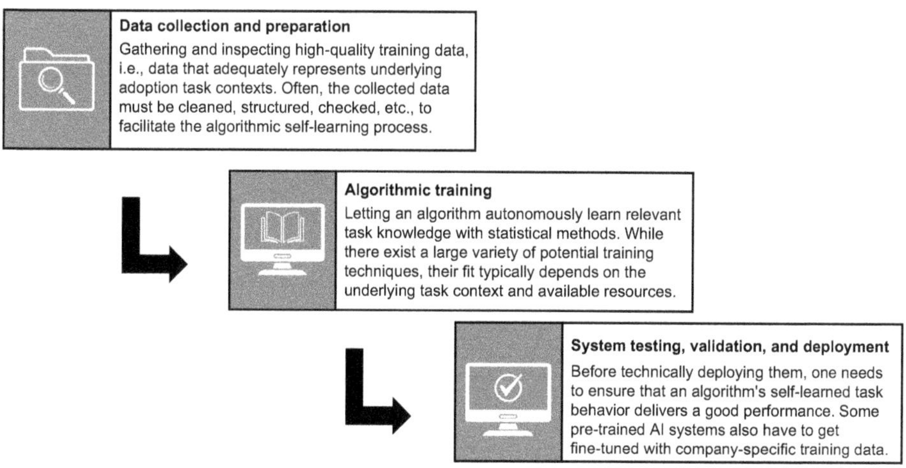

Figure 3.3 How Machine Learning Algorithms Are Trained

be market or product research firms, as well as specialized business analytics or IT system providers.

As mentioned earlier, the quality and quantity of the training data are crucial for model performance. They directly influence the model's ability to learn meaningful patterns. Hence, good training data must sufficiently represent underlying task structures for which a machine learning algorithm should be developed and deployed. Unfortunately, collecting high-quality training data is often difficult since it is not always available or technically and legally accessible because of infrastructure needs or data privacy limitations.

Equally important is the adequate preparation of collected data for the subsequent training intervals. An algorithm can only learn effective task behavior when the training data is correct, unbiased, aggregated, and purposefully structured. Accordingly, data preparation may involve cleaning the data by manually inserting missing parameters, standardizing and normalizing values, checking for potential biases, or restructuring columns and rows. It could also mean encoding explicit categorical data variables that can be effectively recognized by machine learning algorithms, which is known as feature engineering. Additionally, data preparation may require identifying outliers, correcting inconsistencies, and double-checking whether the data is really relevant to the task at hand.

To collect and prepare training data, firms need a systematic plan, often called a data strategy.[33] A well-defined data strategy aims to generate as much high-quality task data as possible. This means not only training data for current development projects. Instead, it should incentivize employees to collect task data well in advance to proactively prepare a firm for future machine learning opportunities. The success of AI adoption often hinges on the strength of a data strategy, making it an essential component for any profound AI transformation.

3.3.2 Algorithmic training

With the data ready, the focus shifts to the actual algorithmic training. There, a machine learning algorithm typically learns its probabilistic task behavior from the training dataset by applying some kinds of statistical methods.[34] Learning, in that sense, means that the algorithm iteratively modifies its task knowledge (i.e., its machine learning model) with each training period in which it is exposed to new datasets. It scans the underlying data for correlations among different parameters and puts them together in a specific task model, reflecting its worldview.[35] The more correlations are found, the more it can learn. The stronger the correlations among parameters, the more they influence the algorithm's behavior.[36] Big datasets with cleaned variables that convey many correlational relationships foster algorithmic learning strongly.

While there are very different machine learning techniques, choosing the right one(s) is typically not that easy.[37] One requires technical expertise and a profound digital infrastructure. One should also consider the underlying task problem at hand to check which technique is most promising, thus creating a so-called task-technology fit.[38] Since we do not want to become too technical, let us briefly cover four prominent training techniques (Table 3.2). It is essential to note that these techniques deal with different concepts and cannot be compared. Still, these techniques can also be combined very successfully.[39]

Supervised learning

First, one can distinguish whether machine learning algorithms are trained with or without human supervision.[40] In supervised learning, humans proactively label the data that algorithms are trained on. This means the model learns to map known data input parameters to known data output parameters (input–output data pairs).[41] For instance, supervised learning is often used in image recognition. An animal detector might be trained on images explicitly labeled with animal names. With well-prepared training data and

Table 3.2 Summarizing Prominent Machine Learning Techniques

Supervised learning	• Humans actively label the underlying training data • An algorithm knows what kinds of variables it processes • The technique is applied when classified task outputs are required
Unsupervised learning	• Humans do not actively label the training data • An algorithm does not know what kinds of variables it processes • This approach helps explore new or unknown phenomena
Reinforcement learning	• An algorithm learns to make decisions by interacting with a physical or virtual environment • Based on its actions, it receives performance feedback through rewards or penalties • This method is often used to train algorithms with simulations
Deep learning	• An algorithm learns its task behavior with a complex, multi-layered artificial neural network architecture • This approach particularly excels with large, complex datasets • Deep learning has driven many advancements in fields like computer vision and natural language processing

fitting statistical methods, the algorithm learns to identify patterns regarding shapes, textures, colors, etc. In the end, with several learning periods, the algorithm should be able to correctly classify animals it has previously learned about in new images it has not seen before.[42]

Unsupervised learning

In unsupervised learning, on the other hand, humans do not label the training data. Thus, an algorithm identifies patterns it cannot precisely name.[43] In other words, the analyzed variables are unspecified. In the case of our animal detector example, this would mean that the algorithm can successfully differentiate between animals but cannot name them. Unsupervised learning provides many beneficial applications, such as in cybersecurity. For anomaly detection, unsupervised machine learning systems can give an alarm if they identify unusual network activities, potentially resulting from unauthorized access. Such functions are very useful because human IT specialists cannot label all types of potential fraud attempts in advance.

Reinforcement learning

A different approach, which can be either supervised or unsupervised, is reinforcement learning.[44] In this training technique, algorithms learn task knowledge by receiving data feedback from the physical or virtual task environment, including humans. Using a mathematical point maximization function, the algorithm learns by seeking positive feedback that provides point rewards and avoiding negative feedback that would bring point penalties.

Prominent application examples of reinforcement learning are robotic areas, particularly concerning complex physical movements. For instance, autonomous vehicles are predominantly trained with reinforcement learning techniques in virtual driving scenarios to avoid too early real-world tests. Volkswagen aimed to accelerate its autonomous driving developments with simulations to minimize dependence on scarce real-world data and reduce costly physical tests.[45] The AI system improves driving behavior over time through continuous virtual feedback in each simulation round. Only when the vehicle system has reached a certain level of driving performance can physical training take place on real-world (test) streets.

Deep learning

A fourth key concept is deep learning, which refers to algorithms built on complex but powerful multi-layered neural network architectures.[46]

Artificial neural networks, loosely inspired by the human brain, comprise multiple layers of interconnected information-processing nodes, often called neurons. During training, the algorithm repeatedly adjusts the strength of the connections between these nodes, which are called weights, based on how well the network performs for a dataset. Over multiple training iterations, this process allows the network to form a complex internal representation of correlations among task variables.

Deep learning is compelling for training large-scale machine learning systems. For example, due to the size and complexity of human language, the LLMs developed by Google, Microsoft, Meta, and others are usually trained using deep learning techniques in the form of so-called transformer-based architectures. These, in turn, are deep learning models that use a mechanism called self-attention to understand how words in a sentence relate to each other, even if they are far apart in a text. Self-attention makes LLMs especially good at handling complex language tasks like translation, summarization, and human-machine conversation.

3.3.3 *System testing, validation, and deployment*

After training, the algorithm should undergo substantial performance testing. For this, a separate test dataset, which the model has not seen during training, is used to assess key metrics regarding an algorithm's task performance. The procedure helps determine whether a machine learning model's behavior can generalize to new, unseen task data or whether it requires further training.[47] That is an essential prerequisite for its practical application because an implemented AI system must continuously deal with new data inputs.

In some cases, it is necessary to gain a deeper understanding of the task knowledge acquired by an AI system in order to validate whether it has learned the correct behavior or not. Due to the probabilistic nature of self-learning algorithms, this can be an extremely challenging task. We explicitly address these "black box" issues in Section 3.7.

Some algorithms also might need to be fine-tuned before being applied. In general, fine-tuning is about adapting the behavior of a pre-developed machine learning model to its unique implementation context by feeding it with additional task-specific training data. Fine-tuning is especially required if firms acquire pre-trained machine learning systems from external vendors. As an example, many firms fine-tune large language models with company-specific information so that the AI system can effectively work in organizational task environments. AI-based knowledge management systems, for instance, must be able to deal with firm-specific abbreviations, technical documents, organizational structures, etc.

Finally, developed machine learning systems must be technically implemented into the existing digital infrastructure. Moreover, organizations must monitor adopted systems and potentially retrain them with updated data if task environments substantially change over time. Retraining would mean restarting the development circle, at least to some extent. This is natural, as each AI model has its own individual life cycle.

3.4 PREDICTIVE AND GENERATIVE AI MODULES

As stated before, machine learning systems are nowadays majorly applied for tasks benefiting from prediction-making (predictive AI), content generation (generative AI), or a combination thereof.[48] For each task an AI system is trained for, it is equipped with a "module" that represents the specific, underlying machine learning (sub-)model. If a system predicts something for a task, it has a predictive AI module. If it generates content, it has a generative AI module. If it combines both for a task, it has a combined AI module. Since AI systems can be trained for multiple deployment tasks, an AI system can consist of several modules, usually one for each kind of task. In such a case, the different machine learning (sub-)models are aggregated into an overall model, representing the entire AI system.

3.4.1 *Predictive AI modules*

From its beginnings, machine learning scholars have focused on all kinds of prediction-making tasks. Predictive AI modules generally leverage historical data to forecast potential outcomes of a particular phenomenon or classify objects based on specific characteristics. More specifically, a self-learning system predicts the most likely output value or classification type for given input parameters.[49] This can range from numerical forecasts, such as cost or sales projections, to categorical classifications, like identifying customer segments or diagnosing critical process weaknesses with business analytics tools. It can also facilitate managerial decision-making by computing different scenarios or providing direct suggestions.

In retail, for instance, predictive AI can forecast consumer demand, allowing businesses to optimize inventory and pricing. In healthcare, it can predict patient treatment success rates or anticipate infection likelihoods. In manufacturing, predictive models compute optimal production schedules on assembly lines or order lead times, reducing waste and ensuring sufficient machine capacities. Similarly, AI algorithms identify patterns that suggest fraudulent customer claims in insurance, and forecasting stock trends or categorizing investment options into different risk levels can greatly improve financial decision-making tasks in investment management.

3.4.2 Generative AI modules

In contrast, generative AI modules focus on producing new content in various formats, such as text, images, video, audio, or code. Essentially, at its core, a generative AI module uses statistical predictions, too.[50] Such types of machine learning algorithms determine the most likely sequences of elements, whether words in a sentence, pixels in an image, or code snippets in a software program.

While the subfield of generative AI has existed for much longer than 2022, it gained significant attention through breakthroughs in natural language processing, enabling humans to create algorithmic content with text or speech commands via prompt engineering. These prompts are direct human commands specifying what a desired algorithmic output should look like. In ChatGPT, for instance, a prompt gives contextual information to steer the output of an algorithm toward an anticipated text reply, the creation of an image, or the suggestion of software code. Ultimately, the more contextually precise the prompts, the more accurate the resulting content outputs.

As such, generative AI modules are widely used to centralize, for example, a firm's knowledge management landscape, assist in complex software development projects, or reshape customer-product interactions with verbal communication interfaces. Moreover, it is frequently employed to assist marketers in creating attractive and informative social media campaigns or to support engineering firms in designing novel technical product concepts.

3.4.3 Combined AI modules

Machine learning systems can also combine predictive and generative AI models if they can create more value together for a task than individually. To develop such a combined AI module, one connects a pre-trained predictive and a pre-trained generative machine learning model. For instance, this could mean that an AI system uses its predictive part to analyze a phenomenon and its generative part to formulate fitting verbal recommendations. Many chatbot solutions use this approach today. For example, a service chatbot would identify and analyze a customer's problem. Afterwards, it would formulate individual advice.

Notably, AI systems can also combine different modules to be applied to multiple task contexts. Often, various modules are stored within an AI platform to bundle all related task applications in one place. For example, agricultural technology firm Syngenta released a new AI toolbox app called "Cropwise AI" that unifies predictive and generative AI to help farmers increase their harvest.[51] Predictive AI modules forecast crop growth in a certain farming region or identify risk factors concerning potential pest infestations. Based on that, a generative AI module can provide specific text-based farming advice that builds on the analyzed information.

One can also connect an AI system or individual modules with other digital systems, thus creating an "Internet of Things" (IoT). The goal of an IoT is that all integrated applications mutually share information so that an AI system can constantly learn. This concept is also called the data network effect.[52] Remarkably, the term "AI of Things" (AIoT) was also coined to describe networks that consist of many different machine learning-based AI systems.[53]

Besides, AI modules can be added to existing, traditional information systems, too. Many manually programmed technology systems have been enriched with predictive or generative AI modules over the years. For instance, the modern CRM platform from Salesforce incorporates predictive lead scoring, which uses machine learning to estimate how likely a customer is to convert to a competitor. Similarly, a generative AI module automatically drafts personalized sales email responses. Overall, AI add-ons

Table 3.3 Distinguishing Predictive, Generative, and Combined AI Modules

Predictive AI module	• Can produce statistical forecasts for a specific phenomenon • Can statistically classify objects based on individual characteristics • Is often used to facilitate decision-making tasks through business predictions
Generative AI module	• Statistically predicts the most likely sequence of elements, like words or pixels • Produces new content in formats such as text, images, video, audio, or code • Can be guided during output creation with prompt engineering techniques
Combined AI module	• Unifies predictive and generative AI • Connects different pre-trained (sub-)models to a new aggregated model • Can be powerfully applied to unify algorithmic analytics and verbal communication functions

can significantly increase the power of traditional IT systems and avoid the need to replace an existing technology system with a new one.

3.5 INTELLIGENT AUGMENTATION VERSUS AUTOMATION

AI systems are adopted to automate tasks or task portions to some extent. The more a certain task benefits from predictive, generative, or combined AI modules, the more it can be automated with a machine learning system. In contrast, the more a task relies on human skills, the more a machine learning system should be used to augment human capabilities. The overall aim will always be to purposefully combine the skills of both humans and AI systems so that they can mutually reinforce each other's strengths to maximize the overall task performance.[54] In other words, it is important to identify the optimal combination of humans and AI systems.

As a result, intelligent augmentation and automation span a human-AI collaboration continuum for each task, meaning that very different levels of automation exist.[55] Lower levels indicate more AI augmentation. Higher levels mean outsourcing more task portions to a machine.

Notably, a special but very powerful form of human-AI collaboration is the installation of a so-called AI agent, which is a relatively autonomous human assistant taking care of many interrelated work tasks in parallel. More specifically, whereas AI agents are shaped by higher levels of task automation, they are characterized by their ability to perceive and analyze their environment, make logical decisions, and take corresponding actions in line with pre-defined goals. AI agents can become especially powerful when they are able to process natural language. For instance, in customer support, an AI agent can automatically resolve routine inquiries and escalate complex issues to human staff if necessary. Alternatively, in project management, it can track task progress, remind team members of deadlines, and adjust action schedules to prevent critical bottlenecks.

The most appropriate automation level depends on whether a human or an AI system owns the necessary skills for a good task performance (one has, of course, also to consider cost aspects for each type).[56] Since humans and AI systems come with very different strengths and weaknesses, let us highlight some crucial skills of each that help you indicate whether higher or lower levels of automation should be preferred for a use case.

3.5.1 *Potentially relevant skills of machine learning-based task agents*

Machine learning-based task agents are any technology systems equipped with a self-learning ability, including but not limited to classic AI agents.

First, they are effective in handling massive amounts of information and in reducing task complexity. Whereas humans often struggle to deal with high dimensionality and information overload, a self-learning AI system can, with sufficient technological infrastructure, learn many important insights, maybe even those that human experts are unaware of. Imagine an application designed to predict customer churn for the telecommunications company Vodafone.[57] The system is trained on millions of customer records containing various data points such as call duration, billing history, customer complaints, service usage, and demographic information. Unlike a human analyst, who might struggle to analyze and identify patterns in this complex dataset, a machine learning-based task agent system can learn from it to provide accurate churn predictions or suggest retention tactics tailored to individual customers.

Relatedly, a further skill of machine learning is its information processing speed because, with the proper digital infrastructure, it can provide complex outputs in seconds. Payment service provider PayPal, for example, uses machine learning systems to detect fraudulent transactions.[58] AI's data processing speed allows PayPal to rapidly flag suspicious transactions in real time, including spikes in transactions from unfamiliar locations or purchases deviating from a customer's typical spending behavior.

A third relevant skill of machine learning is its logical consistency. Intelligent machines can significantly reduce human errors arising from conflicting decisions, counterproductive actions, or inertia. Self-learning algorithms form their task knowledge with statistical methods from data, and their acquired task behavior follows self-created, probabilistic if-then rationales.[59] Take a cancer diagnosis system, for example. Whereas a human physician may be influenced by fatigue, biases, or inner conflicts, an AI system always investigates cancer suspicions with the same standards. However, logical consistency is not always beneficial, as stated in the following sections.

3.5.2 *Potentially relevant skills of human task agents*

Human task agents still possess many skills that intelligent machines cannot equally imitate yet. For instance, individuals are often seen as better at dealing with novel and unforeseen future task scenarios through improvisation and gut feelings.[60] Conversely, since algorithmic training data reflects only past events, machine learning systems often have substantial difficulties in such scenarios. Strategizing, for instance, is a task in which one has to thoroughly anticipate potential environmental change and alternative scenarios.

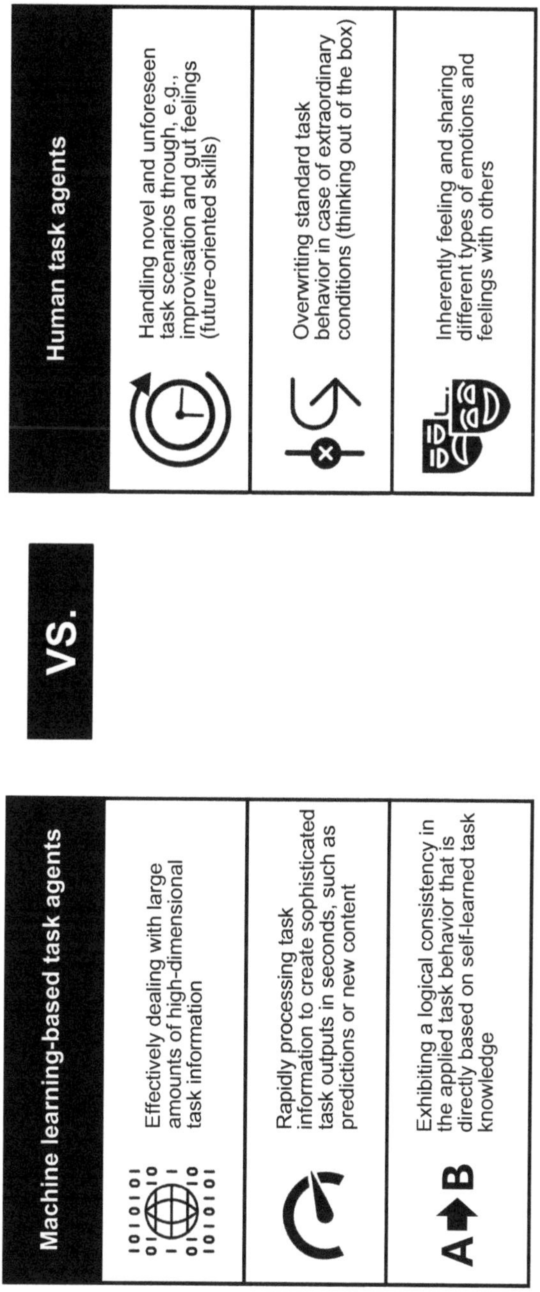

Figure 3.4 Potentially Relevant Task Skills of Different Agent Types

Second, human task agents often outperform algorithms with their context awareness. This term describes an individual's present ability to overwrite standard behavior in case of extraordinary task conditions. A different term for this is thinking out of the box. For example, a human supervisor might directly understand that an employee's productivity decreases because of mental health issues like depression or burnout. A performance evaluation algorithm, in turn, would probably be less able to do so.

A third human task skill is related to empathy, which is often fundamental for socio-emotional interactions with other humans or animals. While humans can perceive and physically show feelings to others, artificial machines can only simulate rather than genuinely experience or share them.[61] Truly understanding and expressing emotions would require a level of machine self-awareness that remains far beyond current technological capabilities.[62]

3.5.3 *Exemplary automation levels*

At this point, we would like to give some examples of appropriate augmentation and automation levels. For instance, the task of addressing severe customer complaints is often more prone to AI augmentation as it usually requires strong socio-emotional communication skills to resolve the issue with highly involved individuals. Still, an AI-based sentiment analysis tool can support the process by identifying highly dissatisfied customers early on. This process allows employees to intervene proactively and reduce response times perceivably.[63]

On the other hand, quality inspection is a task that can often be extensively automated.[64] Unlike humans, computer vision machines can detect even the most minor optical defects with high precision, flag anomalies, and raise alarms in case of errors. However, humans are still observing the accuracy of the algorithm from time to time. Alternatively, due to its capacity, speed, and logical consistency, a machine learning-based AI agent can automate various procurement tasks in parallel, such as selecting suppliers, placing orders, and monitoring deliveries.[65]

Remarkably, it is necessary to stress that humans or organizations always remain responsible for algorithmic task outcomes. Autonomous systems are trained and deployed by humans, so they cannot be held accountable for errors or task failures.[66] Organizations must assign clear responsibilities to qualified individuals for each AI system, independent of whether it is developed internally or acquired externally.

3.5.4 *Some notes on AI's current technological capabilities*

Although there exist a growing number of powerful AI use cases, universally applicable AI systems are not technologically possible today. Usually, AI systems excel at specific tasks or task portions by unfolding their self-learning ability. Humans, however, often support or supervise them. It is crucial to understand that we still do not live in a world where everything can or should be made AI-driven.

In the future, some experts expect that we could reach a level of so-called artificial general intelligence involving technology systems that can seriously compete with humans in all types of cognitive tasks.[67] Moreover, some of them believe that one day we will be able to develop a level of artificial super intelligence, which is about applications that outcompete humans in every, literally every task domain.[68] Nevertheless, even though the field of AI continuously progresses, it remains questionable whether we can or want to reach such levels of machine intelligence.

3.6 ETHICAL CONCERNS

Like every powerful technology, the application of machine learning-based AI can also evoke different ethical concerns. While ethical concerns mainly result from a firm's responsibility to human or organizational stakeholders when deploying an AI system,[69] whenever they arise, they should be thoroughly eliminated or at least adequately mitigated. Otherwise, substantial trust, reputation, cost, or even legal damage can occur. While we will show how to deal with ethical concerns through AI governance practices in Section 6.1.2, let us briefly highlight some frequent ethical issues.

A critical example is using self-learning algorithms for immoral business tasks, since technology should not be misused to create harm. For instance, the training of face recognition or human classification systems is to some extent restricted by governmental policies.[70] The EU AI Act, for example, prohibits using machine learning to scan biometric properties in real time remotely.[71] However, regulatory policy scope, auditing, and enforcement vary widely across countries, leading to ongoing debates about global standards for ethical AI development. Companies located in countries with less strict regulations can have perceivable training advantages over those in countries with more strict laws (e.g., through different data collection or system application rules).

Furthermore, as intelligent machines can learn a lot about the inherent behavior of individuals, one must respect if stakeholders do not want their personal data to be analyzed by an AI system. Data consent, transparency, and sovereignty are often essential to maintain trust and protect individual rights. Similarly, the generation of novel algorithmic outputs raises intellectual property questions. In addition, a progressing AI transformation evokes several cybersecurity threats, can negatively impact the environment by extensive energy consumption, and opens a vital discussion about labor displacement and human skill degradation.

Further ethical concerns refer to who is accountable if an AI system makes consequential mistakes. Think of diagnosing cancer suspicions. Physicians must carefully balance the extent to which they are willing to rely on technologies to make critical medical decisions. A wrong diagnosis can destroy the life of a patient. Furthermore, cancer suspicions should be communicated with emotional sensitivity. While AI systems can enhance diagnostic accuracy and efficiency, relying on them for high-stakes judgments may challenge traditional notions of professional responsibility and patient trust.

Avoiding algorithmic discrimination in terms of gender, age, race, sexuality, education, etc., is also of outstanding relevance. While algorithmic biases typically result from biased training data, they can reinforce existing social inequalities and unfairly (dis-)advantage individuals. For instance, Apple's credit scoring system prompted a legal investigation because the algorithm granted some women only a fraction of the credit limit awarded to their husbands, despite both parties having similar financial backgrounds.[72] Another case was the image generator Stable Diffusion, which depicted Middle Eastern men usually as bearded, with dark skin, and wearing only traditional clothes.[73]

Finally, algorithmic transparency is a vital ethical topic as well. However, due to its relevance, we will discuss this more specifically within the next section.

3.7 PROBLEMATIC BLACK BOX PERCEPTIONS

A fundamental characteristic of probabilistic machine learning systems is that humans often perceive them as black boxes, including AI experts.[74] Sophisticated AI systems typically learn their algorithmic behavior by autonomously identifying complex task patterns in training data. Hence, self-learning AI tools are often challenging to understand, rendering the underlying system opaque to human stakeholders. Interestingly, black box perceptions can vary significantly. Reasons for this can be found in different levels of technology expertise and the complexity of the underlying statistical model. Powerful deep learning techniques are particularly seen as relatively less understandable.

While we will learn how to better deal with opaque AI systems in Section 6.2.2, black box perceptions evoke serious technology management problems for firms. In the following, we discuss the two most important ones.

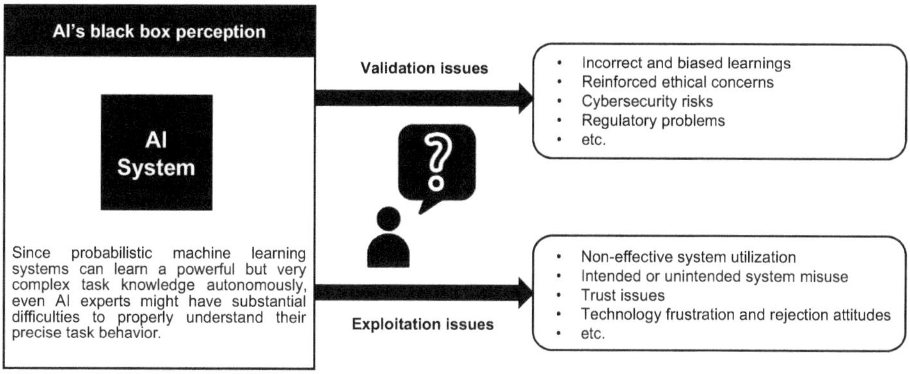

Figure 3.5 Common Black Box Problems

3.7.1 System validation issues

In the case of very complex machine learning algorithms, firms' AI experts might be unable to validate whether a technology system works correctly, reliably, and robustly for a task.[75] They might also have difficulties monitoring it over time. Due to a machine learning model's probabilistic nature, this could even include systems that AI experts have trained themselves. However, validating self-learning algorithms is often crucial, particularly in high-stakes task contexts, since they might also have learned wrong task knowledge, resulting in incorrect or unusable outputs.

Regarding predictive AI modules, this includes inaccurate and biased forecasts or classifications. A warning example is the US real estate company Zillow, which experienced a substantial financial loss due to wrong algorithmic home price forecasts.[76] Zillow's algorithm strongly overestimated the actual value of real estate, so the company had to make write-downs worth more than $500 million over a few days.

On the other hand, regarding generative AI modules, unvalidated models can evoke inadequate or false content. For instance, natural language processing systems like chatbots can exhibit so-called hallucinations, that is, erroneous, misleading, or nonsensical texts that may initially seem plausible but, upon closer inspection, lack any grounding in factual reality or context.

Besides incorrect outputs, validation problems can substantially reinforce ethical concerns about algorithmic biases or offensive behavior. One of Google's image recognition software became publicly known when it labeled black people systematically as gorillas.[77] While many people felt offended by the racist classifications, Google's technology experts were unable to find and fix the corresponding mistake in the algorithm.

Other types of validation problems could be centered around cybersecurity or governmental regulations. For example, firms might have to understand how an AI system communicates with external IT devices or whether it collects data from trustworthy and legally correct sources. System impairment and copyright affairs should be prevented, too. If AI experts cannot eliminate such issues, an AI system should not be applied to its designated task context in its current shape.

3.7.2 *System exploitation issues*

Black box problems matter not only for AI experts but also for individuals without deep technological backgrounds, meaning AI laypeople. When inexperienced stakeholders of an AI system, who are often end-users, do not sufficiently understand its self-learned working behavior or outputs, the system is less effectively utilized, which strongly impedes its exploitation. Besides internal employees, such understandability issues could also concern external customers, suppliers, partners, or auditors.

Black box perceptions can even foster the risk of system misuse. Individuals could use an AI system differently than intended, consciously or unconsciously. For example, in 2023, Samsung employees uploaded sensitive software code to publicly usable generative AI tools as they were unaware of the AI system's working mechanisms.[78] As a consequence, Samsung banned the usage of specific generative AI tools at that time until its internal security standards were modified.

On top of that, humans often have trust issues when they do not sufficiently understand algorithms, especially when they are personally involved or affected by their outputs.[79] Imagine you are applying for an urgently needed bank loan, but a machine learning-based creditworthiness scoring system refuses your request without indicating any reasons for the decision. As with many others, you would probably create an intense technology frustration or rejection attitude regarding algorithm and bank. Due to the increasing adoption of probabilistic AI systems, human trust perceptions have become an enormous research topic over the last years.

3.7.3 *Explainable AI as a remedy*

To counteract black box problems, the subfield of explainable AI has evolved. This research area focuses on making algorithmic AI models much more understandable for humans, including both technology experts and laypeople. Explainable AI aims to ensure that algorithmic decisions can be traced, justified, and trusted, especially in high-stakes task contexts. As mentioned earlier, we will explicitly deal with explainable AI in Section 6.2.2.

High-performing models based on complex statistical training techniques, such as deep learning, are the most difficult ones to validate. This issue highlights the existence of a potential performance-understandability trade-off for self-learning technology systems.[80] Human system validations can be in a trade-off with an algorithm's ability to fully leverage its self-learning ability. The consequence is that explainable AI approaches must thoroughly balance both sides so that intelligent machines can be effective but also validated when necessary.

3.8 CHAPTER SUMMARY

- Whereas the research field of AI has seen many ups and downs, today's AI systems predominantly rely on *machine learning* techniques, enabling an algorithm to learn task knowledge autonomously.
- In contrast to manually programmed information systems, machine learning applications are *probabilistic.* They learn task knowledge by statistically detecting correlated data patterns.
- The power of machine learning algorithms mainly depends on the *quality and quantity* of their *training data.*
- There exist very different machine learning training techniques. We discussed the four most prominent ones, which can also be combined:
  - In *supervised learning,* humans actively label the training data on which an algorithm learns. Hence, the algorithm knows what it processes.
  - In *unsupervised learning,* data is not labeled. Hence, the algorithm does not know what it processes.
  - In *reinforcement learning,* algorithmic task behavior is steered by providing rewards and penalties for its decisions. The system learns by maximizing rewards and minimizing penalties.
  - *Deep learning* builds on artificial neural network architectures. These are especially powerful when training an algorithm with large amounts of complex datasets.
- Today's AI systems can be equipped with *predictive*, *generative*, or *combined AI modules.* Whereas a machine learning system can be trained for one or multiple tasks, it owns a corresponding AI module for each.
- AI systems can be used for task automation or human task augmentation. The focus should be on leveraging *human-AI collaboration* so that both types of task agents mutually support each other when beneficial.

- Probabilistic machine learning systems can evoke serious *ethical concerns* and problematic *black box perceptions*, which can both strongly impede AI adoption endeavors. Firms must find adequate handling approaches to deal with both topics purposefully.

3.9 HANDS-ON PRACTICE

Worksheet 3 shall help you identify existing machine learning-based AI systems within your selected case company. In the best case, many systems already exist that make a perceivable business impact. For such a scenario, we recommend concentrating on the 3–5 most prominent ones or those you personally work with. If you are unaware of any AI systems, try to reach out to colleagues or think about hypothetical use cases for the future.

Importantly, you do not necessarily have to search for stand-alone AI systems. Check whether existing IT systems have some generative, predictive, or combined AI modules. If you do not find any existing applications, try to discover prominent ones from other firms that could interest you or your firm.

	Example 1	*Example 2*	**My AI system 1**	**My AI system 2**	**My AI system 3**	**My AI system 4**	**My AI system 5**
What is the (internal) name of your AI system?	*Intelligent inventory*	*Hybrid AI food vision*					
Where is my AI system implemented? *(process/product)*	*Internal logistic / production department (business process)*	*Household refrigerator (customer product)*					
What is my AI system doing? *(precise adoption task)*	*Optimizing internal production inventories*	*Managing food levels in private households*					
How does my AI system create task value? *(included AI features)*	*Making predictions about material requirements for future production schedules*	*Generate cooking recipes based on available groceries; predict groceries that should be reordered*					
On what data was my AI system trained? *(internal/external data)*	*Historical production schedules, product categories, inventory characteristics, item delivery times, etc.*	*Mainly customer data, such as the consumption of certain groceries*					
What is the level of automation? *(augmentation/automation)*	*High level of task automation. Humans supervise and control prediction outputs*	*Medium level of task automation. The refrigerator suggests options that humans can pursue or not*					
Are ethical or black box problems evident? *(privacy, validation, etc.)*	*Production and warehouse employees would like to better understand the given predictions*	*Some customer do not want that the refrigerator learns about their private behavior*					

Worksheet 3 How AI Transformed Are You Already?

NOTES

1 Parker, C., "Artificial Intelligence Could Be Our Saviour, According to the CEO of Google", *The World Economic Forum*, January 24, 2018, available at https://www.weforum.org/stories/2018/01/google-ceo-ai-will-be-bigger-than-electricity-or-fire/.

2 For more detailed information regarding the history of AI, we recommend the outstanding monography by Russel, S. J. and Norvig, P., *Artificial Intelligence: A Modern Approach* (Upper Saddle River, NJ: Pearson, 2020).

3 Turing, A. M., "Computing Machinery and Intelligence", *Mind*, LIX/236 (1950): pp. 433–460.

4 McCarthy, J., Minsky, M. L., Rochester, N., and Shannon, C. E., "A Proposal for the Dartmouth Summer Research Project on Artificial Intelligence", August 31, 1955, *AI Magazine*, 27/4 (2006): p. 13.

5 The Hanoi Tower game is a mathematical puzzle where the objective is to move a stack of disks from one peg to another, following the rules that only one disk can be moved at a time, and no disk may be placed on top of a smaller disk.

6 Mitchell, M., "Debates on the Nature of Artificial General Intelligence", *Science*, 383/6689 (2024).

7 Agar, J., "What Is Science For? The Lighthill Report on Artificial Intelligence Reinterpreted", *The British Journal for the History of Sciences*, 53/3 (2020): pp. 289–310.

8 Buchanan, B. G. and Smith, R. G., "Fundamentals of Expert Systems", *Annual Review of Computer Science*, 3/1 (1988): pp. 23–58.

9 Implicit task knowledge refers to the unconscious, intuitive understanding and skills gained through experience, often difficult to articulate. Explicit task knowledge, on the other hand, can clearly get articulated, documented, and communicated, often through verbal conversations, manuals, or physical demonstrations.

10 The transfer of implicit knowledge into code is very difficult. Individuals usually apply their implicit knowledge unconsciously or intuitively.

11 See, for instance, Newell, A. and Simon, H., "Computer Science as Empirical Inquiry: Symbols and Search", *Communications of the ACM*, 19/3 (1997): pp. 113–126; or Minsky, M., "Logical Versus Analogical or Symbolic Versus Connectionist or Neat Versus Scruffy", *AI Magazine*, 12/2 (1991): pp. 34–51.

12 Copeland, B. J., "MYCIN", *Britannica*, available at https://www.britannica.com/technology/MYCIN.

13 DEC stands for Digital Equipment Corporation.

14 McDermott, J., "R1: A Rule-Based Configurer of Computer Systems", *Artificial Intelligence*, 19/1 (1982): pp. 39–88.

15 For more insights, have a look at Campbell, M., Hoane, A. J., and Hsu, F.-H., "Deep Blue", *Artificial Intelligence*, 134/1–2 (2002): pp. 57–83.

16 While chess is considered as a very complex game, it has still a finite number of potential moves as the gaming board is an 8×8 matrix.

17 In this book, we use the term machine learning and self-learning for AI systems interchangeably.

18 An excellent article about the nature of machine learning is written by Jordan, M. I. and Mitchell, T. M., "Machine Learning: Trends, Perspectives, and Prospects", *Science*, 349/6245 (2015): pp. 255–260.

19 While machine learning algorithms can learn autonomously, manual coding effort can still be necessary, for example, to purposefully guide algorithmic learning or adjust self-learned task knowledge afterwards.

20 Of course, humans are often still needed to accompany algorithmic self-learning processes (e.g., for data management, model selection, training, or system validation). We will discuss these topics more in detail within the subsequent sections.

21 Notably, there also exist hybrid AI approaches. An example for this might be the combination of expert system and machine learning techniques. See, for instance, Buchanan, B. G., "Can Machine Learning Offer Anything to Expert Systems?", *Machine Learning*, 4/3-4 (1989): pp. 251–254.

22 The machine learning paradigm was already approached much earlier e.g., by Arthur Samuel in the 1950s, who worked on self-learning checker players. See, Samuel, A. L., "Some Studies in Machine Learning Using the Game of Checkers", *IBM Journal of Research and Development*, 3/3 (1959): pp. 210–229.

23 McElheran, K., Li, J., Brynjolfsson, E., Kroff, Z., Dinlersoz, E., Foster, L., and Zolas, N., "AI Adoption in America: Who, What, and Where", *Journal of Economics & Management Strategy*, 33/2 (2024): pp. 375–415.

24 See Hillebrand, L., Raisch, S., and Schad, J., "Managing with Artificial Intelligence: An Integrative Framework", *Academy of Management Annals*, 19/1 (2025): pp. 343–375.

25 Over the last centuries, machines were primarily developed to physically outperform human beings, as they can been stronger, faster, or more precise than individuals in certain tasks. Today, the new focus lies on cognitively outperforming humans.

26 Have a look at Agrawal, A., Gans, J., and Goldfarb, A., *The Simple Economics of Artificial Intelligence* (Boston: Harvard Business Review Press, 2018); as well as Boyacı, T., Canyakmaz, C., and de Véricourt, F., "Human and Machine: The Impact of Machine Input on Decision Making Under Cognitive Limitations", *Management Science*, 70/2 (2023): pp. 1258–1275.

27 We will also discuss issues regarding unfitting, unstructured, or biased data in the following sections.

28 Interested readers find more insights within the AI monography by Russel and Norvig, *Artificial Intelligence: A Modern Approach.*

29 That technological possibility is remarkable because it enables humans to program machines with verbal interactions.

30 A chatbot is a software application designed to simulate text-based conversations with users. A voicebot interacts with users through spoken language, utilizing speech recognition abilities. Many of today's chat- and voicebots are based on retrieval-augmented generation (RAG) techniques, allowing them to combine real-time information retrieval from external sources (e.g., from the internet) with AI-generated natural language responses. Thus, they can provide more accurate and up-to-date answers in both text and voice interactions.

31 Our list is only a short extraction of existing playfields. For example, there also exist AI approaches to investigate olfactory (smelling) or gustatory (tasting) senses. Furthermore, playfields can be combined. A machine learning system can create descriptive texts with natural language processing abilities about what it has detected and interpreted with visual cameras. That means it consists of different AI modules.

32 The detailed development process of machine learning systems is well illustrated in Géron, A., *Hands-on Machine Learning with Scikit-Learn, Keras, and TensorFlow: Concepts, Tools, and Techniques to Build Intelligent Systems* (Sebastopol: O'Reilly Media, 2019).

33 An informative article on data strategies is written by DalleMulle, L. and Davenport, T. H., "What's Your Data Strategy", *Harvard Business Review*, 97/3 (2017).

34 Some examples regarding statistical methods would be about regression analyses, naive bayes, decision trees and random forests, k-means clustering, maximum likelihood estimations, Markov chains, etc. For more precise information about statistical training methods and their purpose, please see Géron (2019), *Hands-on Machine Learning with Scikit-Learn, Keras, and TensorFlow: Concepts, Tools, and Techniques to Build Intelligent Systems*; together with Pearl, J., *Causality: Models, Reasoning, and Inference* (Cambridge: Cambridge University Press, 2000).

35 Jordan & Mitchell (2015), "Machine Learning: Trends, Perspectives, and Prospects".

36 The precise learning procedure and outcome depends on the underlying statistical methods, but also on the manual adjustment of model parameters, which is better known as feature engineering.

37 Model selection must always be aligned with data collection and preparation. Hence, one should think about potentially appropriate machine learning technique(s) for an AI use case from the beginning.

38 The task-technology fit concept was developed by Goodhue, D. L. and Thompson, R. L., "Task-Technology Fit and Individual Performance", *MIS Quarterly*, 19/2 (1995): pp. 213–236.

39 For instance, one can combine supervised learning and reinforcement learning. A model could learn from a dataset of explicitly labeled variables (supervised component) before exploring its environment for actions that evoke rewards (reinforcement component).

40 Experts do also use the term semi-supervised learning when only some variables are labeled (by humans). Further, it exists the term self-supervised learning which means that an algorithmic model learns to predict parts of its input data from other labeled parts.

41 Joshi, A. V., *Machine Learning and Artificial Intelligence*, 2nd edition (Cham, Switzerland: Springer, 2023).

42 Of course, an algorithm cannot identify and label animals it has never "seen" before in its data.

43 Joshi, *Machine Learning and Artificial Intelligence.*
44 Wiering, M. and van Otterlo, M., *Reinforcement Learning: State-of-the-Art* (Berlin, Germany: Springer, 2012).
45 "Reinforcement Learning Speeds Up Autonomous Driving", *deepsense.ai*, no date, available at https://deepsense.ai/case-studies/reinforcement-learning-speeds-up-autonomous-driving/.
46 LeCun, Y., Bengio, Y., and Hinton, G., "Deep Learning", *Nature*, 521/7553 (2015): pp. 436–444.
47 A big problem is model over- or underfitting. Overfitting occurs when a model sticks too much on its training data, including its noise, so that it performs poorly on new data. Underfitting, in turn, happens when a model is technically not able to capture the underlying patterns in its training data, leading to poor performance on both training and test sets.
48 While the realms of predictive and generative AI exist for decades, the traditional focus lied on predictive AI. However, since 2022, this has changed as more and more powerful generative AI systems became available.
49 See Agrawal, A., Gans, J., and Goldfarb, A., *Prediction Machines: The Simple Economics of Artificial Intelligence* (Boston, MA: Harvard Business Review Press, 2018).
50 For more details on the nature of contemporary generative AI, you can refer to Feuerriegel, S., Hartmann, J., Janiesch, C., and Zschech, P., "Generative AI", *Business & Information Systems Engineering*, 66/1 (2023): pp. 111–126.
51 "Syngenta Group Adds Cutting-Edge Generative Artificial Intelligence (GenAI) to Cropwise", *Businesswire*, September 30, 2024, available at https://www.businesswire.com/news/home/20240929730485/en/Syngenta-Group-Adds-Cutting-Edge-Generative-Artificial-Intelligence-GenAI-to-Cropwise.
52 See Gregory, R. W., Henfridsson, O., Kaganer, E., and Kyriakou, H., "The Role of Artificial Intelligence and Data Network Effects for Creating User Value", *Academy of Management Review*, 46/3 (2021): pp. 534–551.
53 An "Internet of Things" (IoT) represents a network of interconnected physical or virtual systems that are mutually connected with each other. An AIoT is a special version of an IoT, often consisting of several machine learning systems as well as traditional IT applications.
54 For more information about potential skills of machine learning agents, see Brynjolfsson, E. and Mitchell, T. M., "What Can Machine Learning Do? Workforce Implications", *Science*, 358/6370 (2017): pp. 1530–1534; as well as Jarrahi, M. H., "Artificial Intelligence and the Future of Work: Human AI-Symbiosis in Organizational Decision-Making", *Business Horizons*, 61/4 (2018): pp. 577–586; and Huang, M.-H., Rust, R., and Maksimovic, V., "The Feeling Economy: Managing in the Next Generation of Artificial Intelligence (AI)", *California Management Review*, 61/4 (2019): pp. 43–65.
55 More insights on the human-AI collaboration continuum are given in Raisch, S. and Krakowski, S, "Artificial Intelligence and Management: The Automation-Augmentation Paradox", *Academy of Management Review*, 46/1 (2021): pp. 192–210; and also in Choudhary, V., Marchetti, A., Shrestha, Y. R., and Puranam, P., "Human-AI Ensembles: When Can They Work?", *Journal of Management*, 51/2 (2023): pp. 536–569; and Raisch, S. and Fomina, K., "Combining Human and Artificial Intelligence: Hybrid Problem-Solving in Organizations", *Academy of Management Review*, 50/2 (2024): pp. 441–464.
56 For details, we recommend Kolbjørnsrud, V., "Designing the Intelligent Organization: Six Principles for Human-AI Collaboration", *California Management Review*, 66/2 (2023): pp. 44–64; and Murray, A., Rhymer, J., and Sirmon, D. G., "Humans and Technology: Forms of Conjoined Agency in Organizations", *Academy of Management Review*, 46/3 (2021): pp. 552–571.
57 Carlesso, R. and Vijayvargia, A., "Vodafone: A DevOps Approach to AI/ML through Cloud-Native CI/CD Pipelines", *Google*, July 18, 2023, available at https://cloud.google.com/blog/products/devops-sre/how-vodafone-uses-cicd-to-speed-up-ml-pipelines?hl=en.
58 "A Guide to Leveraging Data Analytics in Fraud Management", *PayPal*, January 15, 2024, available at https://www.paypal.com/us/brc/article/data-analytics-fraud-management.
59 Every technology system, independent of whether machine learning-based or not, executes task actions in an if-then relationship. The logic is that each specific scenario evokes a corresponding action, which can be either probability-based or rule-based.
60 See Ormrod, J. E., *Human Learning* (Boston, MA: Pearson, 2018); and Sadler-Smith, E. and Shefy, E., "The Intuitive Executive: Understanding and Applying 'Gut Feeling' in Decision-Making", *Academy of Management Perspectives*, 18/4 (2004): pp. 76–91.

61 Huang, M.-H. and Rust, R., "Artificial Intelligence in Service", *Journal of Service Research*, 21/2 (2018): pp. 152–172.
62 Mudrik, L., "Consciousness: What It Is, Where It Comes From – and whether Machines Can Have It", *Nature*, 623/7985 (2023): pp. 25–26.
63 Interested readers can have a look at Kim, J. and Lim, C., "Customer Complaints Monitoring with Customer Review Data Analytics: An Integrated Method of Sentiment and Statistical Process Control Analyses," *Advanced Engineering Informatics*, 49 (2021): Article No. 101304.
64 More details are given in Mangat, A. S., Mangler, J., and Rinderle-Ma, S., "Interactive Process Automation Based on Lightweight Object Detection in Manufacturing Processes," *Computers in Industry*, 130 (2021): Article No. 103482.
65 Nuñez, M., "ZIP Debuts 50 AI Agents to Kill Procurement Inefficiencies – OpenAI Is Already on Board", *VentureBeat*, June 10, 2025, available at https://venturebeat.com/ai/zip-debuts-50-ai-agents-to-kill-procurement-inefficiencies-openai-is-already-on-board.
66 See, for instance, Tschang, F. T. and Almirall, E., "Artificial Intelligence as Augmenting Automation: Implications for Employment," *Academy of Management Perspectives*, 35/4 (2021): pp. 642–659.
67 Goertzel, B., "Artificial General Intelligence: Concept, State of the Art, and Future Prospects", *Journal of Artificial General Intelligence*, 5/1 (2014): pp. 1–48.
68 A very interesting thought experiment is written by Bostrom, N., *Superintelligence: Paths, Dangers, Strategies* (Oxford: Oxford University Press, 2014).
69 This includes both internal stakeholders, who are in most cases employees, but also external ones like suppliers, competitors, partners, customers, regulators, and others.
70 Madiega, T. and Mildebrath, H., "Regulating Facial Recognition in the EU," *European Parliament*, 2021, available at https://www.europarl.europa.eu/RegData/etudes/IDAN/2021/698021/EPRS_IDA(2021)698021_EN.pdf.
71 Details are given in "EU AI Act: First Regulations on Artificial Intelligence", *EU Parliament*, February 19, 2025, available at https://www.europarl.europa.eu/topics/en/article/20230601STO93804/eu-ai-act-first-regulation-on-artificial-intelligence.
72 The precise case is described by Nedlun, E., "Apple Card Is Accused of Gender Bias. Here's How That Can Happen", *CNN*, November 12, 2019, available at https://edition.cnn.com/2019/11/12/business/apple-card-gender-bias/index.html.
73 AlDahoul, N., Rahwan, T., and Zaki, Y., "AI-Generated Faces Influence Gender Stereotypes and Racial Homogenization", *Nature – Scientific Reports*, 15 (2025): Article No. 14449.
74 A good overview about black box perceptions is given by Guidotti, R., Monreale, A., Ruggieri, S., Turini, F., Giannotti, F., and Pedreschi, D., "A Survey of Methods for Explaining Black Box Models", *ACM Computing Surveys*, 51/5 (2019): pp. 1–42.
75 Lebovitz, S., Levina, N., and Lifshitz-Assa, H., "Is AI Ground Truth Really True? The Dangers of Training and Evaluating AI Tools Based on Experts' Know-What", *MIS Quarterly*, 45/3 (2021): pp. 1501–1526.
76 The full Zillow debacle is summarized by Metz, R., "Zillow's Home-Buying Debacle Shows How Hard It Is to Use AI to Value Real Estate", *CNN*, November 9, 2021, available at https://edition.cnn.com/2021/11/09/tech/zillow-ibuying-home-zestimate/index.html.
77 See Hern, A., "Google's Solution to Accidental Algorithmic Racisms: Ban Gorillas", *The Guardian*, January 12, 2018, available at https://www.theguardian.com/technology/2018/jan/12/google-racism-ban-gorilla-black-people.
78 Gurman, M., "Samsung Bans Staff's AI Use after Spotting ChatGPT Data Leak", *Bloomberg*, May 2, 2023, available at https://www.bloomberg.com/news/articles/2023-05-02/samsung-bans-chatgpt-and-other-generative-ai-use-by-staff-after-leak.
79 Details on human-AI trust are provided by Glikson, E. and Woolley, A. W., "Human Trust in Artificial Intelligence: Review of Empirical Research", *Academy of Management Annals*, 14/2 (2020): pp. 627–660; and Vanneste, B. S. and Puranam, P., "Artificial Intelligence, Trust, and Perceptions of Agency", *Academy of Management Review*, forthcoming (2024).
80 Rai, A., "Explainable AI: From Black Box to Glass Box", *Journal of the Academy of Marketing Science*, 48/1 (2020): pp. 137–141.

Part III

THE AI BUSINESS STRATEGY FRAME©

4

HOW TO INITIATE YOUR AI BUSINESS STRATEGY

"The path to the intelligence age is paved with compute, energy, and human will."[1]
—Samuel Altman, CEO of OpenAI

AI-oriented business strategies must be initiated, formulated, and implemented in line with a firm's overall objectives. As we have learned all the required basics about business strategies and machine learning-based AI in the previous chapters, it is time to start with the first step of our framework – initiating your AI business strategy. Accordingly, this chapter will show you how to identify your own AI ecosystem (Section 4.1) and deal with the various types of AI signal sources (Section 4.2). In addition, we explain how to purposefully evaluate the strategic relevance of detected AI signals with competent technology strategists (Section 4.3). The outcomes of the strategy initiation step should build a rich information base for the subsequent strategy formulation part.

4.1 IDENTIFYING YOUR AI ECOSYSTEM

The field of AI is vast, highly branched, and continuously progressing. The recent breakthroughs in the area of generative AI or the rise of autonomous AI agents, for example, have just highlighted this. Indeed, many scholars and practitioners have been surprised by the explosive availability of powerful algorithmic content creation and task assistance tools. Further, the AI landscapes of companies are rapidly growing and getting increasingly

DOI: 10.4324/9781003673170-7

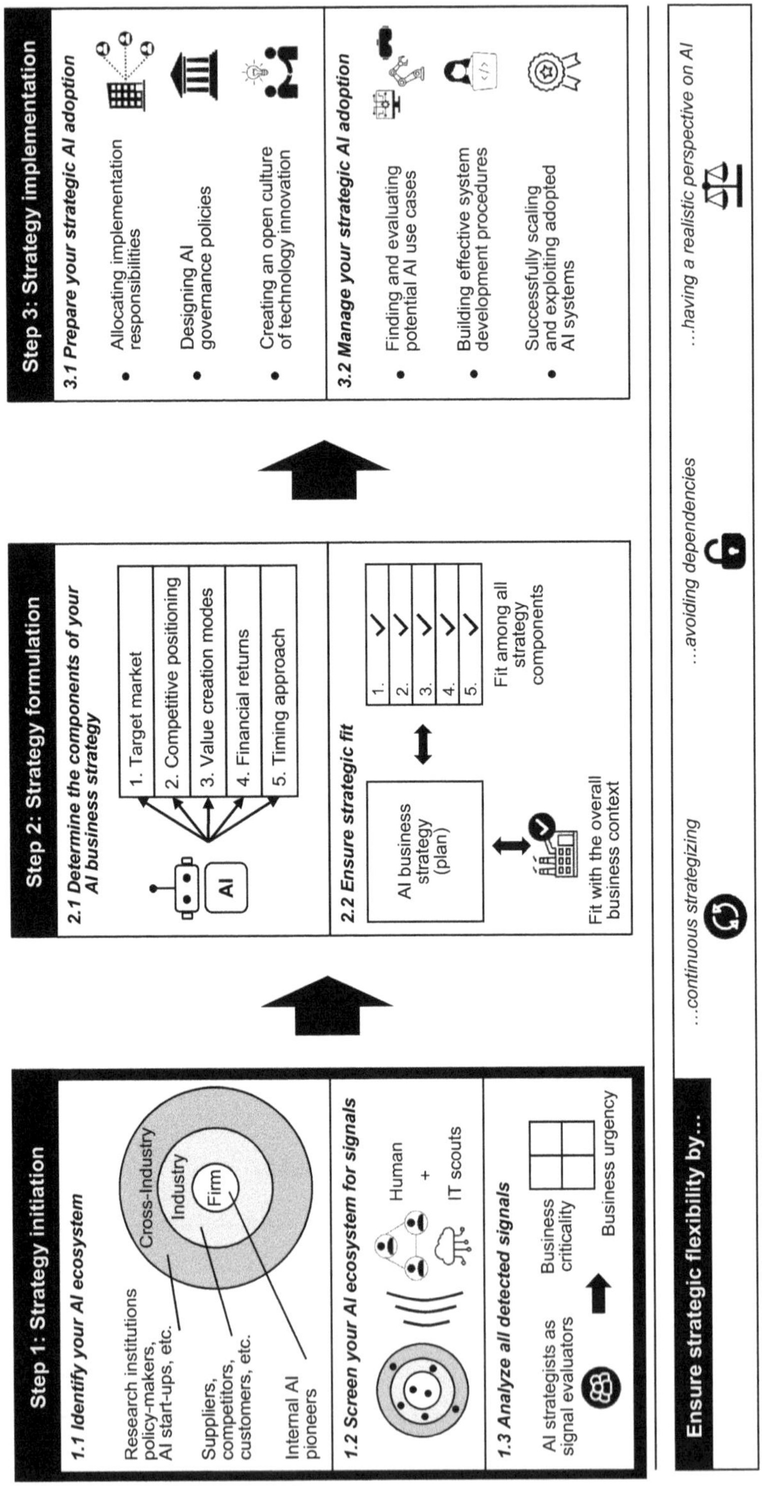

Figure 4.1 The AI Business Strategy Frame© – Step 1

complex. Given the numerous technological opportunities, more and more companies, public institutions, governments, universities, and even individuals are actively engaging with or contributing to the field, thus shaping AI's future development and corresponding business opportunities.

The consequence is that it becomes increasingly challenging for firms to identify and observe their environmental AI landscapes comprehensively. However, doing so is crucial to gaining strategically relevant information for creating an AI business strategy. Without perceiving or, by actively ignoring environmental information, one cannot draft a purposeful strategy that effectively deals with competitive uncertainty.

As we have learned in Section 2.4, all types of possible information sources can send out distinctive, strategically relevant signals.[2] While signals can be about very different themes, they are of strategic interest if they directly affect at least one of the five business strategy components. Hence, to initiate an AI business strategy, a firm is asked to reliably detect and appropriately evaluate relevant signals that reveal how internal and external firm environments currently deal with AI topics. Corresponding AI signals can be about themes like use case ideas, market opportunities, regulations, customer trend shifts, competitor actions, partnerships, technological change, and many other aspects. We will give more signal examples in the following sections.

To detect relevant AI signals, the first step is to systematically identify one's own AI ecosystem, bundling all potentially relevant AI signal sources in a systematic way. In this book, we split an AI ecosystem into three distinctive environmental layers that are well-manageable for every type of company (see Figure 4.2). More precisely, we divide an AI ecosystem into a firm's internal environment, its within-industry environment, and its cross-industry environment. Each of the three layers typically consists of multiple signal sources (that firms might weigh differently). Nevertheless, because of unique business contexts, varying organizational structures, and individual preferences, AI ecosystems can differ significantly among firms.

4.1.1 Finding internal AI signal sources

Internally, relevant AI signals usually originate from two types of employees: those with a technology focus and those with a business task focus (some individuals also combine both attributes). These two types of internal pioneers can provide helpful considerations for shaping an AI business strategy, such as deriving valuable use case ideas (we will explicitly deal with use case identification later in this book), suggesting novel algorithmic

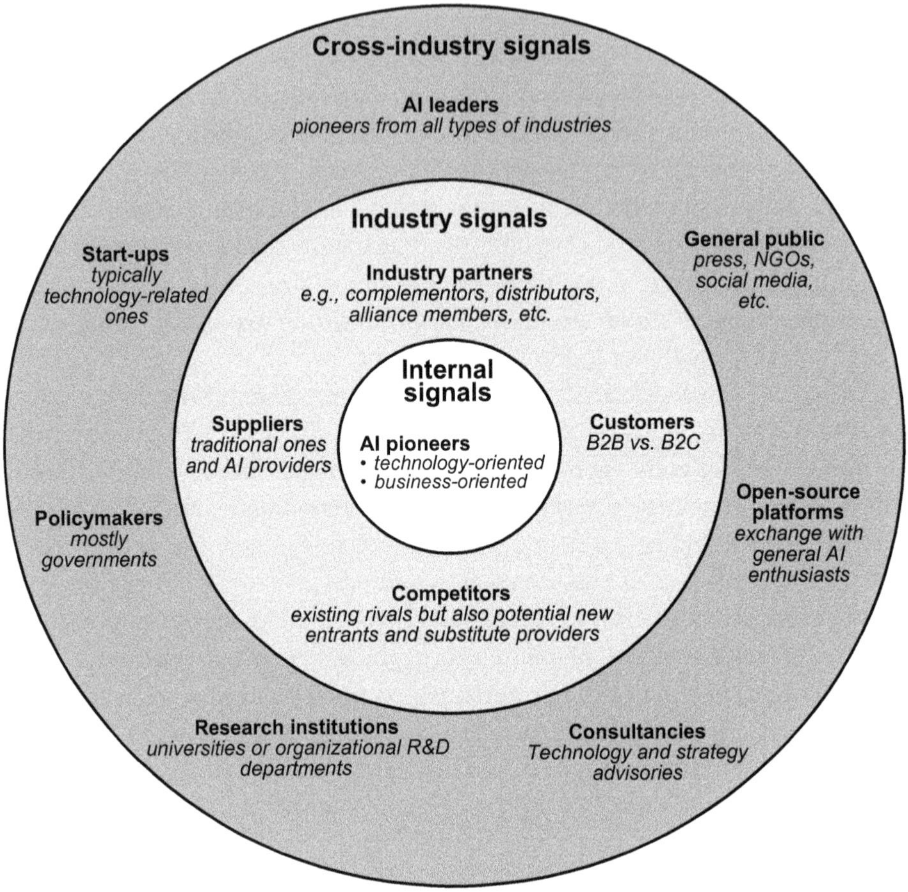

Figure 4.2 Three Environmental Layers of an AI Ecosystem

training methods, or learning about relevant technology management practices. The larger, more diversified, and more international a corporation is, the more pioneers usually exist globally. Firms should generally leverage their company-wide network to identify and engage as many technology- and business-oriented AI pioneers as possible.

Technology-oriented AI pioneers

Technology-oriented AI pioneers are often software developers, IT architects, data scientists, application managers, R&D engineers, system designers, digital transformation managers, etc. Since these groups of employees are typically characterized by their solid IT background, they can, for instance, develop valuable use case ideas to improve organizational processes or enrich market offerings with new technology features. They are also the ones who can perceive technical signals from a firm's IT infrastructure, such as cybersecurity threats, or initiate the internal software development process. The R&D experts of aircraft manufacturer Boeing worked on concepts for accelerating complex product prototyping with digital engineering solutions to provide more convenience for pilots and passengers.[3] These initiatives clearly steered Boeing in line with its AI transformation ambitions, including AI-driven R&D processes and innovative aircraft features to differentiate from competitors.

To encourage AI-driven innovation, some companies establish so-called AI labs where employees from different departments can collaborate, experiment, and co-develop together. These labs can involve participants from various global locations to maximize knowledge-sharing across the organization. An alternative approach is to host internal AI conferences at rotating company spots to foster regular exchange. Another measure is a hackathon. The social media company Pinterest, known for its creativity and art platform, invites internal AI experts to a company-wide hackathon in which different teams develop and pitch their ideas to the management.[4] The most promising ideas are getting a realistic chance for implementation.

Business-oriented AI pioneers

While business-oriented pioneers are the ones dealing with similar tasks daily, they can appear in each functional or regional department worldwide. Hence, they are usually the most capable experts in identifying improvement potentials for a task enabled by self-learning technologies. For that reason, one should actively listen to pioneers who propose improvement

Table 4.1 Examples of Internal AI Signals

Technology-oriented AI pioneers	• An R&D team suggests integrating generative AI modules into existing analog products or legacy software systems • IT experts come up with self-developed algorithms for their own tasks or perceive substantial cybersecurity threats in a certain technology application
Business-oriented AI pioneers	• Employees use available AI systems in innovative ways, although they were initially adopted for other business tasks • Employees find improvement potential with AI for existing inventory management processes and suggest implementing a new AI software feature

ideas, especially for business-central tasks requiring many organizational resources. The same is true if they propose novel product concepts.

A compelling example comes from the global law firm Dechert, where legal professionals recognized that the skills of a machine learning agent could viably support screening potential miscarriages of justice.[5] These pioneers initiated the development of an AI system capable of analyzing vast amounts of legal documents, trial transcripts, and other case records to detect inconsistencies, procedural errors, and overlooked evidence. As a result, Dechert was able to accelerate such legal review processes significantly.

Another interesting case is Google, which actively encourages employees from all types of company units to foster internal innovation. More precisely, Google has a 20% initiative, allowing employees to work 20% of their weekly work time on side projects that interest them but are not directly related to their work. Many of these projects refer to hypothetical process improvements, product ideas, or collaboration synergies.[6] For example, Google AdSense, the online algorithmic advertisement tool, resulted from the 20% time procedure.

4.1.2 Finding industry-specific AI signal sources

Beyond internal sources, firms must also monitor potential AI signals emerging from their industry environment, known as the micro-environment. Since industries consist of multiple key players, each can generate strategically relevant signals that influence the content and outcomes of an AI business strategy.[7] In the following, we briefly discuss the most essential ones, including suppliers, competitors, customers, and partners.

Suppliers

Suppliers typically send out signals about new offerings or collaboration opportunities. For example, introducing a new AI-based inventory management system by a supplier might offer the potential to better organize one's inventory by initiating just-in-time deliveries. Another example is a supply-chain disruption. For instance, the global semiconductor chip shortage triggered by the COVID-19 pandemic posed heavy challenges for many electronic device manufacturers that integrated AI modules into their products. Proactively anticipating such risks allows firms to act quickly or prepare in advance.

Relatedly, in the technology realm, it is necessary to look at competency providers or IT vendors offering pre-trained machine learning models, consulting services, and infrastructure like cloud computing. Over the last few years, more and more technology suppliers have appeared in industry markets. For example, fashion retailer Victoria's Secret acquired a Google chatbot solution, helping to suggest personalized product recommendations and facilitate online shopping processes.[8] While many suppliers claim to have the best AI products or services, we always recommend thoroughly assessing them and their offerings. Avoid initial long-term commitments. Start with testing or piloting phases before signing long-term contracts.

Competitors

Other critical signals come from competitors trying to strategically adopt and leverage AI systems to gain competitive and financial advantages over you. Therefore, it is crucial to proactively observe their plans and ongoing activities to avoid bad surprises. One way to do so is benchmarking, which compares your core business processes and market offerings with those of industry competitors. Some guiding questions could be: "Where is competitor X currently using AI?", "What have they announced to do with AI in the future?", "How do we differentiate?", or "What else could they do that they have not announced yet?". Remarkably, the ignorance or rejection of a competitor to invest in a particular AI product function or competency could also be a very relevant signal, implying first-mover opportunities.

However, competitor signals are not just about AI adoption but about every AI-related topic thinkable. For instance, an M&A deal might signal that a competitor aggressively leverages its internal knowledge in a particular technology domain. US fashion retailer Gap Inc. acquired a promising AI start-up that worked on improving sales and inventory management processes with machine learning.[9] Other fashion firms responded with comparable acquisitions over time. Another signal could be a new flagship partnership between a competitor and specific technology providers, as seen in the Victoria's Secret example. Similarly, one should be alarmed when multiple competitors sign a strategic alliance to pool training data[10] or share other types of AI resources. Volkswagen and Ford have entered into such a partnership to co-develop autonomous vehicles.[11] Whereas competitors will try not to disclose their strategic AI endeavors, getting a realistic idea of what competitors are doing with AI and what they are not doing is crucial.

Competitor signals might also result from potential new entrants as well as firms that are planning to enter an industry with the help of AI. Technology-enabled diversifications are particularly observable for big tech firms. Amazon, for example, has intensively entered the healthcare industry over the last few years. It has embedded Amazon One Medical, a membership-based primary care service that combines in-person clinics with AI-powered telehealth solutions to provide convenient and personalized healthcare offerings remotely.[12] Predictive, generative, and combined AI modules are used for appointment scheduling, virtual consultations, the generation of treatment plans, and data-driven patient analyses.

Firms producing potential AI-driven substitutes can be of interest, too. For instance, technological functions can sometimes make analog products and services obsolete, at least to some extent. An AI-powered language app makes traditional language tutoring services less relevant.

At this point, we would like to highlight the need to be aware of the signals that your firm sends to competitors. In other words, one must be careful not to disclose strategically relevant signals about oneself. Sending out signals, consciously or unconsciously, might significantly threaten the realization of strategic advantage, as competitors can better prepare themselves or start imitating you.

Customers

Business (B2B) and private customers (B2C) are fundamentally relevant signal sources. For example, market preferences and societal trends are powerful indicators of where R&D investments should be directed. Many consumers actively seek AI-driven technology functions to enhance convenience, personalization, entertainment, simplification, and so on, highlighting their increasing preference for intelligent machines in their daily lives. By closely monitoring customer behavior and feedback, firms can extract existing and upcoming needs of regional and global markets. Ways to do so are conducting customer surveys, exhibiting at industry fairs, analyzing social media comments, or connecting to lead users, that is, consumers who experience emerging wishes and desires ahead of the broader market.

An illustrative example of incorporating customer signals comes from the photography industry. Software company Adobe recognized a growing demand for AI-powered tools to simplify photo editing.[13] In response, it developed several predictive and generative AI modules that allow users to remove unwanted objects, insert new things, or automatically adjust lighting conditions in images. Today, these features are in high demand and are continuously advanced by Adobe with iterative customer feedback loops.

Industry partners

Signals can also come from industry partners, including firms that offer, for instance, research or sales partnerships. Another partner option is the complementor, a company that offers products or services that enhance the value of another firm's products or services when both are used or consumed together. When complementors introduce AI functionalities into their products, new opportunities arise for seamless AI integration and data network effects. Nike designs running shoes with embedded sensors that can be synchronized with sports smartwatches. This complementation allows athletes to accurately track real-time performance metrics like pace and distance.

4.1.3 Finding cross-industry AI signal sources

Lastly, critical AI signals can also emerge outside an organization's core industry, better known as its macro-environment. This means expanding one's own perspective outside the regular business to detect relevant cross-industry trends. Since firms should identify and monitor several macro-environmental signal sources, let us quickly review the most common ones.

Table 4.2 Examples of Industry-Specific AI Signals

Suppliers	• A supplier installs a new AI system with which the procurement or logistics department might be able to connect • A new AI service provider with better or cheaper offerings appears
Competitors	• The biggest competitor announces substantial investments to digitize its internal R&D department to develop innovative AI-based products • Competitors create a joint venture to pool algorithmic training data
Customers	• A customer survey reveals an increasing demand for complementary AI services that increase the value of analog products • Lead users specify how a digital product should look in the future
Industry partners	• Complementors create a novel AI platform that might enable data network effects with existing offerings • Distributors are open to sharing customer data to improve algorithmic sales planning and production schedules

AI leaders

An important group within the macro-environment represents AI leaders, including all firms that are at the forefront of digital transformation. From these AI leaders, one can identify promising best practices and impactful use case ideas, learn competencies, or perceive other relevant lessons for an AI business strategy. It is essential to consider that AI leaders are not limited to big tech companies like Amazon, Google, Microsoft, Alibaba, and Tencent. Many AI front-runners exist in other types of businesses, such as Tesla in automotive, Siemens in industrial engineering, and JPMorgan in financial services. They all drive AI innovation by integrating advanced machine learning into their core processes and market offerings.

Technology start-ups

Technology start-ups, particularly those located in interconnected clusters, are impactful AI trailblazers. Their agility and entrepreneurial mindset often lead to cutting-edge AI applications that disrupt existing market offerings or internal business operations. By leveraging rapid experimentation and a willingness to take business risks, start-ups push the boundaries of AI innovation in ways that larger, more established firms may struggle to match. In other words, they are a breeding ground for innovations. Many established firms collaborate or experiment with start-ups to foster innovation outside the constraints of rigid corporate structures. Further, they are a prominent acquisition target for transferring novel AI competencies or patents in-house.

Policymakers

Also, policymakers like governments can send out critical AI signals. A good example underlining this is the proclaimed EU AI Act.[14] Specifically, this act is a multifaceted regulatory framework introduced by the European Union to ensure the safe and ethically correct development, deployment, and scaling of state-of-the-art AI systems. For example, the act classifies AI systems based on regulatory risk levels, ranging from minimal to high-level risk. Based on that, algorithmic standards regarding transparency, bias mitigation, and cybersecurity must be committed to and reported. High-risk task contexts, such as health care or law enforcement, are especially affected by the EU AI Act.

Research institutions

Staying connected with public and private research institutions, especially those specializing in AI, can be highly beneficial. Observing ongoing academic and industry research can provide early insights into emerging technological breakthroughs and innovative adoption ideas. This means staying tuned for academic publications or conferences. Furthermore, collaborating with leading technology or management universities can offer knowledge advantages and valuable recruitment opportunities to grow internal AI competencies.

Partnering with the research departments of private technology firms can enable knowledge sharing and resource pooling as well. Over the years, many companies with a strategic interest in AI have formed official partnerships with major tech firms. For example, consumer goods giant Unilever partnered with Microsoft to enhance virtual global laboratory services to streamline its biochemical R&D initiatives.[15]

Consultancies

In addition, it is valuable to watch out for news from prominent technology and strategy consultancy firms. Due to their continuous project business, consultancies typically have a good understanding and overview of industry-independent best practices and the most critical challenges. Connecting with them through partnerships, industry events, or research collaborations can help firms gain insights into emerging technology trends, innovative business models, and practical system implementation. Moreover, consultancies often provide thought leadership on regulatory developments and ethical considerations, ensuring companies stay ahead of compliance requirements and societal changes. Besides, they can offer good recruiting opportunities as well.

Open-source platforms

Engagement with open-source platforms allows firms to connect to interdisciplinary technology experts to exchange novel ideas, data, or model components. These platforms not only facilitate knowledge sharing but also enable firms to experiment with AI models, often for free. By tapping into a global or local community of technology experts, companies can accelerate their AI development and stay ahead of emerging field trends, similar to a lead user approach.

Interestingly, technology firms sometimes share information or AI models on open-source platforms, too. For example, by releasing TensorFlow, a widely used machine learning library, Google has significantly contributed to the tech community. The TensorFlow ecosystem provides pre-trained models, example code, and access to popular training datasets, allowing developers and researchers to build AI systems efficiently without starting from scratch. By openly sharing knowledge and software development tools, firms support technological progress, establish themselves as experts, attract top talent, and encourage responsible use of AI across different sectors.

Table 4.3 Examples of Cross-Industry AI Signals

AI leaders	• A logistics company implements autonomous transportation trolleys for its distribution centers, which manufacturing firms could imitate • Well-known high-tech companies present their latest AI patents at firm conferences
Start-ups	• A promising technology start-up receives significant venture funding • Multiple start-ups form a resource-sharing technology cluster to mutually exchange their knowledge
Policymakers	• New ethical AI regulations are announced by a government, impacting current compliance practices and obligations • More strict AI auditing and reporting requirements are mandated for businesses
Research institutions	• A university highlights its technological breakthrough in one AI subfield, for example, via academic publications or conference presentations • A growing number of institutions converge on a specific research stream
Consultancies	• A major consultancy published its annual AI adoption report, showcasing the most significant technological trends it has seen in its projects • A consultancy is looking for cooperation partners for conducting a large-scale country survey
Open-source platforms	• A new large language model becomes publicly available on a free platform • Active discussions with enthusiastic AI experts in online communities suggest novel use case ideas
General public	• A public backlash against a company for its unethical AI use reveals reputational risks in the case of mutual collaboration • Social media posts indicate an increasing hype for a specific technology product function

General public

Another signal source is the general public. In fact, public debates or newspaper articles on AI privacy concerns or job displacement fears can shape the way people think about the technology. Additionally, discussions in online forums or on social media platforms can highlight emerging societal expectations and preferences. Even non-governmental organizations (NGOs) can influence common AI adoption by highlighting individuals' ethical attitudes. One should never underestimate the influence of the general public on how companies develop and deploy AI solutions internally and externally. A negative reputation, for instance, can lead to substantial sales decreases.

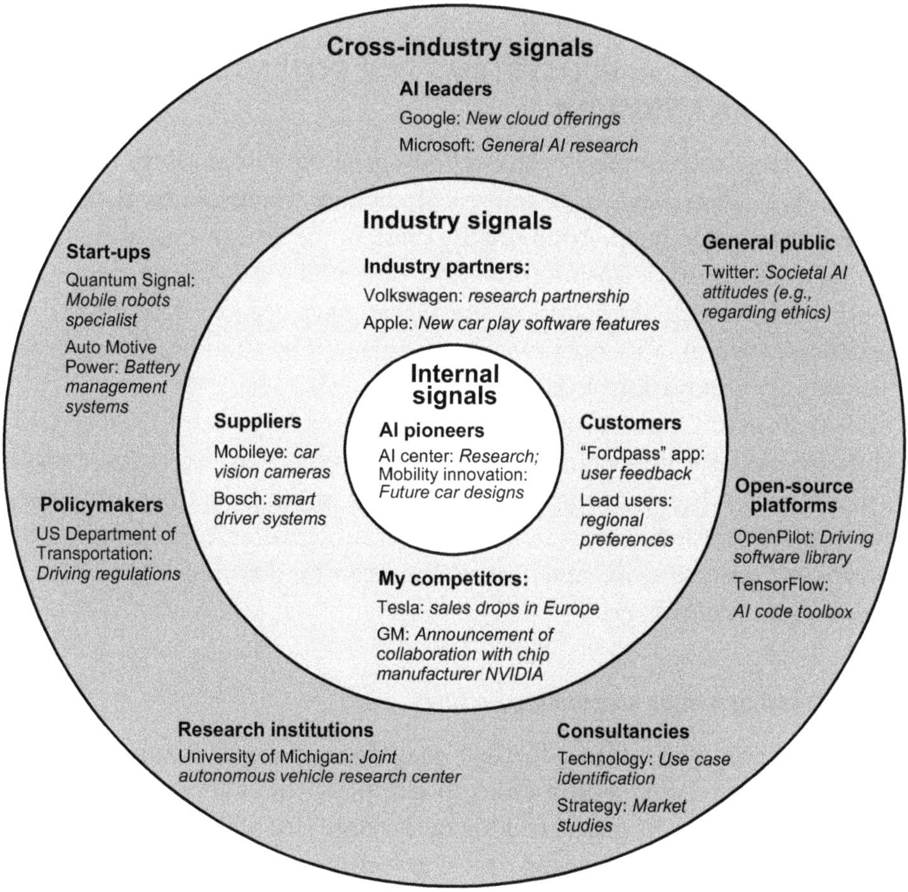

Figure 4.3 Exemplary Signal Sources within the AI Ecosystem of Ford

A real-world example of an AI ecosystem

As an illustration, Figure 4.3 demonstrates a brief overview of some key signal sources in the AI ecosystem of American car manufacturer Ford. While the company's real AI ecosystem is, in reality, even more complex, the examples given are intended to help you better understand and screen your own environments for relevant key players.

Once again, we would like to emphasize that AI ecosystems among firms can vary significantly. While there are often different players for each presented source in the three environmental layers (firms have multiple suppliers, competitors, perceived AI leaders, etc.), firms can weigh their relevance very heterogeneously. We always recommend considering as many signal sources as possible since strategically relevant information could appear everywhere, and the costs of missing important signals could be very high retrospectively.

4.2 SCREENING AI ECOSYSTEMS FOR POTENTIALLY RELEVANT SIGNALS

Typically, large and complex AI ecosystems generate vast amounts of diverse signals. Yet, firms have only limited attentional resources to detect and process them effectively. Additionally, there is the risk of cognitive biases leading to disregard or misinterpretation, potentially skewing strategic decision-making. Overlooking critical signals can have negative long-term consequences, such as a competitive disadvantage when failing to recognize new industry innovations in time.

For that reason, firms require a very structured approach to screen their AI ecosystems for important signals. According to that, we suggest that a firm use both types of scouts to detect signals, meaning human employees and available information systems. Moreover, signal screening must be a continuous process since new information can be detected everywhere in an ecosystem at any time.

4.2.1 *Creating human screening structures*

As a first step, with respect to their available resources, firms must allocate clear screening responsibilities to competent human scouts, who are most often internal AI pioneers. Due to the large size of AI ecosystems, one has to clarify who is responsible for connecting to which type of sources. Generally, one can distinguish between centralized, decentralized, and hub-and-spoke screening structures that humans can build.

Centralized signal screening

A centralized screening structure is characterized by a principal technology scouting department, that is, an AI hub, seeking and bundling all relevant AI signals from internal and external firm environments. This department consists of different technology experts who collectively focus on each of the three ecosystem layers. Thus, the specialized AI hub is the only or most crucial firm entity that tries to ensure that all types of signals are detected and discussed. AI hubs act company-wide, typically on a global basis, and directly report to the middle or top management. Therefore, they are located within or close to the headquarters.

Among firms, central AI hubs have very different names. Examples could be an AI center of excellence, a machine learning hub, an AI innovation cluster, an AI transformation office, etc. While some firms have stand-alone AI hubs, others unify different kinds of innovative technology topics in a central department. For example, the French electrical goods corporation, Schneider Electric, deals with AI topics within its "global center of excellence in innovation," and also with other technology trends like new energy systems or blockchain.[16]

Decentralized signal screening

An alternative approach would be a decentralized screening structure. This approach concentrates on the individual network connections of specific business functions and regional firm departments to perceive potentially relevant AI signals locally. Correspondingly, it is a more flexible screening structure that trusts the competencies and interests of individuals instead of bundling all knowledge in a static hub.

For example, R&D employees can bundle all internal product development ideas company-wide. Individuals from the marketing department might be the best to perceive whether specific competitors are increasingly adopting AI for customer service. Also, IT managers can suggest valuable partnerships with technology providers they have worked with. Legal departments may be best informed about AI-specific regulations that will likely come up in the near future. Amazon, for instance, is proud of its flexible structures as they leave sufficient space for firm departments to drive technology initiatives independently, thus fostering a heterogeneous and creative work culture.[17]

Hub-and-spoke signal screening

A third approach is the combination of both centralized and decentralized structures, resulting in a hub-and-spoke system. This model consists

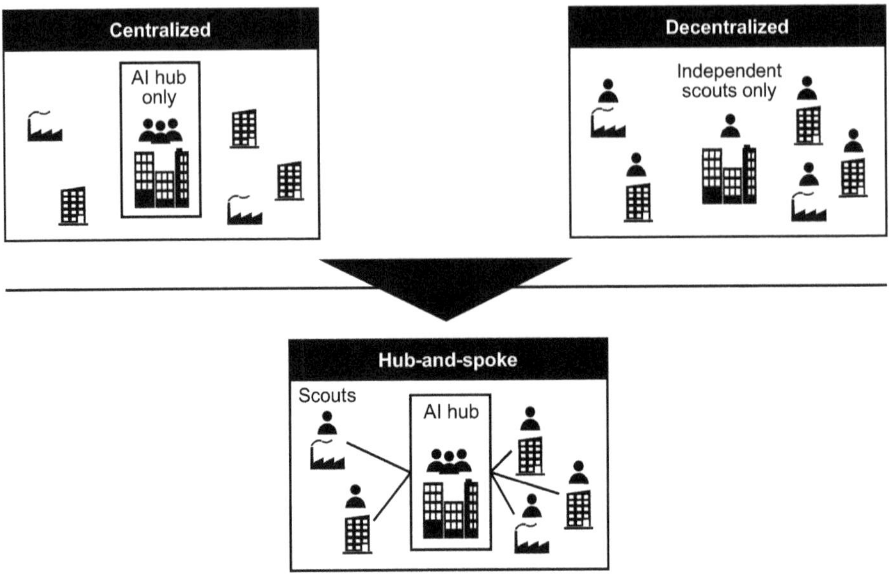

Figure 4.4 Different Signal Screening Structures

of a centralized company-wide technology scouting department that gets additional signal information provided by decentralized experts from different business functions that are much closer to specific ecosystem sources. Hence, it unifies the benefits of centralized and decentralized scouting approaches. Nevertheless, the hub requires strong coordination and communication skills to ensure that all spokes work effectively, are aligned with each other, and frequently forward relevant signals to avoid redundant or inappropriate screening processes.

4.2.2 *Creating supportive technology screening structures*

In addition, firms can also use information systems, AI-driven or not, to support human signal scouts because the usage of digital infrastructure can strongly facilitate signal screening. A firm's various digital IT systems can gather valuable information about potential internal and external environmental changes. Furthermore, one can design novel systems that explicitly focus on signal-screening tasks. Let us explain these ideas in more detail.

Using existing technology systems

On the one hand, a firm should leverage its existing technology landscape to detect potential signals. This includes very different information systems across firm departments, many of which have not been initially designed for signal screening tasks.

For example, an uptick in AI-related discussions within internal knowledge management systems could indicate the emergence of new product opportunities or suggest the need to modify existing products with better-trained AI modules due to potential software bugs. Some firms allow employees to anonymously submit improvement ideas regarding their daily tasks or business processes via electronic mailboxes, often hosted on the company intranet. Furthermore, certain IT interfaces enable direct data exchange with external organizations such as suppliers, partners, customers, and even research institutions or start-ups in the context of collaborations.

However, while externally connected systems can offer valuable insights into potential environmental changes, there may be a trade-off between detecting novel signals and inadvertently disclosing strategically sensitive information to other organizations through this data pipeline. Consider a manufacturing company that connected its supply-chain management system with key semiconductor suppliers to enable real-time inventory updates. Whereas the firm can anticipate raw material shortages early on, this interface could expose new AI product developments, production schedules, customer details, etc., to the supplier. Depending on the supplier, this can be critical. Therefore, one must always consider the consequences of knowledge spillover, cybersecurity, and legal threats.

Acquiring new technology systems

On the other hand, acquiring new technology systems explicitly tailored for signal screening tasks could also be worthwhile. In particular, machine learning systems have proved to be highly applicable to signal screening tasks. Self-learning AI systems can directly learn about ecosystems and, therefore, be applied to observe interesting signal sources and predict future changes, addressing customer trends or promising research avenues.

For instance, according to its text and numerical analysis capabilities, AI agents can be trained to search for important signals in publicly available data on the internet. The AI agent can screen massive amounts of online news, social media posts, discussion forums, press releases, etc. All identified signals can be aggregated, evaluated, and shared with human scouts afterwards.

As mentioned before, humans are typically better at dealing with uncertainty or extraordinary influence factors than artificial machine agents. The result is that human scouts should always be in the lead or have at least the chance to intervene to decide whether a signal is really of relevance for a firm or not.

4.3 STRATEGICALLY EVALUATING DETECTED AI SIGNALS

When a firm has thoroughly screened its AI ecosystem, the next step is to evaluate the strategic impact of each signal. This evaluation is crucial because not all signals convey essential or correct information for formulating an AI business strategy. Some signals may be misleading, outdated, or irrelevant to your business context. The challenge is to filter out non-relevant signals and interpret the key implications of the remaining ones. To do so, one must combine the knowledge of different AI strategists within a firm.

4.3.1 *Finding competent AI strategists*

Effectively analyzing and evaluating potentially relevant signals requires a multifaceted approach incorporating existing strategy, operational process, and technology perspectives. Therefore, involving diverse AI strategists to bundle their knowledge in the signal evaluation process is advisable. Specifically, we suggest including experts from all management levels of an organization, including the lower, middle, and top management.[18] This approach promotes critical reflection and guards against biased or premature interpretations of key signals. You should consider hiring new staff or involving external consultancy support if you lack enough experts within one of these three different management levels.

AI strategists from the lower management

First, one should involve experts from the lower management. These types of AI strategists bring essential hands-on expertise with them, as they directly oversee daily business operations and are deeply familiar with core processes across critical value chain functions. Their insights are crucial for assessing the practical implications of different AI signals, ensuring that strategic decisions align with operational realities.

Additionally, AI strategists within a firm's IT department play a pivotal role in evaluating the benefits, feasibility, and cost implications of AI signals. Their technical know-how allows them, for instance, to assess system integration challenges, infrastructure requirements, or scalability potential. Similarly, the previously mentioned technology scouts located in central AI hubs or within decentralized company functions can provide outstanding evaluation competencies as they are directly interacting with signal sources on a daily basis.

AI strategists from the middle management

Second, middle managers overseeing key value chain functions or large regional subsidiaries are important AI strategists, especially when central to a firm's key value creation modes. With their knowledge, experience, and network, middle managers are most capable of understanding what will work and what will not in their specific firm department. They are aware of best practices, internal competencies, or existing transformation challenges like resource constraints or human technology rejection. Furthermore, their deep knowledge of operational workflows allows them to pinpoint existing inefficiencies for which AI could generate true strategic impact. That could include projects from all areas, such as automating production processes, optimizing supply-chains, enhancing customer service interactions, using AI for internal cost-controlling tasks, and so on.

In sum, the competencies of middle managers help bridge the gap between high-level strategic objectives and day-to-day business processes. They are prone to evaluating the operative and strategic impact of AI signals simultaneously.

AI strategists from the top management

A third relevant group is related to the top management, which usually refers to the management board. In particular, besides CEOs, CIOs and their staff are particularly essential AI signal evaluators because they have the overall strategic responsibility of adopting IT systems. However, due to the rise of intelligent machines, more and more firms have created additional top management or board positions explicitly dedicated to AI technologies, such as

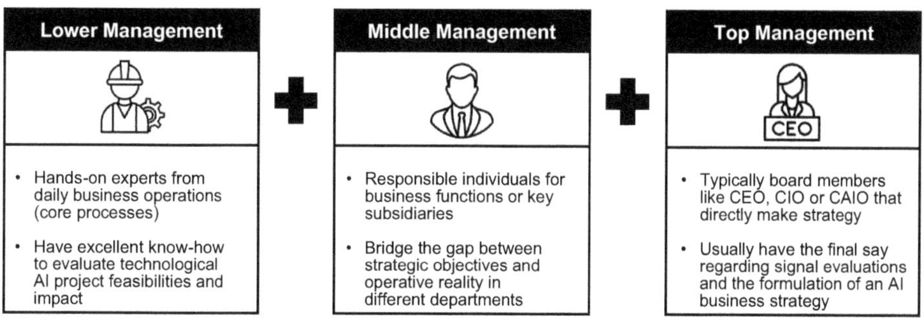

Figure 4.5 Types of Necessary AI Strategists

the Chief AI Officer (CAIO), Chief Data Officer (CDO), and Chief Digital Transformation Officer (CDTO).[19]

While the top management and their strategy offices usually have the final say, they must continuously stay in direct exchange with other signal evaluators from the lower and middle management, as their time and attentional capacity is limited. Overall, the interplay of lower, middle, and top managers should consider both bottom-up and top-down directions. Whereas the bottom-up approach allows the consideration of operative business knowledge regarding central activities, the top-down approach ensures a strategic alignment with the overall business goals of a firm.

4.3.2 Assessing the strategic relevance of signals

Not all detected AI signals provide important information for formulating an effective AI business strategy. Only with a team of competent AI strategists from the lower, middle, and top management in place one can systematically assess the strategic relevance of the detected insights (this information will become crucial for formulating an AI business strategy, as shown in Chapter 5). Ultimately, we suggest the usage of two key dimensions to determine the strategic relevance of an AI signal (see Figure 4.6).

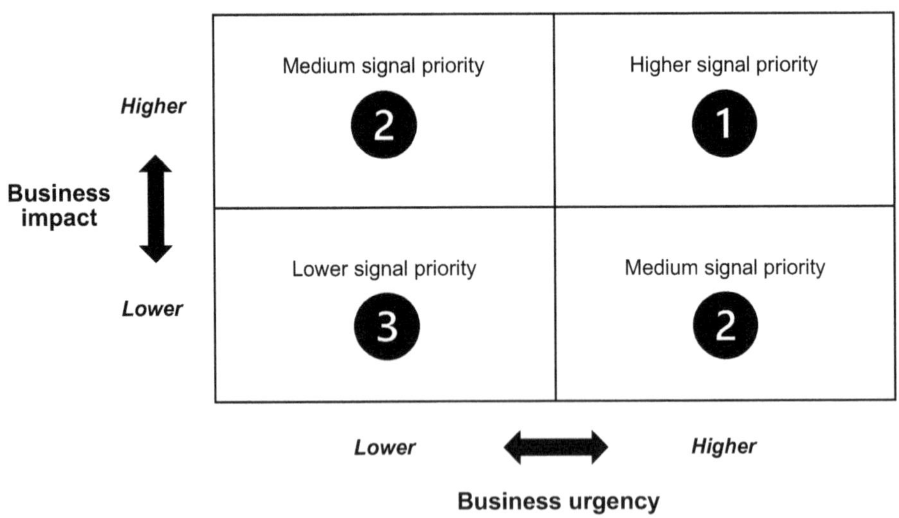

Figure 4.6 The AI Signal Evaluation Matrix

Signal evaluation criteria

One suggested criterion is the level of business impact, determining the extent to which an AI signal has the ability to disrupt the components of an existing business strategy or provide opportunities to create a novel technology-driven one (e.g., for entering a new market). The greater the extent to which an AI signal influences one or multiple strategy components, the higher its overall business impact and implications for strategy-making.

A second criterion is the level of business urgency, which reflects the time-criticality required for a firm to respond appropriately to a certain AI signal. Whereas some signals require immediate action, others might highlight long-term developments that one should be aware of but have no immediacy to act on. The faster one has to respond to a signal, the higher its overall business urgency. Very urgent signals might need a response within the next days or weeks. In contrast, one could wait months or even years for less urgent signals, depending on the prioritization of other signals and available resources.

As a result, one obtains a 2×2 matrix when combining the two dimensions. Ultimately, AI signals characterized by higher levels of both business impact and urgency have the highest strategic priority. In other words, an AI business strategy must be thoroughly built on the information these signals communicate. Afterward, those signals characterized by either a higher impact or urgency should be approached as they typically have a medium priority. However, the largest signal group is usually shaped by a lower business impact and urgency, presenting a lower priority level. Nonetheless, these signals can still provide insights for an AI business strategy today or gain much more relevance over time.

To further illustrate the signal evaluation process, we will provide some examples for each of the four matrix fields (see Figure 4.7). Let us go through them sequentially.

Examples of signal evaluations

An example of an AI signal characterized by both higher levels of business impact and urgency can be technological breakthroughs or the market availability of new types of AI systems. When, in November 2022, OpenAI released its first version of ChatGPT, many firms were surprised by its technological capabilities. From there on, a fast-paced race started to immediately implement novel generative AI modules to gain product or process-related first-mover advantages.

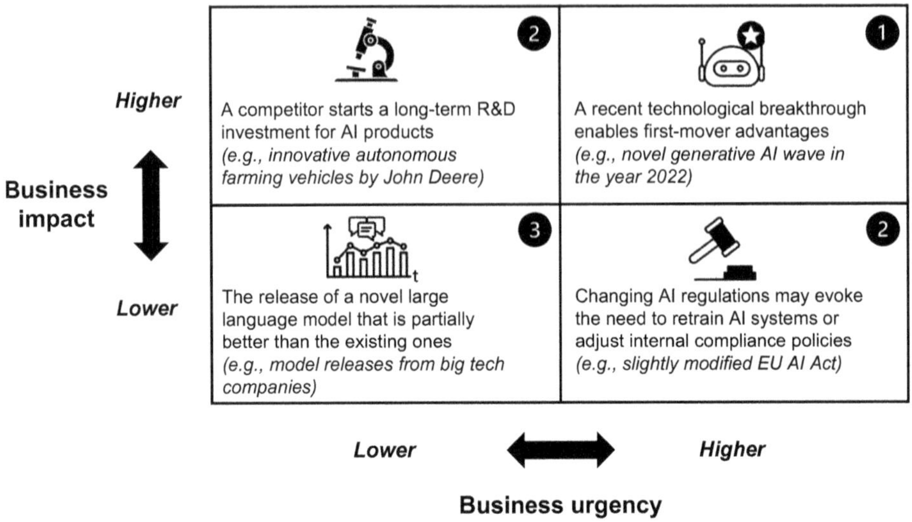

Figure 4.7 Exemplary Evaluation of AI Signals

A signal shaped by higher levels of business impact but lower levels of business urgency could be a competitor's announcement to start long-term R&D investments into new AI innovations. While it will often take time for the competitor to launch very new technology offerings, if successful at all, it could significantly impact the market share of a focal firm in the long run. For example, agricultural technology company John Deere started to undergo long-term investments focusing on autonomous farming vehicles, forcing competitors to think about similar endeavors.[20]

In contrast, a signal with a lower business impact but higher urgency might be about slightly changing AI regulations. When adjusted data protection or transparency standards become mandatory, firms must modify their existing or planned AI systems for compliance, especially in the case of a machine learning system trained on data that must not be used anymore. Consequently, changing regulations could indicate significant retraining efforts or eliminating new use case ideas.[21] Such issues have already happened with AI systems trained on social media content or personal customer data without the explicit permission of affected individuals.

An example of an AI signal characterized by both lower business impact and urgency could be the release of a novel large language model with slightly improved performance compared to its predecessors or competing alternatives. In many cases, transitioning to a newer model does not profoundly affect strategic planning. Still, as large language models become increasingly integrated into firm applications such as chatbots, document search tools, or customer support automation, adopting a new model can provide operational benefits that one should consider.

4.4 CHAPTER SUMMARY

- Firms must identify their individual *AI ecosystem* to extract strategically relevant information from internal and external environments. While AI ecosystems can look very different, we recommend observing three distinctive environmental layers:
  - *Internal signals* typically result from technology- and business-oriented AI pioneers within the firm.
  - *Industry-specific signals* are primarily detected from suppliers, competitors, customers, or partners.
  - *Cross-industry signals* are derived from research institutions, technology and strategy consultancies, open-source platforms, technological AI leaders from any industry, technology start-ups, policymakers like governments, and the general public.
- Firms should use *human scouts* supported by available *technology systems* to detect potentially relevant signals from ecosystem sources.
  - Human screening agents can be installed in *centralized* (e.g., AI hub) and *decentralized* (individual firm functions) *screening structures.* A combination of both in the form of a *hub-and-spoke structure* is also possible.
  - Firms can use their *existing IT systems* and acquire *new IT systems* (incl. machine learning systems) that are explicitly designed for signal screening tasks.
- To assess the strategic relevance of detected signals, one needs to find *competent AI strategists* who check signals for their strategic relevance.
  - Fitting strategists should be found in *lower*, *middle*, and *top management* positions.
  - AI signals should be evaluated for their *business impact* and *business urgency*. The results provide essential information on what to concentrate on when formulating an AI business strategy.

4.5 HANDS-ON PRACTICE

Please identify the individual AI ecosystem layers of your selected case company (Worksheet 4). You should find multiple relevant internal, industry-specific, and cross-industry signal sources. Whereas you can use the Ford example as an inspiration (see Figure 4.3), we encourage you to take time and collect as many potential signal sources as possible. That effort is worth it because missing relevant signals may impede strategy formulation or implementation later on.

AI ecosystems should be screened continuously. Hence, your next task is assigning clear screening responsibilities for all identified signal sources in your existing AI ecosystem (Worksheet 5). For this, think about appropriate human screening structures (i.e., centralized, decentralized, or hub-and-spoke structures) and how existing or new technology systems can support human scouts. We have also included a column for this worksheet where you can note some exemplary detected signals.

Worksheet 6 is about the evaluation of detected signals with competent AI strategists. Start by identifying individuals or teams from the lower, middle, and top management responsible for strategically dealing with AI or who have the necessary competencies and a strong motivation. The identified pool of individuals should sufficiently represent all three management groups.

As soon as competent AI strategists are found, it is time to evaluate the strategic relevance of your detected AI signals. Accordingly, fill out the 2×2 matrix that includes the dimensions of business impact and business urgency. Doing so substantially helps you prioritize each signal's relevance for the strategy formulation phase in the next chapter.

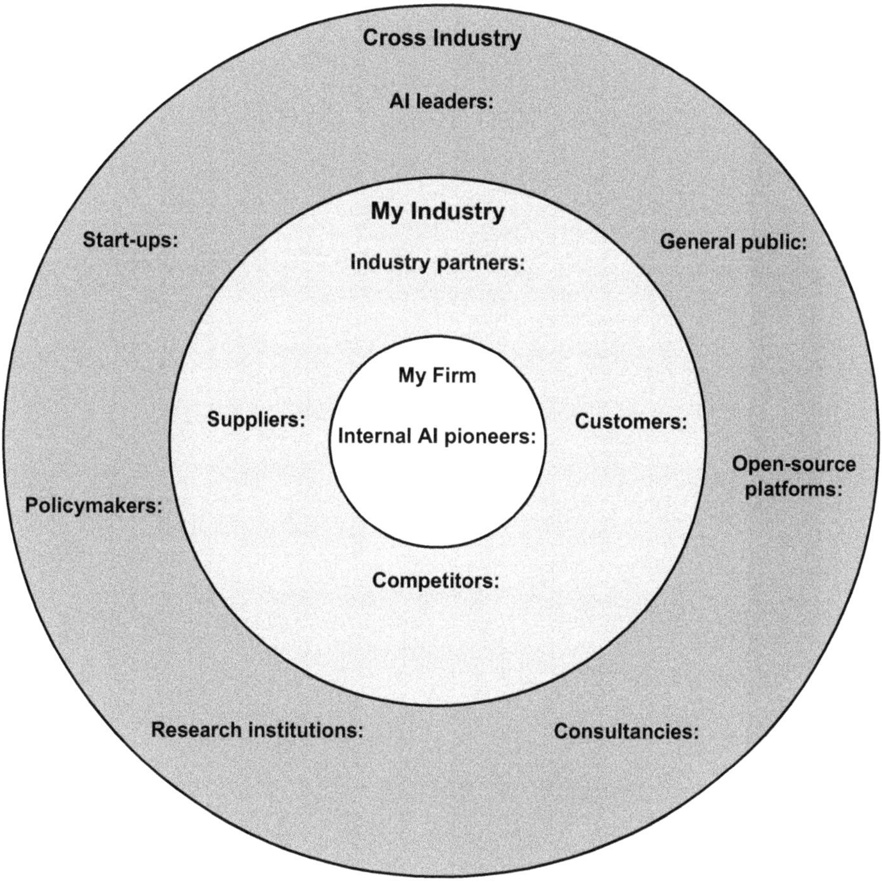

Worksheet 4 What Is Your AI Ecosystem?

Ecosystem layers	Signal sources	Responsible human scouts *(e.g., divisions, teams, individuals)*	Supporting IT systems *(existing or new ones)*	Detected signals *(short description)*
Internal environment	Technology-oriented AI pioneers			
	Business-oriented AI pioneers			
Within-industry environment	Suppliers			
	Competitors			
	Customers			
	Industry partners			
Outside-industry environment	AI leaders			
	Start-ups			
	Policy-makers			
	Research institutions			
	Consultancies			
	Open-source platforms			
	General public			

Worksheet 5 Who Screens Your AI Ecosystem for Signals?

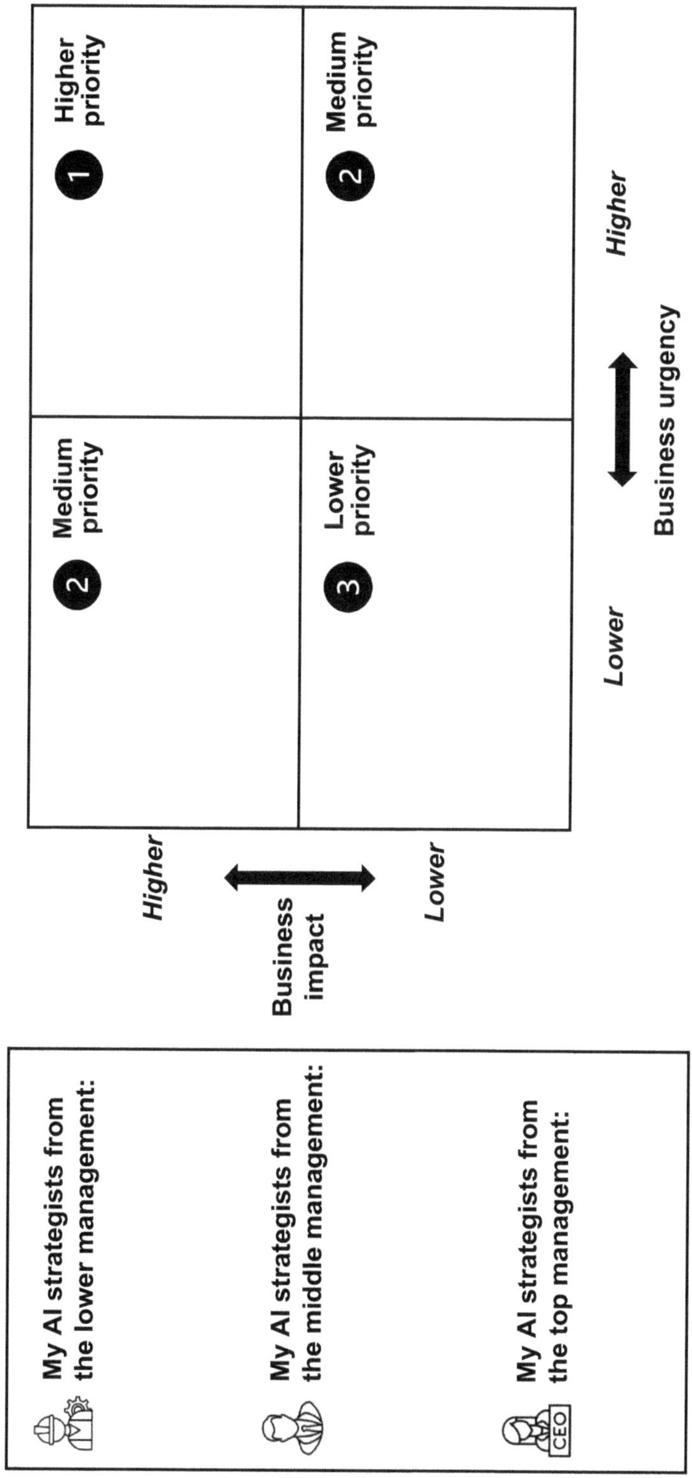

Worksheet 6 How Do You Evaluate Your Detected AI Signals?

NOTES

1 Werner, J., "Pondering Sam Altman's Age of Intelligence Essay", *Forbes*, September 24, 2024, available at https://www.forbes.com/sites/johnwerner/2024/09/25/pondering-sam-altmans-age-of-intelligence-essay/.
2 Signal sources can send out very different messages, all of which might be of higher or lower strategic relevance for a firm.
3 See "Let's Connect: Digital Thread Advances Manufacturing", *Boeing*, October 28, 2022, available at https://www.boeing.com/innovation/innovation-quarterly/2022/10/let-s-connect-digital-thread-advances-manufacturing.
4 Chandonnet, H., "When Pinterest Needs New AI Tools, Employees Can Have a Part in Creating Them", *Business Insider*, May 21, 2025, available at https://www.businessinsider.com/pinterest-hackathons-makeathon-employees-lead-generative-ai-tools-innovation-2025–5.
5 More details on the case are provided by Arnold, H., "Intrapreneurs: The Insiders on a Mission to Change Law Firms", *Financial Times*, December 10, 2024, available at https://www.ft.com/content/cf319e9a-575a-4c27-bce6–099afd5d7a63?.
6 Aksu, H., "Google's Innovation Culture: Fueling Creativity and Disruption in the Digital Age", *Digitopia*, October 4, 2024, available at https://digitopia.co/blog/google-innovation-culture/.
7 For more information about different industry players, see Porter, M. E., *Competitive Strategy: Techniques for Analyzing Industries and Competitors: With a New Introduction* (New York: Free Press, 1980).
8 Meisenzahl, M., "Google Cloud Releases Generative AI Tools for Retailers", *Digital Commerce 360*, January 12, 2024, available at https://www.digitalcommerce360.com/2024/01/12/google-cloud-releases-generative-ai-tools-for-retailers/.
9 "Gap Inc. Acquires AI Startup CB4", *Gap Inc.*, October 4, 2021, available at https://www.gapinc.com/en-us/articles/2021/10/gap-inc-acquires-ai-startup-cb4.
10 Data pooling is the process of combining potential training data from multiple sources or organizations to create a larger, more comprehensive dataset. Each participant can make use of this data pool to train better machine learning algorithms.
11 "Ford-Volkswagen Expand Their Global Collaboration to Advance Autonomous Driving, Electrification and Better Serve Customers", *Ford*, July 12, 2019, available at https://media.ford.com/content/fordmedia/fna/us/en/news/2019/07/12/ford-vw.html.
12 Healthcare services of Amazon are listed at "Get Care, Virtually Anywhere", *Amazon*, no date, available at https://health.amazon.com/onemedical.
13 Moreno, J., "Adobe's All in One AI: Debuts New Firefly AI Models for Creatives", *Forbes*, October 10, 2023, available at https://www.forbes.com/sites/johanmoreno/2023/10/10/adobes-all-in-on-ai-debuts-new-firefly-ai-models-for-creatives/.
14 See "EU AI Act: First Regulations on Artificial Intelligence", *EU Parliament*, February 19, 2025, available at https://www.europarl.europa.eu/topics/en/article/20230601STO93804/eu-ai-act-first-regulation-on-artificial-intelligence.
15 "Future R&D: How Unilever Is Transforming Innovation with Microsoft", *Unilever*, June 18, 2024, available at https://www.unilever.com/news/news-search/2024/future-rd-how-unilever-is-transforming-innovation-with-microsoft/.
16 "Get to Know Our AI Hub", *Schneider Electric*, no date, available at https://www.se.com/ww/en/work/solutions/artificial-intelligence/hub.jsp.
17 "Innovating Across Borders: How Amazon's Worldwide Teams Drive Global Impact", *Amazon*, October 10, 2024, available at https://www.aboutamazon.eu/news/company-news/amazon-international-innovation-map–2024.
18 To some extent, AI strategists can also be external consultants, especially when a firm is less experienced with AI, which is often the case at the beginning of its strategic transformation. However, due to the increasing importance of the technology as a strategic instrument, we strongly recommend that, at least over time, some AI strategists become internal employees, either by hiring or by developing competencies inhouse.

19 For more details about the importance of boards and top managers for strategic AI adoption, please have a look at Li, J., Mengxiang, L., Xincheng, W., and Bennet Thatcher, J., "Strategic Directions for AI: The Role of CIOs and Boards of Directors", *MIS Quarterly*, 45/3 (2021): pp. 1603–1644.

20 Lambert, K., "How Deere Is Preparing for a Fully Autonomous Farm by 2030", *CNBC*, December 1, 2023, available at https://www.cnbc.com/2023/12/01/how-deere-is-preparing-for-a-fully-autonomous-farm-by-2030.html.

21 Interestingly, for this type of problem the subfield of "machine unlearning" has evolved. The idea is that it might be potentially less effort to let an algorithm eliminate its own task knowledge itself instead of fully retraining it again.

5

HOW TO FORMULATE YOUR AI BUSINESS STRATEGY

"Harnessing machine learning can be transformational . . . This means understanding that when machine learning changes one part of the business – the product mix, for example – then other parts must also change."[1]

—Erik Brynjolfsson, Professor and Senior Fellow at the Stanford Institute for Human-Centered AI

With relevant AI signals at hand, we can enter the next strategy-making step, which is the formulation of your AI business strategy. That means creating a precise plan for achieving your financial and non-financial firm goals with machine learning-based AI systems.[2] Therefore, in this chapter, we systematically analyze the implications of relevant AI signals for each of the five strategy components (Section 5.1)[3] and discuss what impactful AI-oriented business strategies look like. We highlight many different decision options for each strategy component, provide various illustrative real-world company examples, and deal with the topic of strategic fit again (Section 5.2). Furthermore, we introduce two fitting AI business strategies of firms with very different industry contexts that can function as a source of inspiration for you.

5.1 DETERMINING THE COMPONENTS OF YOUR AI BUSINESS STRATEGY

The ultimate purpose of an AI business strategy is to systematically use machine learning as a strategic instrument to succeed in today's increasingly

DOI: 10.4324/9781003673170-8

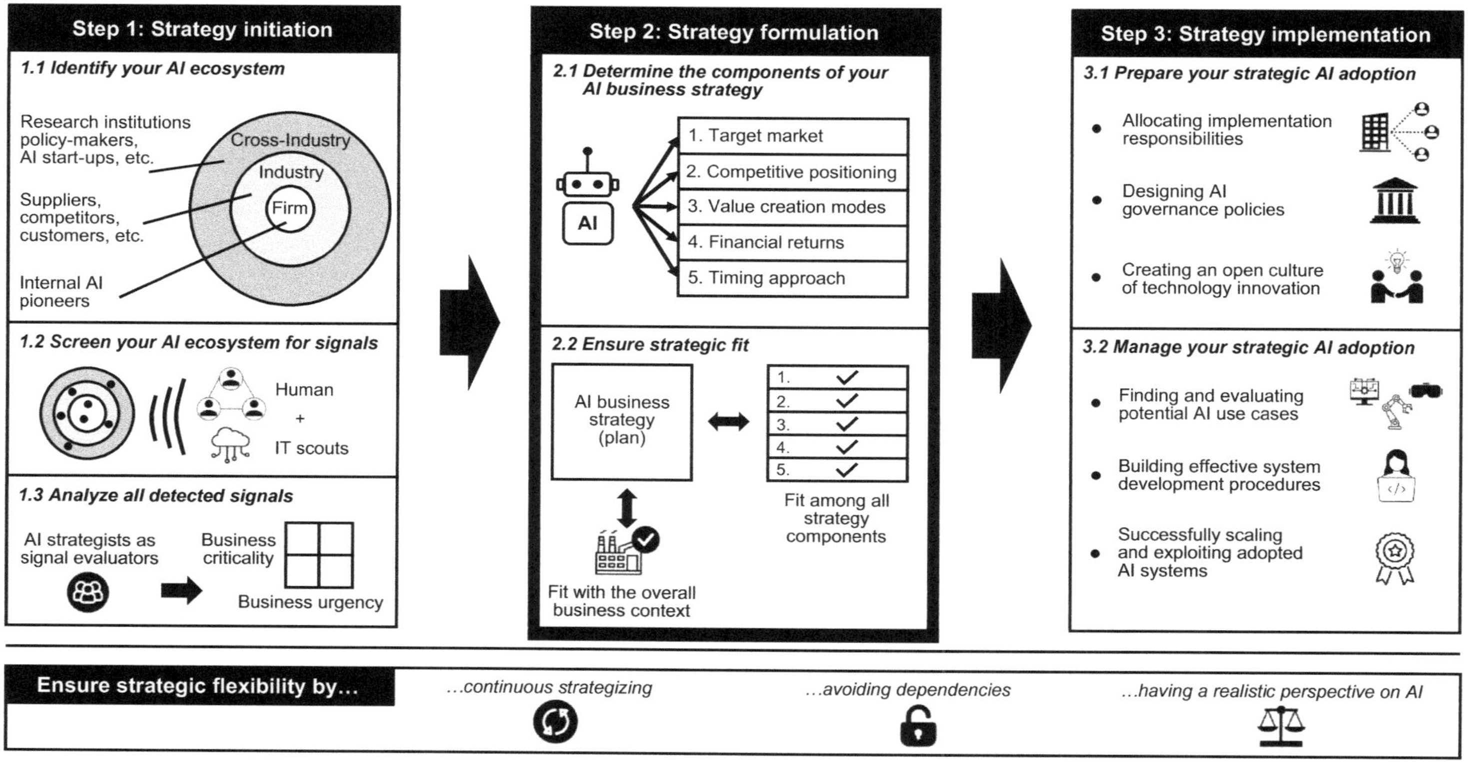

Figure 5.1 The AI Business Strategy Frame© – Step 2

technology-oriented business environments.[4] An AI business strategy must purposefully build on all relevant signals from the initiation phase. Specifically, one has to analyze the implications of AI signals on each strategy component individually.[5] Based on that, while AI strategists typically face multiple different decision options for each component, they should discuss each in line with the information extracted from signal evaluations, implying that AI business strategies can differ fundamentally among firms.

In the following sections, we present step by step instructions on how to systematically integrate machine learning systems into each of the five components of a business strategy based on the analyzed AI signals. While we will introduce various decision options for each component, we provide many illustrative strategy examples of real-world firms that can inspire you for your own business context.

5.1.1 *Target market: discovering strategic AI deployment areas*

The first and most fundamental question to address is where and to what extent a firm should strategically deploy machine learning-based AI systems. While deployment areas significantly influence the markets in which a firm can be or will be active, they represent a firm's precise AI adoption scope(s). In other words, strategic deployment areas determine where a firm primarily searches for impactful use case ideas and, thus, starts to exploit AI's unique self-learning ability.

Overall, two generic types of strategic deployment areas exist: market- and business process-related ones. With the help of intelligent machines, firms can create more attractive customer offerings and strong functional competencies along the value chain, including effective organizational decision-making standards, allowing a firm to strengthen its existing target market focus or expand into new markets. An AI business strategy usually has not only one but multiple different deployment areas. Combining different market- and process-related deployment areas opens truly innovative business opportunities.[7]

Strategic deployment areas are most powerful if they address market offerings and value chain functions that are most critical for the ultimate business success. Simply selecting areas where some kinds of AI use cases have emerged or imitating the use cases of others does, unfortunately, not automatically lead to a perceivable impact. Instead, one should start by concentrating on existing or new core offerings as well as ongoing business processes. Furthermore, in our experience, many valuable and individualized

Strategy components	Decisions to make	Short description
Target market: Discovering strategic AI deployment areas	**Market-related areas**	Enhancing existing and/or creating new products and services with AI
	Business process-related areas	Enhancing existing and/or creating new core competencies along the value chain with AI
Competitive positioning: Winning the market with AI	**Market differentiators**	Using AI to increase customer value and/or to reduce price-levels
	Market defense mechanisms	Strategically and technologically defending the targeted positioning
Value creation modes: Accessing necessary AI competencies	**Internal developments**	Organically growing AI competencies in-house through experimentation and learning
	Acquisitions	Inorganic growth of AI competencies by buying and integrating external firms
	Outsourcing	Purchasing competencies from external AI providers
	Partnerships	Bundling mutually valuable AI competencies with other firms
Financial returns: Becoming profitable with AI	**Revenue streams**	Enhancing existing and/or creating new revenue streams
	Cost structures	Rearranging resource consumptions by intelligent augmentation and/or automation
Timing approach: Scheduling the AI transformation	**Radically scheduled actions**	Reshaping organizational business activities relatively quickly
	Incrementally scheduled actions	Reshaping organizational business activities step-by-step over a longer period

Figure 5.2 Decision to Make When Formulating an AI Business Strategy[6]

use cases often surface over time, especially when organizations systematically focus on a specific product, service, or company function.

An impactful use case within a strategic deployment area must substantially unfold AI's unique self-learning ability through predictive, generative, or combined AI modules. The more use cases are found within an area, the more business impact can be created with the technology (we will outline some use cases, but explicitly approach the topic in Section 6.2.1). In contrast, the strategic impact of machine learning remains limited when it is applied to tasks that do not fully capitalize on self-learning skills. For example, the US newspaper chain Gannett aimed to leverage generative AI to enhance the quality of internal article writing but faced underwhelming results. Many formats still required human context awareness, empathy, or editorial judgment,[8] indicating that Gannett had to adjust its strategic deployment areas and approach others. In the following, let us go into more detail about both deployment types.

Market-related deployment areas

On the one hand, firms should address market-related AI adoption areas, meaning that intelligent machines should become a vital part of existing or new customer products and services. Focus on market offerings that can really benefit from specific AI modules. To find promising market-related deployment areas, you could analyze AI signals about use case ideas, customer needs, technological feasibility, etc. By analyzing these signals for the target market strategy component, you should be able to answer the question: How can self-learning technology systems directly or indirectly increase the customer value of my products or services?

In reality, there are many ways in which one or multiple AI modules can increase customer value.[9] For instance, enriching an existing electronic product with generative AI could be a quick win, as it enables customer-product communication with verbal exchange based on natural language processing capabilities. Similarly, as a complementary service, Wells Fargo offers generative AI-based chatbots and voicebots to reduce customer waiting times, for example, by answering individual banking questions more quickly.[10] Another example is toothbrush manufacturer Oral-B, which enhanced its products with predictive modules so customers can improve their brushing behavior by receiving direct feedback.[11] Whereas the AI module estimates the extent to which each tooth is successfully brushed, customers can use a complementary app to see their individual performance and learn what to do better next time.

Besides enhancing existing offerings, AI also allows the development of entirely new products or services. Opportunities range from simply digitizing analog products and services to the launch of radical technology-driven innovations. Here are two impressive examples of the latter. JP Morgan, for example, offers novel AI-based financial advisory services, better known as robo-advisors (this can be seen as a specific type of AI agents), to private or business investors.[12] While the algorithm was trained on massive amounts of historical stock and banking data, its investment suggestions can outperform human financial experts in several decision areas. In addition, Facebook's mother, Meta, is designing innovations in the realm of virtual reality. The so-called Metaverse is a virtual space for users to interact, work, and socialize, providing new online collaboration possibilities.[13]

Table 5.1 Examples of Strategic Deployment Areas

Market-related	*Enhancing existing offerings*	• Toothbrush manufacturer Oral-B adopted a predictive AI module to help consumers improve their daily brushing behavior • The bank Wells Fargo installed a complementary AI-based customer service to reduce waiting times
	Creating new offerings	• JPMorgan offers a robo-advisory service in which machine learning algorithms can overtake specific stock portfolio investment decisions • Meta develops an innovative virtual fun and co-working space called the Metaverse
Business process-related	*Enhancing existing core competencies*	• Pharmaceutical company Pfizer improves its R&D competencies to accelerate the discovery of new medical drug patents • Coca-Cola further scales its marketing competencies through generative AI-enabled product advertisements
	Creating new core competencies	• Construction material conglomerate Saint-Gobain wants to mitigate a global lack of talent by applying AI to better find and assess job candidates • Rising Chinese car manufacturers like BYD can outcompete incumbents with competencies in the realm of software-defined vehicles

While multiple AI use cases can exist for a specific market offering, machine learning does not automatically provide value for every product or service a company has or plans to develop. With inappropriate or unnecessary AI modules, customer value can even be destroyed. For instance, some customers value human interaction through personal face-to-face services much more than algorithmic exchange, especially when emotional experiences become a vital part of the customer journey. Another example is related to luxury products. When producing high-end luxury watches like a Rolex, individuals usually value sophisticated human craftsmanship much more than robotic machine work, since the watch is seen as a kind of art.[14]

Business process-related deployment areas

On the other hand, business process-related deployment areas improve existing or create new types of core competencies along a firm's value chain functions, including organizational decision-making skills. Core competencies are outstanding functional firm capabilities that allow an organization to be active in specific markets due to skill advantages compared to rivals.[15] Whereas core competencies can occur in each firm department, they are typically very hard for competitors to imitate due to limited access to specific resources, unique knowledge levels, or strong branding effects.

The systematic adoption of one or multiple AI systems in a critical functional department can be a strong enabler of such organizational core competencies. With the help of AI's self-learning ability, substantial operational process efficiencies can be created. To find suitable process-related deployment areas, we recommend analyzing relevant AI signals to strengthen current but also initiate new, desirable competencies for the future. Let us go through some real-world examples to further illustrate this.

For instance, pharmaceutical corporation Pfizer uses prototyping AI tools to reinforce its core competencies within the R&D department.[16] The adopted AI tools make complex biochemical analyses and simulations to accelerate the development of new medical drug patents. Further, semiconductor chip manufacturer Infineon is aware of its strong supply-chain and production management competencies.[17] Hence, the top management strategically focuses on deploying AI within these two functional areas. Some corresponding use cases have been about internal inventory management or chip quality control based on computer vision. Another example is Coca-Cola, which scales its existing marketing core competencies with generative AI systems to design even more creative product illustrations, customer emails, advertising texts, and social media campaigns.[18]

Alternatively, firms can create new core competencies in functional key departments with AI technologies. For this, we especially recommend investing in business skills that are expected to become crucial in the future. For instance, construction material manufacturer Saint-Gobain wanted to acquire better recruiting skills with AI systems to address the global lack of talent.[19] It adopted multiple AI systems to support human recruiters in finding, approaching, and evaluating the best candidates. On top of that, AI helps to replicate or even surpass the capabilities of competitors. In the automotive industry, the age of software-defined vehicles has started. Cars are increasingly shaped by electronic software components, many of which have some kinds of generative, predictive, or combined AI modules.[20] In fact, software development competencies have become almost equally important as traditional automotive engineering skills, as many motor features are similarly offered by various manufacturers. Software features, however, are also a good way to differentiate, providing many opportunities for emerging technology-oriented car manufacturers like BYD to catch up with or even overtake incumbents.

A teaser of prominent AI adoption use cases

Since use cases can firmly guide the selection of strategic deployment areas, Table 5.2 summarizes some exemplary ones we have frequently seen during our research. They can give you a first orientation for your own deployment areas. However, they should only be seen as a starting point, because you will explicitly learn about systematic use case identification in Section 6.2.1. For now, we provide you with some core questions to find and evaluate strategically relevant use cases. Answer them alone or in collaboration with other experienced AI strategists (for example, establish use case identification task forces).

1. In which areas can AI's self-learning power help overcome existing problems or leverage outstanding strengths (through prediction-making, content generation, or a combination thereof)?
2. Can a machine learning algorithm effectively learn from internal or external data for an intended business purpose (data quality, quantity, and access)?
3. What should be the appropriate level of AI automation for this purpose (augmentation vs. automation)?
4. Which critical adoption constraints must be considered (ethical, legal, social, etc.)?
5. Do the business benefits clearly outweigh the costs of an AI system (development, procurement, implementation, and operating costs)?

Table 5.2 An Overview of Exemplary AI Use Cases

Market-related	*Analog product or service*	• Digitization of analog products/services (e.g., computerization) • Complementary digital app services (e.g., AI-based manuals) • 24/7 customer support with chatbots or voicebots
	Digital product or service	• Customer-product communication interfaces (e.g., search tool) • Self-initiated technical problem reporting to manufacturers • Service customization to consumer preferences and habits
Business process-related	*Supply-chain and procurement*	• Automated supplier selection and order placement through AI agents • Finding optimal transportation routes and modes • Inventory optimization and just-in-time deliveries
	R&D	• Virtual prototyping via product simulations and digital twins • Brainstorming and creative product design support with generative AI • Centralized knowledge management assistants with LLMs
	Production	• Adaptive production scheduling and predictive maintenance • Physical quality inspection and industry robots • Automated customer escalation management
	Marketing and sales	• Product recommendations or the creation/placement of ads • Dynamic pricing to match existing demand and supply • Customer segmentation and sales forecasting
	Recruiting	• CV screening and job skill matching AI agents • Assessment centers through generating/evaluating test questions • Applicant relationship management (e.g., FAQ chatbot)
	IT	• Automated problem ticketing and issue prioritizing • Anomaly detection and system access control for cybersecurity • Self-learning ERP, CRM, or project management systems

The selection of use cases must always focus on aligning target markets with desired competitive positioning. Therefore, the next section will teach you more about differentiating from competitors with impactful AI use cases.

5.1.2 *Competitive positioning: winning the market with AI*

When appropriate deployment areas are found, another step is to consider how intelligent machines can improve a firm's competitive positioning in the selected target market(s) with powerful use cases. Specifically, it means leveraging a firm's value-price ratio with machine learning systems to better attract market customers, which leads, in the best case, to a competitive advantage.[21]

A good competitive positioning aims to differentiate a firm from its competitors. Hence, integrating AI into this strategy component means finding ways in which AI adoption increases customer value and/or reduces internal costs to offer better prices. Nonetheless, a value- or price-oriented differentiator is only helpful if customers sufficiently perceive it in the market. Otherwise, the selected competitive positioning will be ineffective.

Additionally, an outstanding and strongly perceived positioning is likely to be imitated by others. In fact, copying others is typically much easier than elaborating entirely new market tactics. Successful imitations, in turn, would destroy competitive advantages. Further, system manipulations or fraud attacks must be prevented to maintain and improve a positioning over time. As a result, an AI-enabled competitive positioning requires adequate protection mechanisms against hostile forces.

Market differentiators

A firm can differentiate itself from competitors with two different levers, including more customer value and/or more attractive prices. That indicates that the decisions for this strategy component should precisely specify how machine learning systems increase value propositions and/or reduce costs in selected deployment areas with use cases. Ideas for that can be derived from all types of AI signals, such as internal AI pioneers, competitors, customers, AI leaders, and start-ups. We will review some further illustrative AI use cases to give you inspiration for both levers.

While many ways exist to increase customer value with machine learning, a frequently seen example is creating new product features through the digitization of analog offerings. The company Magic Tech infused a mirror with digital fitness features so individuals can have better gym workout sessions at home or correct their body posture while looking at themselves.[22] Another common approach is personalization. Platforms like Booking.com or Airbnb collect user information to suggest customized flight or hotel offerings. While faster delivery services, such as Amazon's innovative drone fleet, are another value driver, product simplifications can increase customers' willingness to pay as well. IKEA, for instance, uses several AI modules to create intuitively understandable product manuals for customers to facilitate assembly at home.[23] On top of that, IKEA also uses gamification as a differentiator. The Swedish furniture corporation applies AI for its interior planning tools, in which customers can design their living rooms, kitchens, bedrooms, or baths in a playful virtual environment.[24]

Nevertheless, one can also adjust the price levels of products and services to differentiate from market competitors and realize outstanding value-price ratios. AI systems are primarily applied to reduce average productivity costs by increasing operational efficiencies. The resulting cost reductions for a task, in turn, can be transferred into better market prices again or to receive a higher profit margin (we will learn more about this in Section 5.1.4). Disney uses generative AI to reduce the need to film movie scenes manually. Instead, it animates them or adds artificial action effects afterward, allowing Disney to offer their movies at competitive prices if necessary.[25]

Table 5.3 Examples of How to Win the Market With AI

Market differentiators	• To increase customer value, the fitness firm Magic Tech digitizes an analog mirror product with AI, Booking.com personalizes travel suggestions, Amazon accelerates delivery services, and IKEA bets on simplification and gamification • To be able to adjust price levels, Disney applies generative AI to reduce the need to manually film movie sequences, as it can similarly animate complex action scenes with AI-based video creators
Market defense mechanisms	• The British BT Group established an AI platform that can detect internal and external cybersecurity threats for telecommunication processes and automatically intervene if necessary • Amazon mutually connects various AI and traditional IT systems to create powerful and complex IT landscapes that are much more difficult to imitate than single applications

Market defense mechanisms

Even though strong market differentiators have been placed, effective market defense mechanisms are necessary to establish a long-term impact. Without them, competitors will likely imitate your successful positioning. They will try to train similar or even better AI systems, enabling them to copy or surpass a particular positioning. On top of that, system manipulations and fraud attempts could occur. Therefore, in this section, we discuss three effective AI-oriented market defense mechanisms that you should think about to protect your own positioning. Nonetheless, as successful imitation destroys the temporary advantages of other firms, you could also look at those who are more successful than you in certain competitive aspects and try to copy them if beneficial.

One obligatory measure in systematically exploiting machine learning is activating reliable cybersecurity standards. Since data has become a truly strategic resource, unique and big datasets to which a firm has exclusive access must be protected against imitators under all circumstances.[26] In addition, the actual AI system should be safeguarded against potential system manipulations from both internal and external forces. Hacking, blackmailing,[27] or other fraud attempts have significantly increased over the last years. For instance, AI-based deepfake videos were used to steal 25 million USD from the UK-based engineering company Arup.[28] Such issues should be seen as very relevant AI signals for all types of firms, indicating the need to invest substantially in cybersecurity. Consequently, data encryption, access control, or AI-based data stream anomaly detection might be adequate investments to counteract these types of issues practically. Further measures could include implementing robust authentication protocols or controlling system interfaces (i.e., gateways) to prevent unauthorized interference proactively.

Today, organizations are intensively dealing with many types of cybersecurity topics. For instance, the British telecommunication corporation BT Group has launched a new predictive AI-based cyber defense platform called "Eagle-I."[29] This platform enables real-time detection of security incidents such as hacking or system manipulation attempts regarding the internal technology infrastructure. When a threat is detected, it can automatically intervene by blocking external or internal users. Further, Eagle-I has been designed in a way that it can learn from each potential threat detection, enabling continuous system improvement through retraining.

A second defense mechanism is to train employees to better handle confidential data and use the adopted AI systems more effectively. According to a recent survey, more than a third of all employees would require significant training on this topic.[30] Employee coursework can be about very different themes. Still, at the beginning, the focus should lie on teaching the basic principles of machine learning, just like you learn with this book (we will deal more with stakeholder education in Section 6.1.3).

Third, we recommend integrating AI and traditional IT systems to create an Internet of Things (IoT) or AI of Things (AIoT) infrastructure landscape. Higher levels of system interconnectivity make imitation efforts much more complex because it is typically easier to copy a single application than an entire IT landscape. To foster its AI transformation, Amazon tries to connect as many AI-based and traditional IT systems as possible within its logistics facilities, including transportation robots, commissioning systems, quality inspection applications, packaging tools, and inventory management systems, thus creating valuable data network effects. Imitating complex IT landscapes is more challenging than a stand-alone AI system. Hundreds of physical and virtual interfaces exist, all of which must be understood and mutually aligned.

5.1.3 *Value creation modes: accessing necessary AI competencies*

Systematically adopting machine learning-based AI systems to generate competitive benefits requires strong technological capabilities and resources. For that reason, identifying and accessing the necessary AI competencies becomes a critical part of a firm's value creation modes.[31] Without this, an AI business strategy cannot be implemented.

For instance, converting strategic AI deployment into concrete system development and implementation plans requires profound knowledge from human experts regarding data collection, algorithmic training, and adequate validation approaches in case of problematic black box perceptions. Software and hardware solutions are necessary infrastructure investments as well. Some classic examples are physical sensors to collect data, (cloud) computing power, graphics cards, data warehouses, coding interfaces, and other digital IT infrastructure. Ask yourself or your IT department: What hardware and software solutions are needed to enable the development, implementation, and exploitation of machine learning-based AI systems in line with the competitive positioning selected for a target market?

Consequently, firms must either internally or externally access critical technology competencies to implement an AI business strategy. In other words, one has to establish reliable AI-oriented value creation modes. As sketched before in Section 2.2.3, multiple options exist to access AI competencies, and also the combination of different modes can help overcome capability and resource constraints. Nonetheless, since value creation modes substantially define your business costs, all possible value creation modes should be compared to each other. To do so, we recommend looking at the short-term as well as long-term benefits and costs. AI is here to stay, implying that the importance of technology competencies will likely grow further. The following paragraphs will show how to access AI competencies with the four previously introduced value creation modes.

Internal developments

The first option is the internal development of competencies, which means growing internal AI expertise regarding developing, deploying, and exploiting machine learning systems. Whereas internal developments require time and budget to experiment, this approach is primarily recommended for creating very strategic AI competencies that make you less dependent on external firms in the future. Siemens, for instance, internally developed strategic competencies in the realm of industrial AI to differentiate itself from competitors. Specifically, Siemens learned to exploit machine learning for industrial use cases, including digital twins for product designs, generative AI-based machine programming assistants to steer shop floor robotics, and predictive maintenance applications to avoid machine malfunctions.[32]

Hiring technical AI experts, including data scientists, system developers, AI project managers, or IT engineers, could be a good move to foster internal development. Depending on the selected deployment areas, this could also include technology experts in disciplines like production, legal, finance, or marketing. Importantly, also think about new job positions that AI adoption creates. Examples could be a prompt engineer to steer the outputs of generative AI-based systems, an algorithm auditor to check for technology compliance, or an AI business translator that is placed to connect IT experts and IT laypeople. Since AI talent is often rare, investments in good staff typically pay off in the long run. Do not wait too long to hire competent individuals because others will try to do so, too.

Acquisitions

A further value creation mode option is about acquisitions. Because self-learning AI applications differ significantly from traditional information systems, many firms lack sufficient technology experience to create all necessary competencies solely in-house. Therefore, integrating an external firm with solid expertise in a certain AI domain can be a worthwhile shortcut, particularly if very detailed or rare knowledge is required. For example, Airbus acquired the company Infodas in 2024 to enhance its cybersecurity competencies against the frequent hacking attempts in the aerospace industry.[33] Other examples are Bosch, which acquired the autonomous driving start-up five.AI in 2022, but also Amazon, which bought the robotic warehouse expert Kiva Systems in 2012.[34] This underlines that acquiring start-ups is an excellent way to transfer innovative knowledge into another firm.

Outsourcing

Third, outsourcing technological competencies can be beneficial, which refers to purchasing AI systems or modules (AI as a service – AIaaS), technological infrastructure (infrastructure as a service – IaaS), platform access (platform as a service – PaaS), knowledge in the form of consulting support, or any other service from one or multiple external providers.[35] Today, cloud computing providers like Google, AWS, Microsoft, and others are of outstanding relevance for many business strategies. Cloud providers are often called hyperscalers as they operate a massive data center infrastructure that can quickly scale global computing resources up or down, thus dynamically meeting the precise infrastructure demands of millions of users simultaneously. Besides cloud services, customers can also often book additional predictive or generative AI modules like business analysis tools, automatic report creators, or chatbots within such cloud environments. Similarly, pre-trained large language models are often purchased from external providers and then fine-tuned with company-specific task data.

Medium-sized and smaller companies that do not have the budget to hire many AI developers for the long run often outsource their machine learning operations to a large extent. Such outsourced activities are usually related to use case identification, model training, fine-tuning, system implementation, monitoring, and technical maintenance. Nevertheless, while outsourcing can access necessary AI competencies quite quickly, it can also create strong external dependencies (see Section 7.2). Firms should always try to learn more and more competencies over time in-house, to work more independently in the future, especially for very strategic technology skills.

Partnerships

A fourth technological value creation mode is a partnership, which can take various forms. The most prominent partnership type is a technology

Table 5.4 Examples of How to Access Necessary AI Competencies

Value creation modes	*Internal developments*	• Siemens learned how to exploit machine learning for industrial use cases on a large scale in-house
	Acquisitions	• Airbus acquired the AI cybersecurity specialist Infodas to quickly enhance its cybersecurity competencies
	Outsourcing	• Many firms rely on external cloud environments from hyperscalers like Google, AWS, and Microsoft to accelerate technology access
	Partnerships	• Baker Hughes and the AI firm C3.ai founded a joint venture to collectively innovate the oil and gas industry

joint venture, allowing firms to share risks while combining knowledge and infrastructure resources. Baker Hughes, a subsidiary of General Electric, partnered with the AI firm C3.ai to establish a joint venture focusing on innovative AI solutions in the oil and gas industry.[36] Combining both firms created deep knowledge synergies. Another partnership type could be data pooling. PepsiCo, for example, collaborates with major retailers to share product, inventory, and customer data, aiming to improve algorithmic sales forecasting and supply-chain efficiency.[37] Partnerships can also exist between independent start-ups and corporations. Many corporations invest in start-ups as they are perceived as a fruitful breeding ground for innovation through technology experimentation. Similarly, firms can merge to create synergies, which can be seen as a mix of a partnership and an acquisition.

5.1.4 *Financial returns: becoming profitable with AI*

It is essential to consider that an effective competitive positioning realized with the selected value creation modes does not necessarily lead to good financial results. Indeed, firms might face difficulty becoming profitable due to unrealized revenue expectations or expensive business operations. Nevertheless, a long-term strategy perspective must always enable profit to fulfill shareholder needs and finance a company's business transformation. IBM, for example, had to sell much of its healthcare AI business after investing significant amounts of financial resources. The business unit remained below its profit goals for years, so the management board saw no choice but to sell it.[38]

Ultimately, exploiting AI's unique self-learning ability should be directly linked to profitability. In other words, enhanced customer value or adjusted price levels must translate into sustainable financial returns. Since profit depends on revenue minus costs, firms have two levers they can address. We recommend quantifying the estimated revenue increase and/or cost reductions to analyze and decide on this strategy component. This can also be a valuable indicator of whether pre-selected deployment areas can really create sufficient financial impact as intended or not.

Revenue streams

A successful AI business strategy generates one or more suitable revenue streams, enabling sufficient income and cash inflow over time. To realize this with AI, think about scaling existing streams or creating new ones. A classic example of increasing established revenue streams is the usage of personalized product recommendations.[39] E-commerce vendors are well known for letting algorithms learn about individual customer preferences. These systems learn users' buying habits to suggest additional items that customers might not have considered before but could be interested in. Another example of leveraging existing revenue streams is to improve the match of supply and demand in platform-based business models. Ride-hailing company Uber employs AI systems to predict optimal driver locations and pick-up times across the city, reducing average passenger waiting durations, particularly during rush hours. Additionally, Uber utilizes AI-driven dynamic pricing systems that adjust ride prices based on weather conditions since customers are more willing to pay when it rains than when the sun is shining.[40]

Firms can also create new revenue streams instead of focusing on existing ones. For instance, many companies offer additional bookable AI modules to their basic products or services. The commercial image and video provider iStock offers a generative AI-based premium service, allowing users to prompt tailored pictures, icons, graphs, etc., for commercial uses.[41] Tesla customers, in turn, can unlock autonomous driving assistance features only with premium subscriptions.[42]

Cost structures

Rearranging internal cost structures increases profitability by obtaining new configurations of (machine learning-based) AI and human resources that are more efficient than humans combined with traditional information systems.

Table 5.5 Examples of How to Become Profitable With AI

Revenue streams	*Enhancing existing streams*	• E-commerce vendors like Amazon or Alibaba use personalized product recommendations to leverage existing sales streams • Uber uses a dynamic pricing model based on a predictive AI module to consider different weather conditions
	Creating new streams	• Commercial picture provider iStock offers an image generator as an additional bookable AI function • Customers from Tesla can only unlock autonomous driving assistants with a premium subscription
Cost structures	*Intelligent automation*	• Japanese insurance company Fukoko Mutual Life automated the analysis of medical patient data to save costs • Mobile phone provider O2 automates customer service hotlines with AI-based voicebots
	Intelligent augmentation	• Consumer product conglomerate Unilever applies AI to help human recruiters assess specific skills of job applicants • Software company Salesforce developed an AI system called Einstein to augment salespeople with real-time customer intelligence, thus increasing their productivity

More specifically, the strategic adoption of AI can help create cost advantages by improving operational efficiencies through human–AI collaboration (e.g., augmentation) or task automation. It is important to consider that full automation is not always the best choice or technically feasible. As stated before, automation and augmentation should be viewed as a collaboration continuum between AI systems and humans. Effective collaboration means that each of them should be able to unfold its strengths to compensate for each other's weaknesses.

Due to their relative observability, repeatability, and controllability, routine tasks are especially fitting for higher levels of automation. The Japanese insurance company Fukoko Mutual Life replaced dozens of office workers with an AI system developed for the monotone task of analyzing medical patient data.[43] Another popular routine task suitable for automation is telephone-based customer service, which mobile phone provider O2 does.[44]

For this task, an automated voicebot can efficiently handle basic inquiries and resolve common issues without human intervention.

In contrast, Unilever uses machine learning to augment the skills of human recruiters to facilitate the identification and evaluation of job applicants. AI tools can screen CVs or generate assessment center questions to estimate the match between applicant competencies and required job skills. Correspondingly, humans can concentrate on other recruiting tasks that better fit their individual skills, including manually checking an applicant's motivation or team fit in personal interview rounds.[45] Another augmentation use case concerns salespeople who can perform much better when an AI system analyzes client information in real time through customer analytics.[46] Salesforce, for example, has developed several AI modules in its platform called Einstein. The platform can be used to predict sales success rates and suggest optimal product combinations for individual customers, thus increasing the productivity of salespeople and, in the best case, also impacting revenue simultaneously.

5.1.5 Timing approach: scheduling the AI transformation

Lastly, an effective AI business strategy must carefully reflect the time dimension to schedule the overall AI transformation of a firm in a suitable frame. Many actions are necessary over a specific period to implement an AI business strategy (precise implementation topics are discussed in Chapter 6). When should a company be ready to launch its new AI products in the chosen market? When must the targeted cybersecurity standards be established or the start-up acquisition be completed? When should a potential cost advantage pay off, enabled by high levels of task automation?

Firms can choose between more radical and incremental schedules for all the necessary implementation actions. The faster and more intense the strategic AI transformation, the greater the innovation opportunities, while associated investments and technological implementation risks also increase. This underlines the need to thoroughly assess what actions must be taken immediately and what can wait. Let us have a closer look at these different schedule types.

Radically scheduled actions

On the one hand, firms can select a schedule with more radical actions to realize a short-term transformation. This can mean reshaping organizational business processes or developing novel market offerings relatively quickly, like in one to three years. Radical schedules may enable substantial first-mover or fast-second advantages.[47] For instance, pharmaceutical companies use AI to accelerate product development and register new types of profitable patents. OpenAI, the firm behind ChatGPT, has seen the potential to create first-mover advantages with user-friendly generative AI-based chatbots, as previous applications have not reached such a market-ready performance in natural language processing.[48] Besides gaining advantages, another apparent reason for a radical approach is that competitors are already far ahead with their AI transformation. Then, one has to quickly catch up with them to avoid experiencing substantial competitive disadvantages. Furthermore, radical schedules are a sense-making tool for low-hanging fruit projects to realize quick returns and convince skeptical stakeholders.

Nonetheless, radically scheduled actions also come with several threats. For example, it leaves less space for flexibility as most actions, including investments, are done relatively quickly at the beginning of the transformation endeavor. Also, a radical schedule depends on the availability of existing technological and managerial competencies or capacities. If they are not accessible, no strategy can be successfully implemented. Especially less technology-experienced firms might get easily overwhelmed, indicating that a radical approach is more recommendable when unique opportunities arise, intense competitive pressure exists, or actions are easily implementable.

Table 5.6 Examples of How to Schedule the AI Transformation

Radically scheduled actions	• Pharmaceutical firms aggressively implement AI systems for their medical drug development processes to register valuable patents as soon as possible • OpenAI recognized the potential of creating first-mover advantages with its user-friendly content-generating chatbot ChatGPT
Incrementally scheduled actions	• Car manufacturers like BMW offer autonomous driving functions stepwise to convince customers and finance R&D endeavors for the long run • Apple's credo is to take sufficient time to introduce outstanding AI products instead of rushing with releases

Incrementally scheduled AI adoption

An alternative would be a more incremental schedule, that is, most actions are executed stepwise without much time pressure. Incrementally scheduled actions generally incorporate a long-term perspective, acknowledging that substantial organizational change or the development of complex technology systems takes time. Because an incremental schedule leaves more flexibility to adjust an AI business strategy in line with environmental changes over time, it is often recommended to large incumbents characterized by established, traditional business processes and customer offerings. It allows the gradual integration of AI into existing business activities and, thus, transforms a firm step by step. An incremental schedule is essential for firms targeting the development of extraordinarily complex AI innovations. For such long-term projects, one often has to go through multiple financing rounds to continuously convince shareholders or external investors.

For instance, car manufacturers like BMW cannot, with respect to current technological, societal, and legal circumstances, offer fully autonomous vehicles in just a few years. Still, they substantially invest in research to constantly push the technological boundaries. Meanwhile, to convince shareholders and generate positive financial returns, car manufacturers are releasing more and more AI-based assistance functionalities for each product generation, in line with corresponding regulations and social norms.[49] The procedure proves the long-term vision and self-financing of research activities. Quality instead of speed is also Apple's way. CEO Tim Cook stated that the company's credo for product releases is:

> "Not first, but best."[50]

5.2 ENSURING STRATEGIC FIT FOR YOUR AI BUSINESS STRATEGY

The concept of strategic fit matters for every business strategy, whether AI-oriented or not. Strategists must always build a forward-thinking and coherent plan aligned with a firm's overall objectives. The strategy must adequately address all necessary environmental signals, as demonstrated in the previous sections.[51] In a nutshell, an AI business strategy identifies promising technology deployment areas, explains how to win a market, ensures profit, specifies access to needed technological competencies, and schedules all relevant actions.

Table 5.7 Some Important Characteristics of a Fitting AI Business Strategy

Fit among all strategy components	• Deployment areas are currently or in the future considered business critical • Deployment areas provide differentiation opportunities that can be defended • The selected competitive positioning leaves sufficient space for financial returns by leveraging revenue and/or rearranging cost structures • All necessary AI competencies are reliably accessible and are not too costly, so that they prevent good financial returns • Radically scheduled actions do not depend on incremental ones and consider available competencies or capacities
Fit of a strategy with the business context	• The strategy is well-aligned with other industry and macro-environmental trends • The strategy does consider relevant actions of competitors, customers, suppliers, partners, etc., that do not necessarily deal with AI themes • Functional departments can effectively collaborate during strategy implementation • The strategy can logically achieve not only financial but also non-financial firm goals and reflects all values and norms of an organization and its owners • The strategy is realistically planned from a budget perspective

As you have learned before, strategic fit consists of two dimensions, that is, achieving fit among all five strategy components as well as fit between the business strategy and the overall business context. Let us provide some examples to illustrate what fit could mean in an AI context. In addition to our explanations, Table 5.7 summarizes some exemplary characteristics of a fitting AI business strategy.

5.2.1 *Fit among all AI business strategy components*

First, an AI business strategy must be comprehensive and logically consistent. The decisions for each strategy component must be aligned with all other ones to avoid potential conflicts and impediments. The goal is that each component mutually reinforces the impact of the remaining ones. An AI business strategy must define deployment areas that enable a valuable competitive positioning, ensure access to all necessary competencies, create sufficient financial returns, and stick to a realistic time horizon. If an AI business strategy cannot do so, decisions would be isolated endeavors without a high chance of reaching pre-defined goals.

Here is an example that demonstrates the relevance of mutual fit among components. When focusing on market-related AI deployment areas, as electronic device manufacturers LG and Samsung are trying to, one can effectively differentiate with new smart TV functions that many competitive products do not have yet, thus realizing first-mover advantages. This includes AI-based brightness or sound optimization as well as the integration of chat- and voicebot functions as a steering tool. Based on that, customers might be more willing to pay, which can be capitalized on with new revenue streams. For instance, LG and Samsung offer standard devices without and premium devices with AI features to consider different customer needs. Since developing novel AI features is complex and usually takes a lot of resources, quickly hiring AI experts and accessing external competencies could be more radical actions. Nonetheless, although the previously described approach sounds logically coherent, there is no generic fit approach. Since AI business strategies vary among firms, each plan must be checked for fit individually.

5.2.2 *Fit of an AI business strategy with the overall business context*

Second, one has to align an AI business strategy with a firm's internal and external environments. Doing so not only includes assuring whether decisions rely on the information extracted from analyzed AI signals, but also whether other non-AI-related business information was taken into account. The latter refers to all strategy signals shaped by a high business impact and/or urgency, but have nothing to tell about AI.[52] These are usually the signals you have worked with before initiating an AI-oriented business strategy. If you suddenly start ignoring them, your strategy will fail, as there are many other relevant topics out there, too.

Externally, one can distinguish between within-industry and cross-industry fit aspects. For instance, it is vital to analyze all types of industry customer trends, AI-driven or not, and check whether new value creation potential exists with specific AI modules, opening opportunities for differentiation from competitors. Of course, appropriate suppliers and other partners could be necessary to do so. Relatedly, it can become fruitful to better understand the general behavior of existing customers. Insurance company Allianz, for example, acquired an AI system to forecast average customer claims more accurately throughout the year. The algorithm allows them to improve liquidity planning and unlock more capital for stock market investments. However, you should also reflect on macroeconomic trends to see whether AI is the right technology for a potential deployment area or whether better alternatives exist. Chemical manufacturer BASF also investigates other promising and emerging technology trends, such as nanomaterials (e.g., for sun protection) or energy-efficient production methods.

Internally, a fit with the business context could mean ensuring the strategy sufficiently builds on existing core products and competencies. Doing so is often a quick win when it further increases the gap between you and your competitors. Internal fit also necessitates effective cross-functional collaborations. Suppose process-related deployment areas target the intelligent digitization of internal product manufacturing competencies along assembly lines. In that case, the internal IT department must assist and monitor machine learning implementations and orchestrate the digital landscape for production machines like industry robots. Similarly, the logistics and sales departments must get involved to share valuable customer and supplier data for improved production planning. Alternatively, fit means respecting organizations' or owners' objectives, values, or norms for AI adoption. For instance, some firms announced that they do not diversify into military areas, even though AI offers promising financial opportunities.

5.2.3 Real-world examples of fitting AI business strategies

In the figures below, we provide two fitting AI business strategies as an illustration for you. The first is from the pharmaceutical corporation Pfizer, and the second is from the household appliance manufacturer BSH. While both firms are globally active, they have very different organizational and industry backgrounds, which is why they formulated unique strategy approaches. This is necessary since imitating AI strategy components from other firms is unlikely to yield successful outcomes.

Strategy components	Decisions to make	Short description
Target market: Discovering strategic AI deployment areas	**Market-related areas**	• Creating customized medical drugs • Inventing new types of medical products like a rare disease identifier or surgery robots
	Business process-related areas	• Strengthening existing R&D core competencies with algorithmic biochemical simulations to accelerate drug development times
Competitive positioning: Winning the market with AI	**Market differentiators**	• Accelerating medical diagnoses and treatments • Personalizing medical drugs (e.g., concentration of specific substances)
	Market defense mechanisms	• Enhancing patent enforcement skills • Bundling and protecting exclusive data from different medical trials (e.g., with anomaly detections)
Value creation modes: Accessing necessary AI competencies	**Internal developments**	• Developing product innovations majorly in-house • Designing AI systems for deployment areas as well as cybersecurity solutions mostly independently
	Acquisitions	• Buying pharmaceutical and R&D related AI start-ups
	Outsourcing	• Purchasing cloud computing competencies from hyperscalers
	Partnerships	• Entering research alliances with non-industry partners (e.g., IT firms and universities)
Financial returns: Becoming profitable with AI	**Revenue streams**	• Increasing existing revenue streams with personalized drugs • Creating new revenue streams with new medical offerings (patent-enabled premium margins)
	Cost structures	• Automating biochemical simulations • Augmenting humans in determining potential drug side effects
Timing approach: Scheduling the AI transformation	**Radically scheduled actions**	• Intensively hiring AI and cybersecurity experts
	Incrementally scheduled actions	• Regularly discussing new opportunities enabled by recently adopted AI systems

Figure 5.3 The AI Business Strategy of Pfizer in a Nutshell

Strategy components	Decisions to make	Short description
Target market: Discovering strategic AI deployment areas	**Market-related areas**	• Robotizing existing kitchen devices (ovens, refrigerators, dishwashers, etc.) • Inventing new household appliances such as cleaning robots
	Business process-related areas	• Using AI-based industry robots to create core competencies in production and logistics
Competitive positioning: Winning the market with AI	**Market differentiators**	• Simplifying the usage of household appliances (convenience) • Creating an innovative and environmentally-friendly technology impact (e.g., smart energy savings)
	Market defense mechanisms	• Protecting data with fitting cybersecurity tools like firewalls, data encryption, access control, etc. • Mutually connecting household appliances so that systems can exchange customer preferences
Value creation modes: Accessing necessary AI competencies	**Internal developments**	• Developing robotic AI products in-house • Designing complementary product apps internally
	Acquisitions	./.
	Outsourcing	• Purchasing cloud computing competencies from hyperscalers • Accessing production robot base technology from high-tech leaders
	Partnerships	• Partnering with kitchen assistant start-ups to obtain a safe space for experimentation
Financial returns: Becoming profitable with AI	**Revenue streams**	• Offering AI-based and traditional household appliances to leverage sales • Receiving additional provisions from complementary apps
	Cost structures	• Increasing the level of automation at production facilities
Timing approach: Scheduling the AI transformation	**Radically scheduled actions**	• Implementing robotic production systems in main facilities relatively quickly
	Incrementally scheduled actions	• Integrating more and more AI features into household appliances (step-wise)

Figure 5.4 The AI Business Strategy of BSH in a Nutshell

5.3 CHAPTER SUMMARY

- To formulate an AI business strategy, firms must systematically integrate the implications of AI signals into each of the five components of a business strategy:
  - First, an AI business strategy determines promising deployment areas, that is, where and to what extent a firm plans to unfold AI's self-learning ability. While deployment areas influence the target markets a firm is and could be active in, they can be *market-related* or *business process-related.*
  - Second, an AI business strategy describes how AI systems can enable a promising competitive positioning in a selected target market. For this, a firm must find compelling *market differentiators* to attract customers and establish sound *market defense mechanisms* to protect technology-enabled advantages against potential imitators or fraudsters.
  - Third, an AI business strategy elucidates how a firm can access the AI competencies needed to develop, implement, and exploit machine learning systems. Firms can select one or more of the following value creation modes, including *internal development*, *acquisitions*, *outsourcing*, or *partnerships.*
  - Fourth, an AI business strategy provides sufficient financial returns to achieve profitability goals and finance a firm's AI transformation over time. This involves optimizing *revenue streams* and *cost structures* in line with the competitive positioning.
  - Fifth, an AI business strategy determines the precise timing approach, that is, the sequence of all necessary actions. In general, firms can select between more *radical* or *incremental* timing approaches.
- Like every strategy, an AI business strategy requires strategic fit to be effective. That includes fit among all AI strategy components as well as fit between the formulated strategy and the overall business context.

5.4 HANDS-ON PRACTICE

Now, we encourage you to thoroughly analyze the impact of relevant AI signals on each of the five strategy components (Worksheet 7). To do so, you can build on the material from Worksheet 6. To keep things simple, we recommend a three-step scale for a signal's impact on each strategy component, including lower, medium, and higher impact levels. After finishing the task, you obtain detailed information to formulate a fitting AI business strategy.

Worksheet 8 deals with the actual formulation of your individual AI business strategy. Use the insights from the previous worksheets (especially Worksheets 1 and 7) to make fitting decisions for each strategy component. You can also use the two given strategy examples (Figures 4.6 and 4.7) as an inspiration. The extent to which your formulated business strategy will build on machine learning-based AI depends on you. Whereas there is a continuum from minimal to full AI integration, you can also start with a lower or medium extent and increase the technology's strategic role over time.

Further, we have created a short list with different control questions to check whether you made the right decisions for your AI business strategy (Worksheet 9). If you notice conflicts, inconsistencies, or ineffective decisions after this assessment, we recommend revisiting Worksheets 7 and 8.

Relevant AI signals	Impact on my target market	Impact on my competitive positioning	Impact on my value creation modes	Impact on my financial returns	Impact on my timing approach
Example: *Competitor X starts the long-term development of a new AI product*	***Medium:*** *Such an AI product would partly affect my offerings on the market*	***Lower:*** *I could differentiate with other product features (e.g., comfortability)*	***Medium:*** *I should also invest into my internal AI competencies*	***Medium:*** *Not all customers prefer more technology features*	***Higher:*** *If I would like to develop a similar product, I must start soon, too*

Worksheet 7 What Do Relevant AI Signals Tell You for Each Strategy Component?

Strategy components	Decisions to make	My decisions
Target market: Discovering strategic AI deployment areas	**Market-related areas**	
	Business process-related areas	
Competitive positioning: Winning the market with AI	**Market differentiators**	
	Market defense mechanisms	
Value creation modes: Accessing necessary AI competencies	**Internal developments**	
	Acquisitions	
	Outsourcing	
	Partnerships	
Financial returns: Becoming profitable with AI	**Revenue streams**	
	Cost structures	
Timing approach: Scheduling the AI transformation	**Radically scheduled actions**	
	Incrementally scheduled actions	

Worksheet 8 What Is Your AI Business Strategy?

Strategy components	Decisions to make	Control questions	Check
Target market: Discovering strategic AI deployment areas	**Market-related areas**	• Do customers value AI features within existing products or services? • Is a sufficient demand expected for my AI innovations?	
	Business process-related areas	• Are the targeted core competencies helpful to compete in a certain market? • Are the targeted core competencies important today and/or in the future?	
Competitive positioning: Winning the market with AI	**Market differentiators**	• Is my differentiator really perceived by customers? • Do customers value the selected differentiator?	
	Market defense mechanisms	• Are critical data sources and AI systems adequately protected? • Have different digital systems been mutually connected?	
Value creation modes: Accessing necessary AI competencies	**Internal developments**	• Do I have sufficient resources available to start AI system developments in-house? • Is there a plan B in case of development failure?	
	Acquisitions	• Do acquisition targets exist that can provide valuable AI competencies? • Can these targets be effectively integrated into my firm?	
	Outsourcing	• Are AI provider offerings relatively beneficial? • Can dependency threats be thoroughly mitigated?	
	Partnerships	• Do partners offer valuable AI competencies that can be bundled? • Are partners reliable and trustworthy?	
Financial returns: Becoming profitable with AI	**Revenue streams**	• Is the willingness to pay of different customers considered (e.g., segments, regions)? • Are cross-selling effects possible and without cannibalization effects?	
	Cost structures	• Does intelligent augmentation enhance the skills of humans? • Does intelligent automation build on the skills of machine learning agents?	
Timing approach: Scheduling the AI transformation	**Radically scheduled actions**	• Are potential first-mover advantages identified? • Are potential actions of competitors or future industry changes taken into account?	
	Incrementally scheduled actions	• Is the long-term adoption of AI financially covered? • Are required actions planned in a logical, step-wise sequence?	

Worksheet 9 Have You Achieved High Levels of Strategic Fit?

NOTES

1 Johnson, N., "Fixing the AI Skills Shortage: An Interview With Erik Brynjolfsson", *MIT Initiative on the Digital Economy*, March 22, 2019, available at https://ide.mit.edu/insights/fixing-the-ai-skills-shortage-an-interview-with-erik-brynjolfsson/.

2 Always clearly define your financial (e.g., revenue, expected profit, or company value) and non-financial goals (e.g., market share, branding, or customer satisfaction). Do also note that AI adoption could influence your goals. Siemens, for example, publicly stated that they want to become the worldwide industrial AI leader.

3 AI business strategies must also consider non-AI-related information regarding internal and external firm environments. This is usually all the information that you have collected before dealing with AI topics. As we assume that you are familiar with these types of information, we do focus on AI-related signals in this book.

4 See Hutzschenreuter, T. and Lämmermann, T., "What Is Your AI Strategy? Systematically Integrating Self-Learning Technologies into Your Business Strategy", *Academy of Management Perspectives*, forthcoming (2025).

5 Worksheet 7 will explicitly help you analyze the implications of AI signals on each strategy component.

6 As mentioned earlier, our book builds on the classic business strategy elements of Hambrick, D. C. and Fredrickson, J.W., "Are You Sure You Have a Strategy?", *Academy of Management Perspectives*, 19/4 (2005): pp. 51–62. For the integration of AI into these elements, see also Hutzschenreuter & Lämmermann (2025), "What Is Your AI Strategy? Systematically Integrating Self-Learning Technologies into Your Business Strategy".

7 Deployment areas can be interdependent. A new AI-based product offering, for example, might require AI adoption in R&D, procurement, production, or sales processes in parallel.

8 See Wu, D., "Gannet Halts AI-Written Sports Recaps after Readers Mocked the Stories", *The Washington Post*, August 31, 2023, available at https://www.washingtonpost.com/nation/2023/08/31/gannett-ai-written-stories-high-school-sports/.

9 The integration of AI into products or services can be used to automate customer tasks or to augment human capabilities in line with the human-AI collaboration continuum. For example, AI-powered sports broadcasting with self-directing cameras or a robotic vacuum cleaner demonstrate automation, as these systems perform tasks independently, that is, without human intervention. In contrast, AI-based exoskeletons assist construction workers in lifting heavy objects, and intelligent FAQ chatbots support customers in resolving technical product issues.

10 Refer to Best, E., "Wells Fargo, Artificial Intelligence, and You", *Wells Fargo*, May 21, 2024, available at https://stories.wf.com/wells-fargo-artificial-intelligence-and-you/https://stories.wf.com/wells-fargo-artificial-intelligence-and-you/.

11 Further details are given in Peters, J., "Oral-B's New $220 Toothbrush Has AI to Tell You When You're Brushing Poorly", *The Verge*, October 25, 2019, available at https://www.theverge.com/circuitbreaker/2019/10/25/20932250/oral-b-genius-x-connected-toothbrush-ai-artificial-intelligence.

12 Robo-advisors are AI agents that automate or augment investment management tasks by analyzing financial data, assessing risk profiles, executing orders, etc. For more information, we recommend Scholz, P., *Robo-Advisory: Investing in the Digital Age* (London: Palgrave Macmillan, 2020).

13 See also Randieri, C., "The Metaverse: Shaping the Future of the Internet and Business Through AI Integration", *Forbes*, September 18, 2023, available at https://www.forbes.com/councils/forbestechcouncil/2023/09/18/the-metaverse-shaping-the-future-of-the-internet-and-business-through-ai-integration/.

14 Tekic, Z. and Koroteev, D., "From Disruptively Digital to Proudly Analog: A Holistic Typology of Digital Transformation Strategies", *Business Horizons*, 62/6 (2019): pp. 683–693.

15 Prahalad, C. K. and Hamel, G., "The Core Competence of the Corporation", *Harvard Business Review*, 68/3 (1990).

16 "Artificial Intelligence: On a Mission to Make Clinical Drug Development Faster and Smarter", *Pfizer*, no date, available at https://www.pfizer.com/news/articles/artificial_intelligence_on_a_mission_to_make_clinical_drug_development_faster_and_smarter.

17 "Infineon & You – Driving the AI Revolution", *Infineon*, no date, available at https://www.infineon.com/cms/en/product/promopages/artificial-intelligence/.

18 Marr, B., "The Amazing Ways Coca-Cola Uses Generative AI in Art and Advertising", *Forbes*, September 8, 2023, available at https://www.forbes.com/sites/bernardmarr/2023/09/08/the-amazing-ways-coca-cola-uses-generative-ai-in-art-and-advertising/?sh=28a7877b287-

19 Chevalier, F., "AI in HR: How Is It Really Used and What Are the Risks?", *HEC Paris*, February 10, 2022, available at https://www.hec.edu/en/ai-hr-how-it-really-used-and-what-are-risks.

20 Software-defined vehicles are next-generation automobiles in which critical functions, from driving performance optimization to user experience, are primarily shaped by software features, with AI playing an increasing key role.

21 See, for instance, Kemp, A., "Competitive Advantage through Artificial Intelligence: Toward a Theory of Situated AI", *Academy of Management Review*, 49/4 (2023): pp. 618–635; as well as Krakowski, S., Luger, J., and Raisch, S., "Artificial Intelligence and the Changing Sources of Competitive Advantage", *Strategic Management Journal*, 44/6 (2022): pp. 1425–1452.

22 Schroeder, R., "Can a Fitness Mirror Change One Gym-Phobic Bazaar Editor's Outlook?", *Bazaar*, November 22, 2024, available at https://www.harpersbazaar.com/uk/beauty/mind-body/a61576881/magic-mirror-review/.

23 Bertelsen, V., "Now the AI Creates IKEA Construction Manuals", *Medium*, October 19, 2023, available at https://medium.com/@udart/now-the-ai-creates-ikea-instruction-manuals-117d9da5654e.

24 "IKEA Launches New AI-powered, Digital Experience Empowering Customers to Create Lifelike Room Designs", *IKEA*, July 5, 2022, available at https://www.ikea.com/us/en/newsroom/corporate-news/ikea-launches-new-ai-powered-digital-experience-empowering-customers-to-create-lifelike-room-designs-pub58c94890/.

25 Chmielewski, D. and Hu, K., "Disney Creates Task Force to Explore AI and Cut Costs", *Reuters*, August 10, 2023, available at https://www.reuters.com/technology/disney-creates-task-force-explore-ai-cut-costs-sources-2023-08-08/.

26 Further insights about the strategic relevance of data are given by Hartmann, P. and Henkel, J., "The Rise of Corporate Science in AI: Data as a Strategic Resource", *Academy of Management Discoveries*, 6/3 (2020): pp. 359–381.

27 Blackmailing, in that sense, means the criminal action of demanding a payment or another benefit from someone in return for not revealing sensitive or comprising information (that were often stolen).

28 For more information about the Arup case, please see Ellio, D., "'This Happens More Frequently than People Realize': Arup Chief on the Lessons Learned from a $25m Deepfake Crime", *World Economic Forum*, February 4, 2025, available at https://www.weforum.org/stories/2025/02/deepfake-ai-cybercrime-arup/.

29 "BT Launches Transformational New Security Platform, Eagle-I, to Predict and Prevent Cyber Attacks", *BT Group*, October 14, 2021, available at https://newsroom.bt.com/bt-launches-transformational-new-security-platform/.

30 See "AI Chatbots Spill the Beans on Company Trade Secrets", *PYMNTS*, October 7, 2024, available at https://www.pymnts.com/artificial-intelligence-2/2024/ai-chatbots-could-be-a-trojan-horse-in-the-office.

31 Have a look at Haefner, N., Parida, V., Gassmann, O., and Wincent, J., "Implementing and Scaling Artificial Intelligence: A Review, Framework, and Research Agenda", *Technical Forecasting and Social Change*, 192 (2023): Article No. 122878; and Lee, Y. S., Kim, T., Choi, S., and Kim, W., "When Does AI Pay Off? AI-Adoption Intensity, Complementary Investments, and R&D Strategy", *Technovation*, 118 (2022): Article No. 102590.

32 "Artificial Intelligence in Industry Must Meet Stringent Requirements", *Siemens*, no date, available at https://www.siemens.com/global/en/products/automation/topic-areas/artificial-intelligence-in-industry.html.

33 "Airbus to Acquire INFODAS and Strengthen Its Cybersecurity Portfolio", *Airbus*, March 25, 2024, available at https://www.airbus.com/en/newsroom/press-releases/2024-03-airbus-to-acquire-infodas-and-strengthen-its-cybersecurity.

34 At that time, this was the biggest M&A investment Amazon had ever made.

35 Another type of service that becomes increasingly prominent is cybersecurity as a service.

36 "Baker Hughes, a GE company, and c3.ai Announce Joint Venture to Deliver AI Solutions Across the Oil and Gas Industry", *Baker Hughes*, June 24, 2019, available at https://investors.bakerhughes.com/news-releases/news-release-details/baker-hughes-ge-company-and-c3ai-announce-joint-venture-deliver.

37 More details are given in Naidu, R. and DiNapoli, J., "PepsiCo, Retailers Share Purchase Data to Improve Sales Forecasting, Exec Says", *Reuters*, October 31, 2024, available at https://www.reuters.com/business/retail-consumer/pepsico-retailers-share-purchase-data-improve-sales-forecasting-exec-says-2024-10-30/.

38 The precise case is illustrated by Duffy, C., "IBM Is Selling Off Its Watson Health Assets", *CNN*, January 21, 2022, available at https://edition.cnn.com/2022/01/21/tech/ibm-selling-watson-health/index.html.

39 We see that personalization is a very powerful tool as it can do both improve a competitive positioning and increase revenue streams in parallel.

40 Sahota, N., "Harnessing AI for Dynamic Pricing for Your Business", *Forbes*, June 24, 2024, available at https://www.forbes.com/sites/neilsahota/2024/06/24/harnessing-ai-for-dynamic-pricing-for-your-business/.

41 Shastri, A., "Generative AI by iStock", *Forbes*, April 11, 2024, available at https://www.forbes.com/sites/arunshastri/2024/04/11/generative-ai-by-istock/.

42 "Full Self-Driving (Supervised) Subscriptions", *Tesla*, no date, available at https://www.tesla.com/support/full-self-driving-subscriptions.

43 See McCurry, J., "Japanese Company Replaces Office Workers with Artificial Intelligence", *The Guardian*, January 5, 2017, available at https://www.theguardian.com/technology/2017/jan/05/japanese-company-replaces-office-workers-artificial-intelligence-ai-fukoku-mutual-life-insurance.

44 When a machine is used to automate relatively simple routine tasks, we are in the realm of robotic process automation (AI agents, in comparison, are more adaptive and can execute different more cognitively complex tasks). For an interesting robotic process automation case, please refer to Lacity, M. and Willcoks, L., "Robotic Process Automation at Telefonica O2", *MIS Quarterly Executive*, 15/1 (2016): pp. 21–35.

45 Booth, R., "Unilever Saves on Recruiters by Using AI to Assess Job Interviews", *The Guardian*, October 25, 2019, available at https://www.theguardian.com/technology/2019/oct/25/unilever-saves-on-recruiters-by-using-ai-to-assess-job-interviews.

46 An excellent article about this type of AI use case is written by Jia, N., Luo, X., Fang, Z., and Liao, C., "When and How Artificial Intelligence Augments Employee Creativity", *Academy of Management Journal*, 67/1 (2023): pp. 5–32.

47 Mahidhar, V. and Davenport, T. H., "Why Companies That Wait to Adopt AI May Never Catch Up", *Harvard Business Review*, December 6, 2018, available at https://hbr.org/2018/12/why-companies-that-wait-to-adopt-ai-may-never-catch-up.

48 Bravo, C., "OpenAI's First-Mover Advantage", *Medium*, April 24, 2023, available at https://medium.com/byte-sized-insights/the-bcenefits-of-being-first-85656ea19dee.

49 With every car generation, BMW and other car manufacturers strive for getting closer to fully autonomous vehicles. For more information about BMW's current AI journey, refer to Nolan, S., "BMW Combines Level 2 & 3 Autonomous Driving", *EV Magazine*, August 11, 2024, available at https://evmagazine.com/articles/bmw-combines-level-2–3-autonomous-driving.

50 See Ricker, T., "Not First, But Best", *The Verge*, October 21, 2024, available at https://www.theverge.com/2024/10/21/24275578/not-first-but-best.

51 See again Hambrick, D. C. and Fredrickson, J. W., "Are You Sure You Have a Strategy?", *Academy of Management Perspectives*, 19/4 (2005): pp. 51–62.

52 As stated before, non-AI related signals stay important for an AI business strategy. Not every strategic signal is about AI and it depends on you how deep you will integrate AI into your strategy.

6

HOW TO IMPLEMENT YOUR AI BUSINESS STRATEGY

"There's going to be two types of companies in this world: Those who are great at AI, and everybody else that they put out of business."[1]

—Mark Cuban, American Self-Made Billionaire and AI Investor

The mere formulation of an AI business strategy is insufficient for being successful and achieving pre-defined firm goals. Instead, formulated strategies require efficient implementation mechanisms for all planned actions to progress with the actual organizational transformation. In this regard, smooth implementation mechanisms allow a firm to purposefully adopt and leverage machine learning-based AI systems in line with the five determined AI business strategy components. That being the case, in this chapter, we provide several best practices for effectively preparing and managing a firm's strategic AI adoption endeavors over time. We will discuss allocating important implementation roles, creating an AI governance framework, and fostering an internal culture of innovation (Section 6.1). Afterward, we provide several recommendations to effectively find and evaluate potential AI use cases, develop machine learning algorithms, and scale adopted AI systems company-wide (Section 6.2).

6.1 PREPARING YOUR STRATEGIC AI ADOPTION

Before starting the actual adoption of physical or virtual AI systems in line with your new business strategy, you must thoroughly prepare yourself for the upcoming transformational challenges. An AI transformation means a lot of

DOI: 10.4324/9781003673170-9

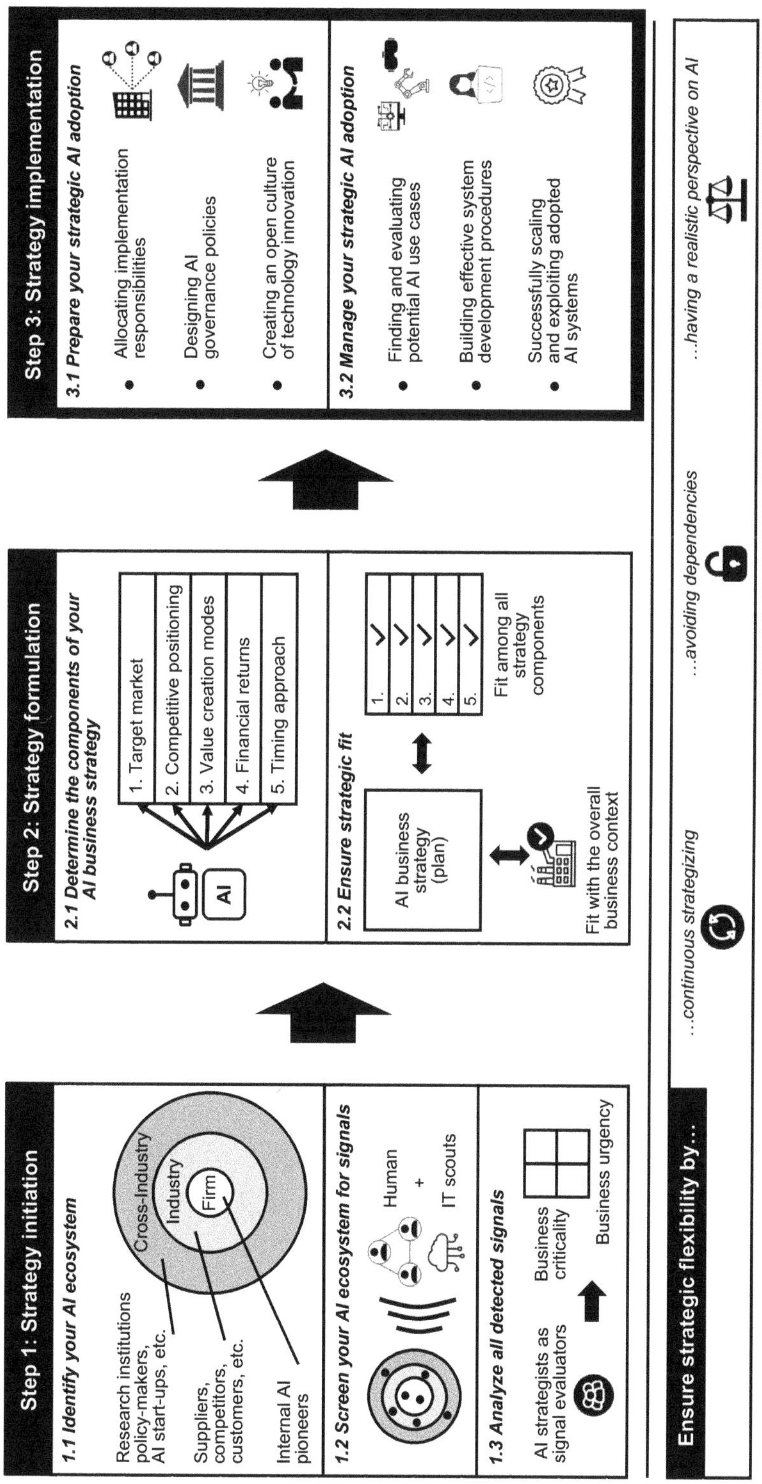

Figure 6.1 The AI Business Strategy Frame© – Step 3

change. Hence, strategy implementation requires various technology management competencies, knowledge, and best practices. Scholars often call companies that have sufficiently prepared themselves "AI-ready."[2] In the following sections, we discuss important aspects of preparing your firm for its strategic AI transformation. Specifically, we will show how to allocate clear responsibilities, design governance policies, and create an innovative work culture.

6.1.1 *Allocating implementation responsibilities*

The first topic for AI readiness lies in properly allocating different strategy implementation responsibilities to competent individuals within a firm. Since the decisions for each strategy component must be adequately implemented, an AI business strategy must be translated into direct operational plans for all value chain functions. An IT department may need to acquire cloud computing resources and install physical technology infrastructure. Recruiting teams could be asked to hire additional AI experts and retrain employees. The R&D department's task may be to design new AI-based product prototypes, for which the legal department would register patents. The marketing department, in turn, could monitor customer reactions to the latest products to better understand which AI modules are genuinely valued and which are not.

Accordingly, since an AI business strategy requires decomposition into precise actions for each company function or subsidiary, you need to allocate five key roles among employees, including AI strategists and other competent individuals. If you do not have suitable strategy implementers, you could also use external parties and resources to some extent. It is generally relevant to mention that individuals are not necessarily limited to only one role. They can take over multiple roles simultaneously if they have the time, knowledge, and no conflicts of interest with their other roles.

Enablers

A first vital role to allocate is what we call the enabler. The primary responsibility of this role is leadership, which means motivating, empowering, and legitimizing individuals from relevant departments and subsidiaries to implement the formulated AI business strategy. This role is typically allocated to the top management. Board members such as CEOs, CIOs, or CAIOs[3] can visibly endorse the formulated strategy, show their confidence in its success, and delegate other key roles to competent business and AI experts globally across the firm.

Siemens' Chief Technology Officer, Dr. Peter Körte, internally and externally promotes the strategic vision of becoming the global leader in industrial AI. For instance, he publicly said:

> "Industrial AI is a game-changer that will create a significant positive impact in the real world across all industries."[4]

Such public statements clearly show internal and external firm stakeholders where Siemens' AI journey should lead and create a shared company vision.

Organizers

Next, so-called organizers are in charge of acquiring and orchestrating all necessary AI competencies for implementing machine learning systems within the selected strategic deployment areas. Organizers are typically AI transformation managers or the responsible project leads for impactful use case endeavors aligned with the formulated business strategy. They initiate use case identification, supervise system training progress, discuss procurement and partnership questions, accompany technical implementation or organizational change management, and so on. In other words, they fully steer strategic AI adoption projects. Due to the impact of these roles, they should be allocated to middle managers from strongly affected firm departments, including senior technology experts from the IT function.

Developers

A third role is the developer, who is mainly responsible for the actual machine learning operations. That includes collecting task data, training an algorithm, validating it, introducing the final system to users, monitoring its effectiveness, and retraining the algorithm over time. Correspondingly, all developers together should be a combination of AI experts and individual task specialists. Whereas AI experts usually represent data scientists, software developers, system administrators, IT project managers, and so on, task specialists could be process or product owners. Notably, developers are sometimes located outside a firm through outsourcing or resource sharing in the case of a technology partnership. Examples are knowledge from AI consultancies, technological infrastructure assistance from cloud providers, or data pooling within a strategic alliance. Given the extensive

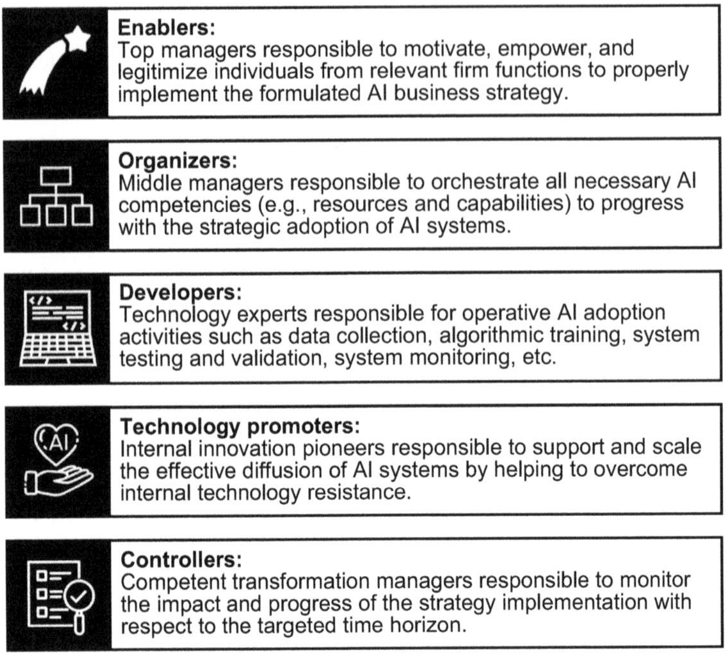

Figure 6.2 Relevant Strategy Implementation Roles to Allocate

technological competencies required for a sophisticated long-term-oriented AI transformation, developers typically represent the largest implementation group.

Technology promoters

The major role of technology promoters is to help progress internally with organizational change. Many of your employees may exhibit resistance or knowledge deficits that impede the effective exploitation of adopted AI systems, thus threatening the actual implementation of the formulated business strategy. Some employees might be more reluctant to embrace new AI technologies, while others may fear being replaced by AI systems or simply distrust their outputs. Such a phenomenon is also known as human algorithm aversion.[5] For that reason, competent technology promoters should be found and installed in all relevant firm departments. Their job will be to actively communicate the benefits of an AI business strategy and machine learning systems, address individual concerns, and support colleagues in effectively utilizing adopted technology systems for designated business tasks if necessary. To some extent, technology promoters can also support external stakeholders, for example, by helping customers understand a new digital product or by showing suppliers the benefits of a technology-driven logistics partnership (see Section 6.1.3).

Strategy controllers

Last but not least, a fifth key role is the strategy controller. In contrast to the other four roles, which actively promote, organize, or execute the strategic adoption and exploitation of AI systems, controllers passively observe the correctness and progress of the strategy implementation with respect to the selected time horizon and quantitative KPIs (such as milestone achievement, on-time delivery, or resource utilization rates). Based on their impressions, they create reports that are shared with all other implementation roles to highlight strengths and areas for improvement. Typically, controllers intervene when significant strategy implementation barriers arise over time or costs increase much more than expected. Hence, this role is in charge of measuring the impact of each strategic action quantitatively and qualitatively.

At this point, we would like to highlight the special role of users, too. While users can be internal and external stakeholders of an AI system, they play only an indirect role in strategy implementation by creating value with adopted technology systems over time. They are not directly responsible for executing an AI business strategy, but must be incentivized to use new technology tools. Nonetheless, if applicable, they can still fulfill one or more of the presented implementation roles.

6.1.2 Designing AI governance policies

Another timely topic today is AI governance. This concept describes the framework of your firm to bundle all company policies needed to ensure the responsible and purposeful development, deployment, and exploitation of machine learning-based AI systems for affected human or organizational system stakeholders.[6] While governance policies are generally rooted in societal norms, regulations, and company values, they represent binding constraints on AI adoption, designed to mitigate different types of risks when implementing an AI business strategy. As data is the driving force behind machine learning, data strategies must be well-aligned with governance topics, too.

AI experts and firm strategists should collectively create the internal AI governance framework. They must cover all types of risks a firm perceives as critical over its transformation journey and find adequate mitigation approaches. It is crucial to note that governance frameworks should be made adaptable when necessary. Responsible AI experts and strategists will have to refine and adjust company policies over an ongoing transformation to address environmental changes if required. In the following, we discuss the most relevant risk factors that an AI governance framework should purposefully address and highlight some potential mitigation approaches.

Ethical responsibility

The first aspect is a firm's ethical responsibility regarding internal and external stakeholders of AI systems. This includes all questions regarding the actual treatment of humans or organizations by self-learning algorithms. For instance, AI adoption should neither focus on morally doubtful tasks nor conflict with firm norms or moral values. IBM, for example, abandoned its facial recognition system as it violated privacy rights.[7] The reason was that modified governmental regulations considered collecting or processing individuals' data without explicit consent to be judicially critical. Besides, machine learning algorithms can acquire very different kinds of biases, leading to discrimination and unfair treatment.[8] There exist cases in which job applicants or internal employees were not only evaluated on the basis of their performance but also regarding their gender, age, race, etc.

Remember Google's image recognition system that mistakenly labeled black people as gorillas, or Apple's credit scoring system, which was found to grant some women significantly lower credit limits than their husbands, even though both had similar financial backgrounds. Since AI systems learn biases from training data, firms should try eliminating them before a machine learning algorithm is deployed for a sensitive product- or business process-related use case. The subsequent removal of biases in self-learned task knowledge is typically much more complex, as seen in Google's Gorilla problem.

Governmental regulations

A related framework aspect concerns governmental regulations. A prominent example is the previously mentioned EU AI Act, which the European Commission introduced as part of its pioneering attempt to regulate the adoption of self-learning AI systems. In the following, we present Article One of the EU AI Act as stated in Spring 2025:

> "The purpose of this regulation is to improve the functioning of the internal market and promote the uptake of human-centric and trustworthy artificial intelligence (AI), while ensuring a high level of protection of health, safety, fundamental rights enshrined in the Charter, including democracy, the rule of law and environmental protection, against the harmful effects of AI systems in the Union and supporting innovation."[9]

To some extent, governmental regulations overlap with a firm's ethical responsibility. For instance, using AI to manipulate individuals or rank them based on some personal traits is both illegal and morally inadequate. Such an overlap helps intrinsically and extrinsically incentivize firms to deal with these critical AI governance topics proactively.

Nevertheless, besides ethics, regulations address many more aspects, like copyright questions for algorithmic outputs. Clarifying whether an external system developer or the adopting firm owns the intellectual property for algorithmic outputs is essential, especially for generative AI modules. In fact, one can create all types of images or videos, including those in which protected content, such as brand products or company names, appears. Further, in some markets, firms are forced to proactively label whether content is created by humans or algorithms.

Algorithmic accountability

A third governance theme is algorithmic accountability. Technology systems like AI applications cannot be held responsible or liable for their outputs. Instead, those organizations that created or applied them for a specific business purpose are usually accountable. Human system developers, owners, or users would act as representatives of a firm entity, which still retains the overall responsibility for the AI systems it provides or exploits. However, an exception could be if humans consciously abuse an AI system.[10] Clarifying accountabilities facilitates internal and external auditing, thereby maintaining the trust and integrity of employees, suppliers, partners, customers, regulators, or the general public.

An interesting measure in the realm of algorithmic accountability is the so-called human-in-the-loop approach, ensuring that individuals remain involved in the decision-making process of an AI system, especially in critical stages where algorithms might produce high-impact or sensitive outcomes.[11]

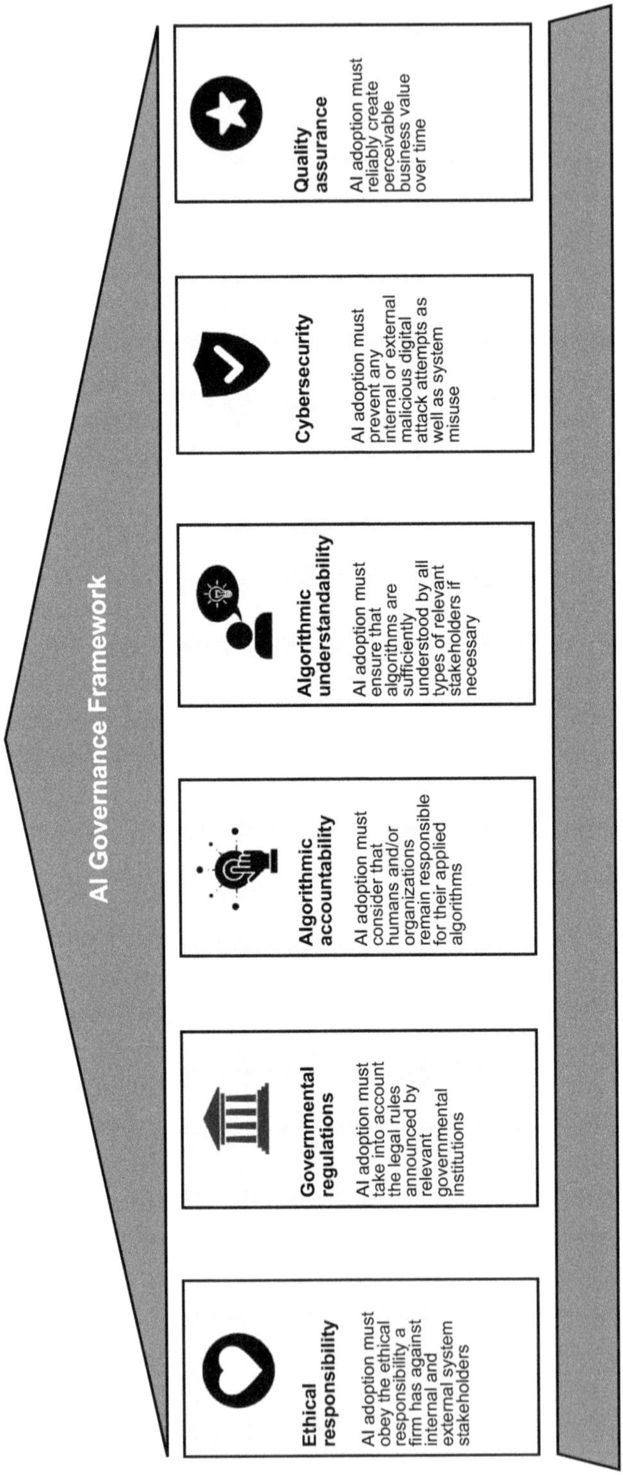

Figure 6.3 Dimensions of an AI Governance Framework

By incorporating human oversight, errors, biases, or other unintended consequences from automated decisions can be caught, analyzed, and corrected early on. System developers and owners are often in the loop.

Algorithmic understandability

Another critical governance issue directly related to potential black box perceptions is the need for algorithmic understandability, which evokes the field of explainable AI.[12] For complex algorithms, humans may struggle to determine whether an algorithm functions correctly, reliably, and robustly for a given task, thus perceiving it as a black box. However, understanding probability-based machine learning agents could be essential for both experts and laypeople.

System developers, for instance, are in charge of ensuring that the task behavior learned by an algorithm is correct and relatively unbiased. Without this cross-check, many AI systems can never be rolled out within a firm. Lay users, in turn, without much IT background, might also need to understand a system's task behavior to gain trust or appropriately use it for designated task contexts. As algorithmic understandability is a unique topic for developing machine learning algorithms, we will explicitly focus on it in Section 6.2.2.

Cybersecurity

Fifth, AI governance frameworks must identify and mitigate critical cybersecurity risks. When AI systems become a central part of a firm's business strategy, their dependency on them increases strongly. System manipulations to imitate powerful machine learning algorithms or data theft attempts can significantly threaten the success of an AI business strategy (compare Section 5.1.2). Therefore, each implemented system must be checked for potential cybersecurity weaknesses, particularly in cases where digital interfaces to external organizations and individuals exist.

To do so, some firms apply the zero-trust approach, which states that no user, device, or external software is considered inherently trustworthy or error-free. Hence, all of them have to be thoroughly evaluated from the beginning and reevaluated in case of changes. This includes, of course, internal users, too. The zero-trust approach assumes that breaches are inevitable, so the focus shifts to minimizing their negative impact through strict access controls, continuous usage monitoring, and real-time threat detection. The clue is that organizations can better safeguard their networks and data against external and internal risks by treating every interaction as a potential threat.

Quality assurance

Lastly, quality assurance matters as a governance dimension as well. Quality assurance already starts with effective data collection, indicating the requirement to establish smooth data identification, accessing, storing, aggregation, structuring, and cleaning routines to avoid unnecessary resource consumption. That implies that defining a clear data strategy that fosters the internal collection and sharing of potential algorithmic training data[13] becomes a must-have.

Moreover, AI experts need to ensure that trained algorithms constantly reach a sufficient level of task performance to reliably create business value and support the strategic AI transformation. The performance of AI systems must be continuously monitored over their lifetimes. To do so, one could frequently create performance protocols that can be analyzed in predefined time intervals. Furthermore, gathering user feedback and specifying transparent processes for when and how outdated AI systems get retrained is worthwhile.

Some exemplary AI governance policies

In Figure 6.4, we have aggregated some potential policy actions that can purposefully address each element of an AI governance framework. However, these are only ideas that should serve as an inspiration for you. Indeed, as each company is different, you should define individual policies yourself. In the best case, the formulated policies impact not only one but multiple different governance dimensions simultaneously.

6.1.3 Creating an organizational culture of innovation

Since the systematic integration of today's AI systems within a firm's business strategy comes with substantial organizational change, there are typically many cultural adoption barriers that one has to proactively approach.[14] Humans often resist change because adjusting their daily work habits is generally seen as effortful. However, successful strategy implementation depends on all employees and critical external stakeholders. All of them must work together toward a common goal.

Consequently, preparing your strategic AI adoption should also focus on creating an organizational culture of innovation in which everybody,

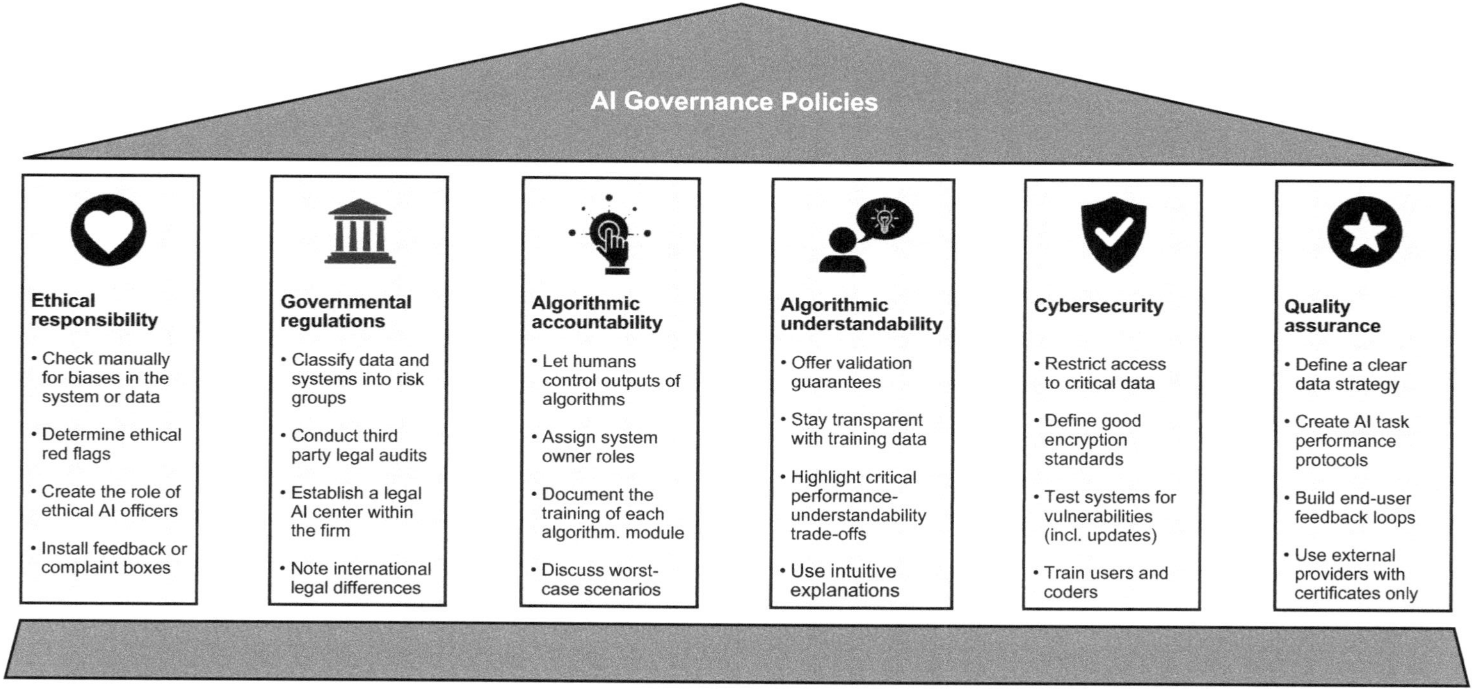

Figure 6.4 Exemplary AI Governance Policies

internally and externally, is convinced of the positive impact of technologies, wants to learn new things, and actively contributes to the progress of the AI transformation. This is underlined by Google CEO Sundar Pichai, who stated:

> "You have to have an optimistic culture, a culture of curiosity."[15]

Different options should be applied in parallel to form a more innovative work culture. Let us describe three powerful approaches for this.

Technological stakeholder education

One crucial way to foster a culture of innovation is the education of key stakeholders, that is, growing a common AI literacy among potentially relevant internal and external stakeholders. For instance, the more knowledge employees gain about how machine learning algorithms can create value, the more they recognize the strategic and operational benefits of the technology. Additionally, they become better equipped to use implemented AI systems more correctly and effectively, thereby increasing operational productivity and reducing task failures. Customers, in turn, may require a clearer understanding of how an AI-driven product functions and what value it offers them. Similarly, suppliers might need to be convinced how a mutually operated AI-based inventory management system would work, and regulators want to see whether technology adoption sticks to all ethical and legal compliance guidelines.

To increase stakeholder education, firms have started to organize internal or external AI workshops in which participants learn the basics of AI technologies and have the chance to train to effectively utilize a firm's available AI systems in a playful environment. Pharmaceutical conglomerate Johnson & Johnson has invited more than 56,000 employees to AI training courses.[16] At the end of each course, participants who pass can get a certificate of expertise to underline their newly gained skills. However, while such educational workshops primarily address technology laypeople, IT experts can also benefit from tailored coursework. Fashion retailer Levi Strauss organizes AI boot camps for IT employees to strengthen their AI knowledge in data collection and algorithmic training.[17] In addition to workshops, internal experimentation in interdisciplinary groups, as seen in hackathons and AI labs, or tolerance for human mistakes at the beginning of system rollouts, can foster long-term AI literacy, too.

User explanations

Another measure is the generation of direct, user-friendly explanations by an AI system, helping laypeople to better understand how the algorithm works and how it directly came up with specific outputs. Explanations can powerfully elevate the trust levels of users, thereby increasing their willingness to apply AI systems on a regular basis.[18] User explanations are usually created by additional generative AI modules in the underlying AI system, such as chatbot interfaces. These, in turn, can provide written or verbal information about the system's purpose and decision-making behavior. Besides text, good explanations can be visualizations, such as graphs and diagrams to show causality, or verbal instructions. In the end, user explanations must always address the individual understandability needs of the target group. For example, a user from the knowledge management department might want to cross-check whether a chatbot has collected correct sources or whether it hallucinated. That being the case, the chatbot can directly insert the links to all crucial sources and explain their selection.

Since most users are usually technology laypeople, explanations must be expressed in an intuitively understandable language, thus avoiding very technical terms.[19] Again, explanations are relevant not only for employees but also for external stakeholders. For example, equipment suppliers may seek to understand why the algorithm suggested extraordinary delivery intervals, or bank customers want to retrace why they were granted only half of their requested loan. To some extent, humans can also provide explanations to other individuals in case of deep human-AI collaborations. Physicians, for instance, should describe how an AI-based surgery robot roughly works, and say that it has a higher precision than human hands in many cases.

Internal and external inspiration

Additionally, an organizational culture of innovation thrives on engaging employees through internal and external inspiration. When employees directly get in contact or even collaborate with highly motivated individuals who are convinced about AI's benefits, they are more likely to develop a positive attitude toward AI adoption. Internally, make use of the allocated implementation roles that can proactively foster a changing work culture mindset. For instance, enablers, including board members and other top managers, can explain their strategic AI vision in public or verbally encourage employees to creatively experiment with intelligent machines, perhaps in interdisciplinary teams. Enablers should also regularly visit company

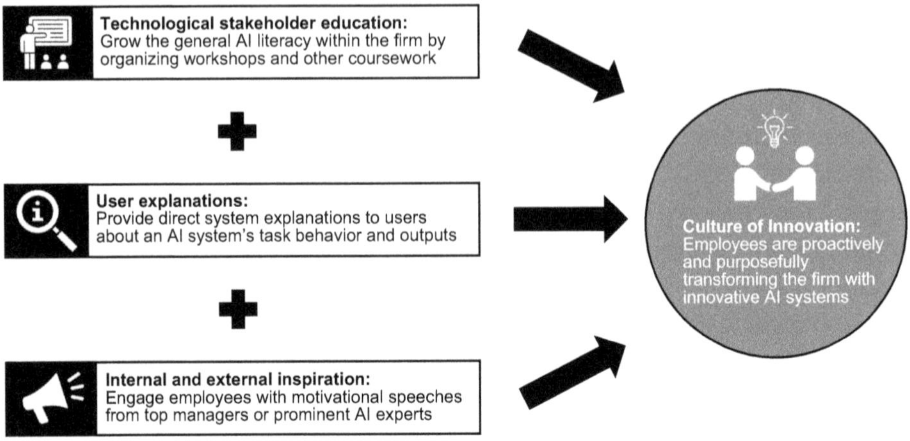

Figure 6.5 Important Drivers for a Culture of Innovation

departments personally and highlight the relevance of each employee, including both managers and frontline workers. Furthermore, technology promoters can increase motivation in each company department, especially in strategic deployment areas.

Regarding external inspiration, it can be valuable to let employees connect with AI experts from other technology-leading firms. Suitable spots can be at conferences, technology fairs, or online discussion forums. Alternatively, external experts can be invited as guest speakers or trainers at internal events. Do this as a special occasion and invite as many employees as possible, so that everybody talks about the event.

6.2. MANAGING YOUR STRATEGIC AI ADOPTION

In addition to helping you properly prepare your firm for strategy implementation, we aim to guide you in effectively managing strategic AI adoption projects over time. Whereas adopting and exploiting machine learning-based AI systems involve multiple overlapping steps, we present several recommendations and best practices for each of them in the upcoming sections. More precisely, we share tips and tricks on effectively identifying and evaluating promising AI use cases, developing machine learning algorithms, and scaling AI systems to exploit them company-wide.

6.2.1 Tips for finding and evaluating promising AI use cases

Impactful use cases are the driving force behind firms' strategic AI transformations. An AI use case is the potential application of an AI system to enhance the performance of one or multiple specific business tasks, by generating content, making predictions, or a combination thereof. While they are important signals on which an AI business strategy should be built, for example, as they help determine strategic deployment areas or create competitive advantage, it is typically not possible or advisable to identify all impactful use cases before or during strategy formulation. Over the transformation journey, new things will be learned, competencies gained, and technological possibilities improved. Hence, one should continuously search for potentially promising AI use cases within strategic deployment areas, as new ideas can pop up everywhere over time.

Unfortunately, because the field of AI is very branched and dynamic, finding and evaluating promising use cases is usually a challenging and time-consuming task. Therefore, we will provide you with three valuable recommendations that can help. The first two recommendations help you find promising use cases, and the third helps you evaluate them.

Recommendation 1: imitate and innovate with AI

First, we recommend deriving use cases from both imitation and innovation approaches. Imitation involves exploring entire AI ecosystems to identify existing use cases. Internally, this can include transferring a use case idea from one business task to a related or entirely different one. While a firm uses chatbots for knowledge management, it might discover that a chatbot is equally valuable for customer relationship management processes. Externally, companies can replicate use cases from other firms, especially competitors. However, looking beyond competitors is essential, too, because inspiration can also be drawn from suppliers, partners, or business customers. One can even transfer ideas from other industries. For example, Amazon's logistics facilities were heavily influenced by robotic use cases from the mobility and transportation industry.[20]

On the other hand, innovation, in our context, describes the identification of novel and unique adoption use cases that have not existed in a particular form before. To do this, one can reach out to internal AI pioneers and brainstorm with them. The ideas of internal employees allowed the Swiss fragrance corporation Givaudan to innovate by developing a unique AI system called Carto, which provides personalized perfume suggestions to customers on demand.[21] Existing use cases from other firms or industries can inspire innovation, too. For example, Siemens Industrial Copilot is a novel generative AI-based product that offers the ability to autonomously program industry machines with natural language processing.[22] Whereas the AI system functions as a direct verbal communication interface between human employees and shop floor machines, this product idea was strongly inspired by the IT industry using generative AI to better code software programs.

Recommendation 2: consider trend and business problem perspectives

Relatedly, firms should also unify trends and business problem perspectives to find use cases. While a trend perspective represents an outside-in approach, a business problem perspective should be seen as an inside-out approach. Since both perspectives are equally important in finding promising AI adoption use cases, we recommend combining individuals from both perspectives when brainstorming potential AI use cases.

A trend perspective analyzes how state-of-the-art machine learning technologies, such as computer vision, natural language processing, robotics, or business analytics, can generally provide value for a company and what customers, the industry, or society might expect in the future. In other words, product or process-related adoption use cases are directly derived from technological opportunities and current hypes. For example, postal service provider DHL maintains a trend radar considering all types of promising technological trends that could become valuable for the firm in the future.[23]

Conversely, a business problem perspective screens whether existing operational challenges can be, at least partially, solved with machine learning agents. Use cases are found by determining whether AI's unique self-learning

Table 6.1 Examples of How to Find Promising AI Use Cases

Imitation vs. innovation	**Imitation:** Scanning the AI ecosystem for existing use cases that can be transferred/copied	Robotic use cases from the mobility and transportation industry heavily influenced the design of Amazon's logistics facilities
	Innovation: Identifying novel use cases that have not existed before	Siemens' Industrial Copilot was inspired by the IT industry, which is using generative AI to code software programs
Trends vs. business problems	**Trend perspective:** Analyzing how available AI technologies and hype ideas can generally provide value for a company	Postal service provider DHL operates a trend radar that aggregates promising technologies and industry hypes
	Business problem perspective: Exploring whether existing business challenges can be (partially) solved with AI	GE Vernova identified that a virtual reality system could help train maintenance engineers for hazardous tasks in advance

ability can significantly impact a focal market offering or internal business tasks. GE Vernova, for instance, uses an AI-enhanced virtual reality system to train maintenance engineers for hazardous tasks, such as dealing with high-voltage equipment.[24] This immersive training approach lets participants learn dangerous and complex tasks in a controlled, virtual environment. Further, extraordinarily high resource consumption for developing a novel product can also be a critical business problem. Correspondingly, many firms have automated product prototyping using digital twins rather than relying on physical testing to save costs.

Recommendation 3: define clear use case evaluation criteria

Each use case requires a thorough evaluation by AI experts and strategists to make sure that it sufficiently aligns with the AI business strategy. For this, they should be assessed in terms of three dimensions: their cost–benefit ratio, technological feasibility, and existing adoption constraints. Some practical guiding questions for you are depicted in Table 6.2.

In general, the cost–benefit ratio of a use case can be determined by applying financial and non-financial metrics. Whereas financial metrics may be about estimated return on investments, revenue growth, or cost reductions, non-financial ones could be related to productivity gains per employee, market share increase, or system stakeholder satisfaction (e.g., employees or

Table 6.2 Important Questions for Evaluating AI Use Cases

Cost–benefit ratio	• Does an AI system provide more value than other IT systems or task restructurings? • What is the cost–benefit ratio for the realization of a use case idea? • Does the use case align with the firm's overall AI business strategy?
Technological feasibility	• Are sufficient resources accessible to implement the use case on time? • Can a certain level of output performance be ensured if necessary? • Was the best provider or AI system identified on the market in the case of outsourcing?
Other adoption constraints	• Does a use case conflict with existing AI governance policies? • Are strategically critical technology dependencies anticipated? • Are potential adoption constraints enforced by other stakeholders, such as employees, suppliers, customers, or partners?

customers). Importantly, always consider the different types of costs that come with AI adoption, such as system development or procurement costs, technological implementation costs (incl. fine-tuning), operating and utilization costs, and organizational change costs. While it is often challenging to estimate cost–benefit ratios, we recommend calculating more conservatively as costs and project times are, at the beginning, frequently underestimated. Never see machine learning-based AI as a plug-and-play technology.

In addition, metrics about technological feasibility evaluate time restrictions, data collection needs, and targeted performance levels for the trained machine learning algorithm. For example, valuable use case ideas for which a firm cannot access sufficient data cannot be realized, even though it has a large budget. Another problem arises when technology experts express their serious doubts about reaching a certain algorithmic performance level. In the case of external value creation modes, like outsourcing, it is worthwhile to compare different providers or partners regarding the technological competencies they offer for their price.

Existing or potential adoption constraints matter, too. For instance, one should avoid use cases with serious ethical concerns or cybersecurity risks as proclaimed in the AI governance framework. Furthermore, in the case of make-or-buy decisions, one should anticipate potentially critical dependencies toward other firms, especially concerning strategic AI competencies needed to run one's own business. Also, some external stakeholders, like customers or suppliers, may have serious objections to AI adoption that must be resolved.

We also want to emphasize that not every potential use case ultimately requires an AI solution. Indeed, other technologies might be cheaper or better for particular business problems, including existing IT systems. In reality, simple task restructurings could often make processes more efficient than costly and complex technology systems.

6.2.2 *Tips for building effective system development procedures*

Once strategically relevant use cases are identified, the next step involves the actual development of machine learning systems, which includes data collection, algorithmic training, and system validation. The exact development steps required depend on make-or-buy decisions. In the case of full outsourcing, the firm would simply purchase ready-to-use AI systems or additional modules for an existing IT application. On the other hand, full in-house development would involve going through the three training steps independently without external help.

In the following paragraphs, we would like to give three further recommendations on how to create effective system development procedures. For this, we highlight the importance of data-sharing principles and algorithmic modularity, stakeholder co-development, and appropriate black box mitigation approaches as suggested by the field of explainable AI.

Recommendation 4: foster internal data sharing and algorithmic modularity

Data is seen as the new oil since it is the driving force for every powerful AI system. It has become a highly strategic resource, and its importance is growing further. For that reason, firms should try to access and aggregate as many available data sources internally as possible. One way to do so, which is a vital part of many firms' data strategies, is the establishment of internal data-sharing principles.[25] This means that data scientists across different firm departments are mutually incentivized to share current process-, structure-, or product-related data. Share everything you have. The more data is shared, the more data becomes available across the organization. This, in turn, can enhance the performance of AI models through better training and facilitate cross-functional collaboration, reducing IT costs through synergy effects.

Ideally, all shared data is consolidated and continuously updated in a centralized data warehouse, enabling system developers to efficiently access and select the specific datasets required for a given use case. While such centralized data storage is often based on cloud services, chatbot interfaces can be integrated to search for particular datasets or variables within the warehouse. However, data sharing must strictly adhere to internal compliance guidelines to align with cybersecurity, privacy, and other regulatory requirements.

Next, we encourage companies to think about strict algorithmic modularity for machine learning algorithms. When an AI system comprises multiple clearly differentiable algorithmic building blocks representing predictive, generative, or combined AI modules, individual components can be more easily replaced or retrained without overhauling the entire system. This procedure can be repeated over a system's lifetime. Strict modularity also enables system developers to efficiently reconfigure existing applications or build new ones using available modules. For this, some companies utilize company-wide model zoos, which are virtual algorithm repositories in which experts can share pre-trained AI model components along with their respective training datasets within the data warehouse.

Algorithmic modularity can also benefit firms looking to differentiate themselves from competitors with AI-based market offerings. Specifically, customers could build their own personalized AI products or services by simply selecting and integrating the predictive and generative AI modules they desire. Individuals or businesses can add or remove system components that are in line with their current needs. Furthermore, modularity allows firms to introduce new technology features incrementally, which is very helpful for adapting to dynamic market demands. As mentioned, car manufacturers developing autonomous vehicles can add new assistance functionalities to each car generation.

Recommendation 5: integrate all relevant system stakeholders in the training process

Another crucial topic we want to discuss is stakeholder co-development, which means ensuring that all critical internal and external system stakeholders are integrated into the development process at appropriate stages when necessary.[26] This procedure allows developers to refine the system based on real-world needs. Overall, we recommend a stepwise, pre-defined co-development process to foster exchange and interdisciplinary AI competencies across the organization.

For instance, when an AI system should be connected to the IT landscape of suppliers, cybersecurity specialists may be involved early on to address potential risks. As the project progresses, legal experts may step in to check legal compliance. Customers can also be integrated into the system

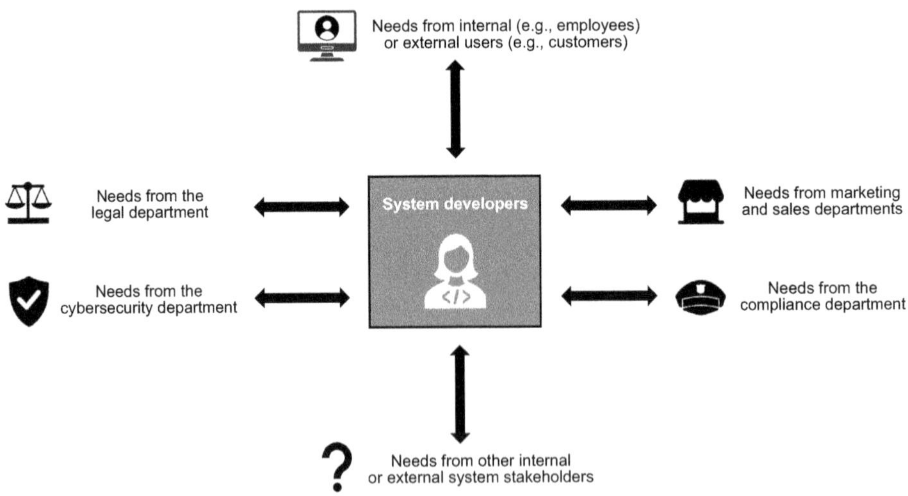

Figure 6.6 Potentially Important System Co-developers

co-development process by providing feedback on usability, functionality, and specific industry requirements, or test an AI system before its official launch. This may be achieved through pilot programs, early-access bug search, or temporary customer advisory boards that help refine AI applications before full deployment.

Recommendation 6: mitigating problematic black box perceptions

This recommendation concerns validating complex machine learning systems, which is necessary if human black box perceptions become critical. Now, we are in the realm of explainable AI. In the following few paragraphs, we will briefly introduce three general approaches that can help mitigate black box perceptions: a performance check, explainability, and interpretability. We strongly recommend using these three handling approaches in line with the criticality of potential system failures in the designated adoption task contexts.[27] Furthermore, we encourage you to combine these handling approaches if applicable.

First, use technical performance metrics to check whether a machine learning algorithm works correctly or not.[28] To do so, a developed algorithm is applied to real-world test cases that were not processed during training. For example, accuracy metrics show how often a machine learning model provides an output that is objectively seen as correct. Reliability metrics, in contrast, indicate how well an AI system produces suitable outputs even though test case conditions change.[29] While performance metrics can help determine if an AI system is ready for deployment, it is essential to remember that AI systems are inherently probabilistic, implying that achieving 100% accuracy or reliability is rarely possible. As a result, relying solely on technical performance indicators does not solve black box perception issues, making this method less recommendable for highly critical business tasks. Use it for task contexts where only the overall task output performance counts, but not for tasks for which single failures can be very consequential.

Another approach is system explainability, which aims to provide post-hoc insights into an AI system's decision-making behavior.[30] In contrast to system explanations for technology laypeople that only summarize key aspects intuitively (e.g., as a measure for stakeholder education), expert explanations go much more into technical details. With the help of an additional generative AI system, the goal is for experts to better understand how a focal algorithm probabilistically derives its outputs. However, explainability only approximates algorithmic behavior with another AI system, so it does not fully solve the black box issue. Therefore, we recommend using explainability for less- or medium-critical business tasks or together with other black box handling approaches.

System interpretability is a third method and refers to achieving inherent transparency for an algorithm. In other words, it enables technology experts to directly trace and understand an algorithm's decision-making processes and how these lead to specific task outputs. A sufficient level of interpretability is particularly crucial for high-stakes task contexts where single-task failures can lead to severe negative consequences for your firm. Examples are big investment decisions, such as those in the Zillow real-estate case, medical cancer diagnoses, or procuring critical production material. To create interpretability, developers often enhance the model training process by identifying and highlighting the most relevant data variables, known as (feature engineering). Other techniques may include manually analyzing datasets or using simpler statistical models. Importantly, interpretability may come at the cost of algorithmic performance. While humans are cognitively limited, strict transparency would mean that an algorithm cannot fully exploit its self-learning ability. At some point, the

Table 6.3 Comparing Black Box Mitigation Approaches

Explainable AI approach	*Description*	*Advantages*	*Disadvantages*
Technical performance metrics	A system is applied to real-world test cases and assessed with selected performance indicators	• Allows AI model benchmarking • Relatively easy to apply • Useful for uncritical tasks	• Does not tackle the black box nature • Does not provide reasons for failures • Less useful for critical tasks
System explainability	A system generates additional explanations to help AI experts understand outputs and task behavior	• Can provide a clear technical justification • Relatively easy to apply • Useful for less and medium critical tasks	• Does only partially tackle black box issues • Explanations can be wrong or inadequate • Less useful for critical tasks
System interpretability	A system is developed in a way that its behavior is inherently transparent to AI experts	• Provides real system transparency • Experts can guide algorithmic learning • Useful for more critical tasks	• Might limit a system's self-learning power • More difficult to implement • Full interpretability is not always achievable

task knowledge would go beyond human capabilities. This performance-understandability trade-off can be a critical challenge for system developers and must be purposefully balanced.

6.2.3 Tips for successfully scaling and exploiting AI systems

When AI systems are developed, validated, and implemented, they should reliably create strategic business value for their deployment tasks. The more they are scaled company-wide, the more impact can be created. In the best case, AI systems can be purposefully rolled out and exploited within every department and subsidiary that handles similar business tasks.

Unfortunately, as experienced by many companies firsthand, scaling and exploiting AI systems over time can come with many complex technology management challenges. Therefore, let us share three further best practices with you.

Recommendation 7: observe virtual and physical system interfaces

Always identify and continuously observe all virtual and physical interfaces of an AI application. Technology systems often operate within complex task environments in which many kinds of virtual and physical system interdependencies exist.[31] In fact, interconnected virtual and embodied systems can significantly influence the behavior and output of a focal AI system. Hence, one must be aware of critical interfaces and monitor whether and how they change over time.

Virtual interfaces, for instance, typically refer to other digital systems, AI-based or not, that provide input, utilize output, operate in parallel, or offer underlying infrastructure services. If an IT system malfunctions, the performance of a connected AI system may suffer, too. Conversely, a physical interface could be the interaction of robotic and natural human movements in storage or production facilities. Similarly, physical room conditions can influence algorithmic performance. An illustrative example comes from a civil engineering company. The firm applied an object detection system based on computer vision to identify erroneous product components along assembly lines. One day, production management decided to replace the existing lighting system with a novel, much brighter one. However, this simple environmental task change caused a substantial performance drop in the AI tool as the algorithm was not trained to work under these new light conditions. The result was a temporary production stop until the system was retrained under the new lighting system.

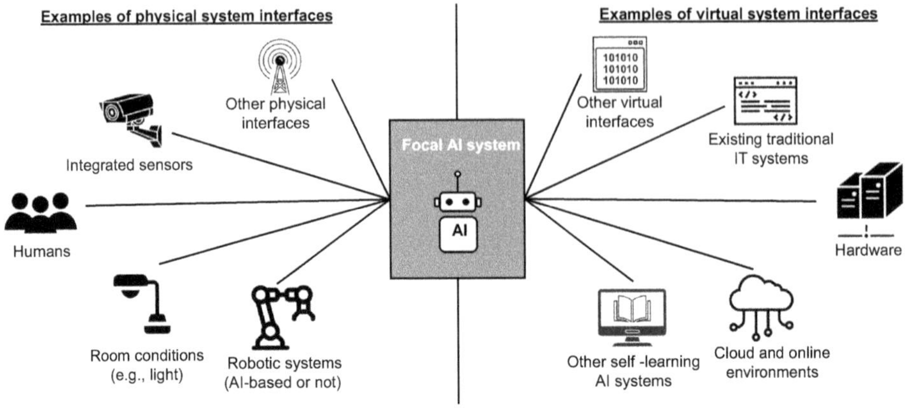

Figure 6.7 Examples of Potential System Interfaces

Given the potential impact of environmental system interfaces, it is crucial to anticipate and observe all of them in parallel. For instance, one can explicitly monitor task environments with sensors that indicate physical changes. Similarly, anomaly detection software can discover changes at virtual interfaces. Proactively observing physical and virtual task environments helps maintain a stable system landscape and ensures the smooth exploitation of AI systems over time.

Recommendation 8: install automatic retraining mechanisms

The next best practice is directly related to the retraining of machine learning models in case task environments have substantially changed. In such a scenario, the task behavior of an AI system might not be adequate anymore, as previously seen with the lighting example. Outdated and inconsistent task knowledge negatively influences algorithmic outcomes. The consequence is that one has to retrain an AI system or at least specific algorithmic modules (see Figure 6.8). This should be done with the latest training data to ensure that a self-learning algorithm can be modified to better meet the recently changed task conditions.

The optimal remedy for task changes would be installing an automatic system retraining mechanism. Practically speaking, an AI system would be capable of autonomously detecting environmental changes at its virtual and physical interfaces. If task conditions have substantially changed, the model gets instantly updated with the latest data, thus without requiring manual intervention, but only supervision. That being the case, firms should create

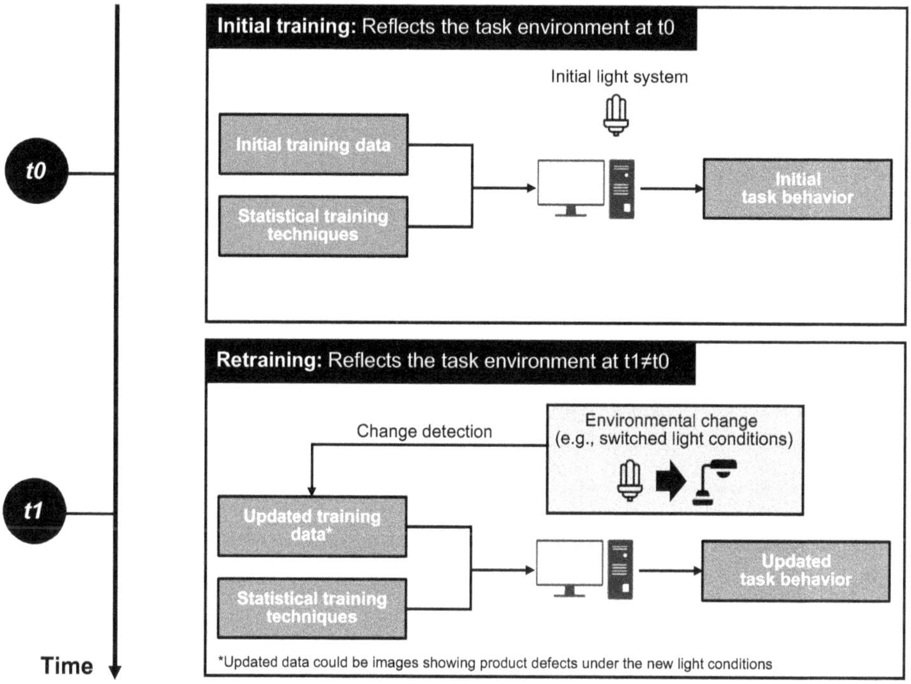

Figure 6.8 System Retraining Mechanisms

automated data pipelines to guarantee that critical AI systems are continuously fed with the most up-to-date task data. Netflix, as an illustration, continuously collects user data to offer fitting movie suggestions because customer preferences or available movie content constantly change over time. Whenever you switch your watching behavior, you will get updated movie suggestions.

Recommendation 9: always try to create data network effects

Scaling self-learning technology systems can create strong data network effects for firms.[32] The more individuals, such as employees or customers, use a system, the more data can be collected from them. This data, in turn, can be utilized to further improve the performance of underlying machine learning modules, so that even more users might be attracted. For instance, AI-enhanced platforms like Airbnb's vacation booking portal particularly benefit from data network effects. The more customers use the platform to search for destinations, book accommodations, or provide host feedback, the more Airbnb can refine and customize its offerings, leading to a better user experience. That, in turn, can attract even more users to join the platform. This virtuous cycle strengthens the platform's value and accelerates its growth.

Data network effects can also emerge when different machine learning and traditional information systems are interconnected, enabling them to exchange potential training data in an IoT or AIoT setting. This interconnectedness can enhance overall system performance as AI models refine their accuracy and adaptability through continuous data flows. Realizing technology-enabled data network effects can be a potent booster for scaling an AI system's overall task performance and deploying it company-wide.

6.3 CHAPTER SUMMARY

- Firms must sufficiently prepare themselves to effectively implement their AI business strategy over time. We have demonstrated the allocation of implementation responsibilities, created an AI governance framework, and learned how to foster a culture of innovation:
  - Five different implementation roles should be allocated, including *enablers* that motivate and empower employees, *organizers* that orchestrate AI implementation projects, *developers* focusing on machine learning operations, *technology promoters* that foster internal technology diffusion, and *strategy controllers* responsible for monitoring the progress of the AI transformation.
  - Clear AI governance policies are required to ensure responsible and purposeful AI adoption. An AI governance framework should mitigate risk factors related to *ethical responsibility, governmental regulations, algorithmic accountability, system understandability, cybersecurity,* and *quality assurance.*
  - To establish an innovative work culture, it is worthwhile investing in *stakeholder education* via workshops, *system explanations* that help laypeople understand algorithmic behavior and outputs, and *inspiration* transferred from internal or external AI strategists to all types of employees.
- For effectively progressing with strategy implementation, firms need well-elaborated processes regarding identifying and evaluating use cases, algorithmic training, and the company-wide scaling of adopted AI systems.
  - Firms should search for use cases by *imitation and innovation*. While imitation means copying use cases from other firms, innovation involves creating entirely new ones. Besides, firms should adopt *trend and problem perspectives* to combine technology-oriented outside-in and business-oriented inside-out use case search approaches. Ultimately, we recommend that experts evaluate the *cost–benefit ratio, technological feasibility,* and potential *adoption constraints* for detected use cases.

- One should install internal *data-sharing principles* and strive for *algorithmic modularity* to facilitate algorithmic training procedures. To appropriately handle potentially problematic black box perceptions, firms must balance *technical performance, explainability,* and *interpretability* methods in line with the criticality of task failures. *Stakeholder co-development* is helpful as well in proactively considering all necessary system requirements.
- Lastly, to successfully scale and exploit AI systems for their designated task contexts, one should identify and observe all *virtual and physical system interfaces*, embed *automatic system retraining* mechanisms, and try to realize *data network effects.*

6.4 HANDS-ON PRACTICE

The competent and timely implementation of your formulated AI business strategy requires allocating clear responsibilities. Therefore, please determine which individual (or team) should be an enabler, organizer, developer, technology promoter, or strategy controller (Worksheet 10). While you typically need several individuals for each role, allocating different roles to the same person is possible but not always suitable. To help you with this worksheet, we have noted some potentially fitting job positions for each role. Nevertheless, please acknowledge that each firm has different job titles.

As a next step, you get the chance to note important ideas and restrictions for your individual AI governance policies (Worksheet 11). While Figure 6.4 provides some possible policy examples, take your time to note everything you have in mind. Since machine learning-based AI systems can affect your organization and corresponding stakeholders on many different levels, especially policies that address multiple governance dimensions simultaneously are the goal.

An organization that does not appreciate innovation will have fundamental problems implementing an AI business strategy. Thus, please elaborate on how to proactively convince people to support your AI journey, thereby creating a culture of innovation (Worksheet 12). Again, we have added some examples on the worksheet to give you a first orientation for the task.

To steadily progress with your strategy implementation, you need to adequately manage AI adoption projects. For that reason, we have created a checklist that will help you to identify potential bottlenecks of your firm, that is, areas where you should put an explicit management focus on or need more resources (Worksheet 13). Since companies should, at least to some extent, internally learn how to deal with AI over time, we recommend this worksheet to firms that are (partially) outsourcing machine learning operations as well.

My enablers:	*For example: CEO, CIO, CDO, CAIO, etc.*
My organizers:	*For example: Functional directors, technology strategists, transformation managers, head of AI / technology,, etc.*
My developers:	*For example: Data scientists/engineers, software developers, IT project managers, product/process owners, etc.*
My technology promoters:	*For example: Change management agents, project management offices, innovation managers, etc..*
My controllers:	*For example: Strategy offices, internal and external consultants, financial controllers, etc.*

Worksheet 10 Who Is Responsible for Your Strategy Implementation?

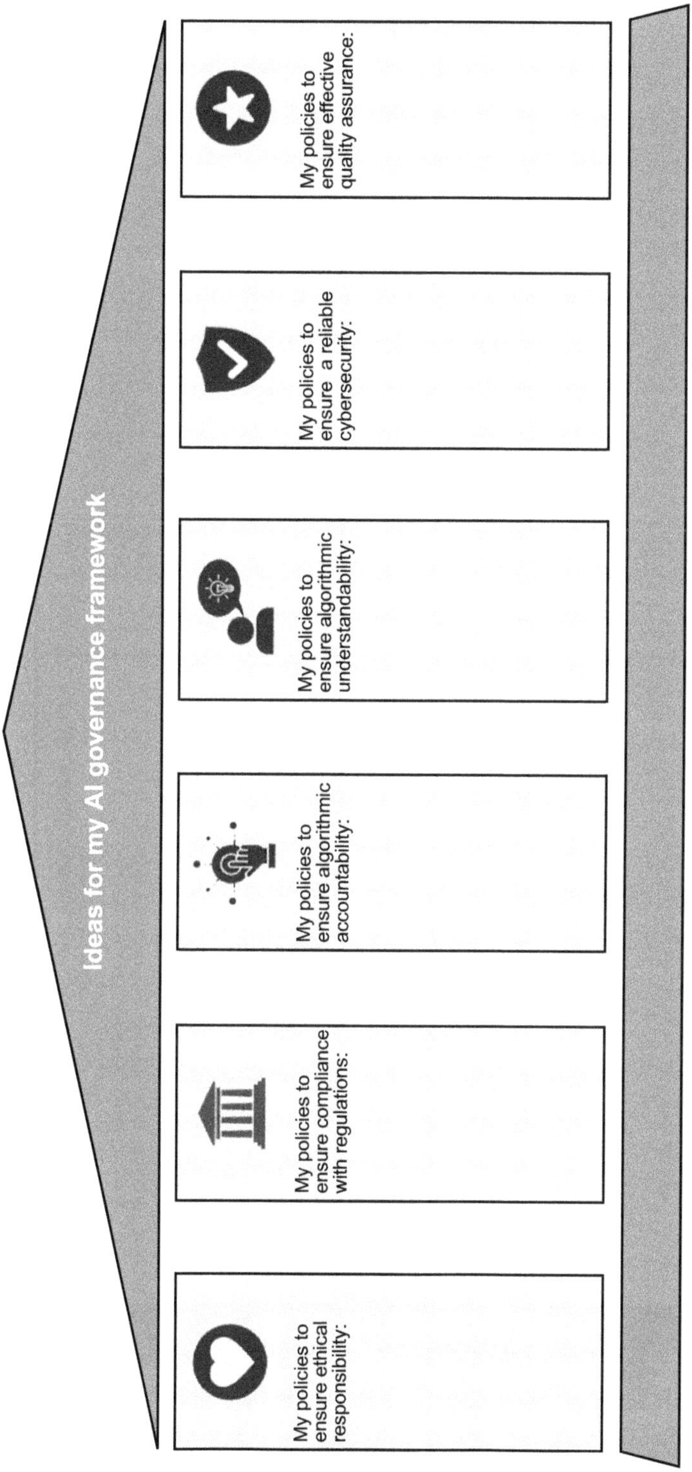

Worksheet 11 What Is Your AI Governance Framework?

	**Technological stakeholder education:** • Which type of AI course could I offer? *(e.g., AI fundamentals, user trainings, effective prompting, etc.)* • Who will be invited? *(e.g., regular staff, managers, developers, customers, partners, etc.)* • What will participants do differently after the course? *(e.g., understanding AI basics, good system handling, better compliance, etc.)*	**My answers**
	**System user explanations:** • Which human stakeholders should receive explanations? *(e.g., specific types of users only or everybody)* • How should the system technically provide explanations? *(e.g., pop-up texts, chatbots, illustrations, verbal speech, etc.)* • What should the explanations be about? *(e.g., decision-making behavior, reasons for a specific output, etc.)*	**My answers**
	**Internal and external inspiration:** • Which employees benefit the most from inspiration in my firm? *(e.g., internal entrepreneurs, AI laypeople, data scientists, etc.)* • Who could internally share the firm's strategic vision? *(e.g., CEO, CIO, head of AI, system owners, etc.)* • Which external AI experts could inspire employees? *(e.g., consultants, start-ups, tech companies, scholars, customers, etc.)*	**My answers**

Worksheet 12 How Do You Create a Culture of Innovation?

	Recommendations	Control questions	Check
Finding and evaluating use cases	Imitation vs. innovation	• Can I copy use cases internally or from external firms? • Can I transfer a use case from another industry into my own industry? • Have I brainstormed to find entirely new approaches of using AI?	
	Trends vs. business problems	• Am I familiar with current technological AI trends? • Am I familiar with my currently biggest business problems? • Have I combined both perspectives in use case discussions?	
	Evaluation criteria	• Have I sufficiently evaluated the value creation potential of a use case? • Have I sufficiently evaluated the technological feasibility of a use case? • Have I considered every potential adoption constraint?	
Developing AI systems	Data-sharing and algorithmic modularity	• Are my employees incentivized to proactively share training data? • Do I run a central data warehouse? • Are my developers incentivized to build machine learning systems in modules?	
	Black box mitigation	• Have I understood the criticality of a task for my business? • Am I using the right black box mitigation approach? • Am I not suffering under a potential understandability-performance trade-off?	
	Stakeholder co-development	• Have I identified all relevant system stakeholders? • Have I identified the individual needs of my relevant system stakeholders? • Do I integrate all relevant stakeholders as co-developers in the development process?	
Scaling and exploiting AI systems	Task interdependencies	• Have I identified all critical physical system interfaces? • Have I identified critical virtual system interfaces? • Do I continuously observe all identified interfaces for potential change?	
	Automatic retraining	• Do I reliably detect environmental task changes? • Do I steadily have the latest task data available for my AI systems? • Can I automatically retrain my AI systems if applicable?	
	Scaling and data network effects	• Do I have scaled my AI systems company-wide? • Do I mutually connect existing AI systems? • Do I mutually connect existing AI systems with other IT systems?	

Worksheet 13 Do You Effectively Manage Your AI Adoption Projects?

NOTES

1 Huddleston Jr., T. and Sauer, M., "Mark Cuban: Companies Can Either Be 'Great at AI' or Risk Being 'Put Out of Business'", *CNBC*, March 15, 2025, available at https://www.cnbc.com/2025/03/15/mark-cuban-companies-that-dont-embrace-ai-may-be-put-out-of-business.html.

2 The AI readiness concept is, for example, well discussed in the articles by Holmström, J., "From AI to Digital Transformation: The AI Readiness Framework", *Business Horizons*, 65/3 (2022): pp. 329–339; and Jöhnk, J., Weißert, M., and Wyrtki, K., "Ready or Not, AI Comes – An Interview Study of Organizational AI Readiness Factors", *Business & Information Systems Engineering*, 63/1 (2021): pp. 5–20.

3 In case of the existence of a CDO (Chief Data Officer), CDTO (Chief Digital Transformation Officer), or similar top manager positions, these can also be very fitting candidates for the role of enablers.

4 "Industry Insider Focus: Should You Believe the Hype on Industrial AI", *Siemens*, no date, available at https://www.siemens.com/uk/en/company/stories/industry-insider-focus-should-you-believe-the-hype-on-industrial-ai.html.

5 Algorithm aversion is the tendency for people to distrust or avoid using algorithms, especially after observing mistakes or when the algorithm's decision-making process remains very unclear. Further details on this concept can be found in Dietvorst, B. J., Simmons, J. P., and Massey, C., "Algorithm Aversion: People Erroneously Avoid Algorithms after Seeing Them Err", *Journal of Experimental Psychology: General*, 144/1 (2015): pp. 114–126.

6 See Attard-Frost, B., Brandusescu, A., and Lyons, K., "The Governance of Artificial Intelligence in Canada: Findings and Opportunities from a Review of 84 AI Governance Initiatives", *Government Information Quarterly*, 41/2 (2024).

7 Bajarin, T., "Why It Matters that IBM has Abandoned Its Facial Recognition Technology", *Forbes*, June 18, 2020, available at https://www.forbes.com/sites/timbajarin/2020/06/18/why-it-matters-that-ibm-has-abandoned-its-facial-recognition-technology/.

8 The following article is an excellent discussion regarding AI-related algorithmic biases: Mehrabi, N., Morstatter, F., Saxena, N., Lerman, K., and Galstyan, A., "A Survey on Bias and Fairness in Machine Learning", *ACM Computing Surveys*, 54/6 (2022): pp. 1–35.

9 This citation reflects the EU AI Act as of Spring 2025. For more details, see "Article 1: Subject Matter", *EU Artificial Intelligence Act*, February 2, 2025, available at https://artificialintelligenceact.eu/article/1/.

10 The precise liability situation depends on contract details, country-specific laws, etc.

11 For more information, see Aoki, N., "The Importance of the Assurance that 'Humans are Still in the Decision Loop' for Public Trust in Artificial Intelligence: Evidence from an Online Experiment", *Computers in Human Behavior*, 114 (2021).

12 As stated in Section 3.6, the field of explainable AI investigates how to create more understandable machine learning systems. Nonetheless, in this field, terms such as understandability, explainability, transparency, or interpretability are often mixed or used in varying contexts. Therefore, we will constantly use the term understandability in this book (see Section 6.2.2).

13 This includes both data that was collected internally but also externally.

14 More details are given in Enholm, M., "Artificial Intelligence and Business Value: A Literature Review", *Information Systems Frontiers*, 25/5 (2022): pp. 1709–1734.

15 Benito, A., "Sundar Pichai: Google's AI Vision Takes Center Stage in Dubai", *CIO Magazine*, February 16, 2025, available at https://www.cio.com/article/3825674/sundar-pichai-googles-ai-vision-takes-center-stage-in-dubai.html.

16 Kell, J., "How Pharmaceutical Companies Are Training Their Workers on AI", *Business Insider*, March 10, 2025, available at https://www.businessinsider.com/pharmaceutical-companies-embrace-ai-in-drug-discovery-efforts-2025-3.

17 More details are given in "Employee Takeaways from Our Machine Learning Bootcamp", *Levi Strauss & Co.*, May 24, 2021, available at https://www.levistrauss.com/2021/05/24/employee-takeaways-lsco-machine-learning-bootcamp/.

18 Different stakeholder roles and their needs are explained by Meske, C., Bunde, E., Schneider, J., and Gersch, M., "Explainable Artificial Intelligence: Objectives, Stakeholders, and Future Research Opportunities", *Information Systems Management*, 39/1 (2022): pp. 52–63.

19 See also Miller, T., "Explanations in Artificial Intelligence: Insights from the Social Sciences", *Artificial Intelligence*, 267 (2019): pp. 1–38.

20 Uddin, R., "Amazon Steps Up Use of Robotics in Warehouses", *Financial Times*, March 11, 2025, available at https://www.ft.com/content/31ec6a78-97cf-47a2-b229-d63c44b81073.

21 "Givaudan Fragrances Launches 'Carto', Its Artificial Intelligence Powered Tool to Reinvent the Way Perfumers Create", *Givaudan*, April 3, 2019, available at https://www.givaudan.com/media/media-releases/2019/givaudan-fragrances-launches-carto-its-artificial-intelligence-powered-tool.

22 Kramer, A., "Siemens Industrial Copilot: AI for Factory Systems", *Heisse Online*, January 7, 2025, available at https://www.heise.de/en/news/Siemens-Industrial-Copilot-AI-for-factory-systems-10229316.html.

23 "Logistics Trend Radar 7.0", *DHL*, no date, available at https://www.dhl.com/us-en/home/innovation-in-logistics/logistics-trend-radar.html.

24 "Virtual Reality Training", *General Electric*, no date, available at www.gevernova.com/grid-solutions/products/brochures/vr_training-transformers-brochure-en-2019-07-grid-ser-1676.pdf.

25 DalleMulle, L. and Davenport, T. H., "What's Your Data Strategy", *Harvard Business Review*, 97/3 (2017).

26 Weber, M., Enger, M., Schaffer, N., Weking, J., and Krcmar, H., "Organizational Capabilities for AI Implementation – Coping with Inscrutability and Data Dependency in AI", *Information Systems Frontiers*, 25 (2022): pp. 1549–1569.

27 A good summary of relevant task-related understandability measures can be found in Doshi-Velez, F. and Kim, B., "Towards a Rigorous Science of Interpretable Machine Learning", *arXiv* (2017).

28 To learn more about algorithmic performance indicators, we recommend reading the previously mentioned machine learning monography by Géron, A., *Hands-on Machine Learning with Scikit-Learn, Keras, and TensorFlow: Concepts, Tools, and Techniques to Build Intelligent Systems* (Sebastopol: O'Reilly Media, 2019).

29 This is comparable to a sensitivity analysis.

30 "Some exemplary technical methods include SHAP and LIME approaches. The SHAP approach (Shapley Additive Explanations) quantifies how much each data variable (feature) contributes to a specific model output. In contrast, the LIME approach (Local Interpretable Model-Agnostic Explanations) approximates the behavior of a complex model locally by perturbing input data and observing the resulting changes in predictions. For more interested readers, we recommend the book by Bhattacharya, A., *Applied Machine Learning Explainability Techniques: Make ML Models Explainable and Trustworthy for Practical Applications Using LIME, SHAP, and More* (Mumbai: Packt Publishing, 2022).

31 An excellent paper about the transformational complexity evoked by systematic AI adoption is Agrawal, A., Gans, J. S., and Goldfarb, A., "Artificial Intelligence Adoption and System-Wide Change", *Journal of Economics & Management Strategy*, 33/2 (2024): pp. 327–337.

32 For more details on AI-driven network effects, please have a look at Gregory, R. W., Henfridsson, O., Kaganer, E., and Kyriakou, H., "The Role of Artificial Intelligence and Data Network Effects for Creating User Value", *Academy of Management Review*, 46/3 (2021): pp. 534–551.

7

HOW TO STAY STRATEGICALLY FLEXIBLE FOR AI

"What's dangerous is not to evolve."[1]

—Jeff Bezos, Founder of Amazon

In the previous three chapters, we have shown how to initiate, formulate, and implement an AI business strategy. However, given that internal and external firm environments constantly change, there is an ongoing need to stay strategically flexible to adjust an AI business strategy if necessary. For that reason, this chapter demonstrates the idea of a continuous strategizing routine (Section 7.1). Besides, we elucidate that one can strongly increase strategic flexibility by mitigating critical provider and system dependencies to avoid high switching costs and potentially consequential lock-in effects (Section 7.2). Similarly, we show that firms have to develop a realistic view of the technological possibilities of today's machine learning systems because AI must be understood as a powerful strategic instrument but not as an ultimate business dogma (Section 7.3).

7.1 CONTINUOUS STRATEGIZING

Creating an AI business strategy is not a one-time endeavor but a continuous, often iterative strategizing approach (see Figure 7.2). The process typically gets reinitiated when new AI signals are detected, or existing signals increase or decrease their relevance.[2] For instance, competitors could devise

DOI: 10.4324/9781003673170-10

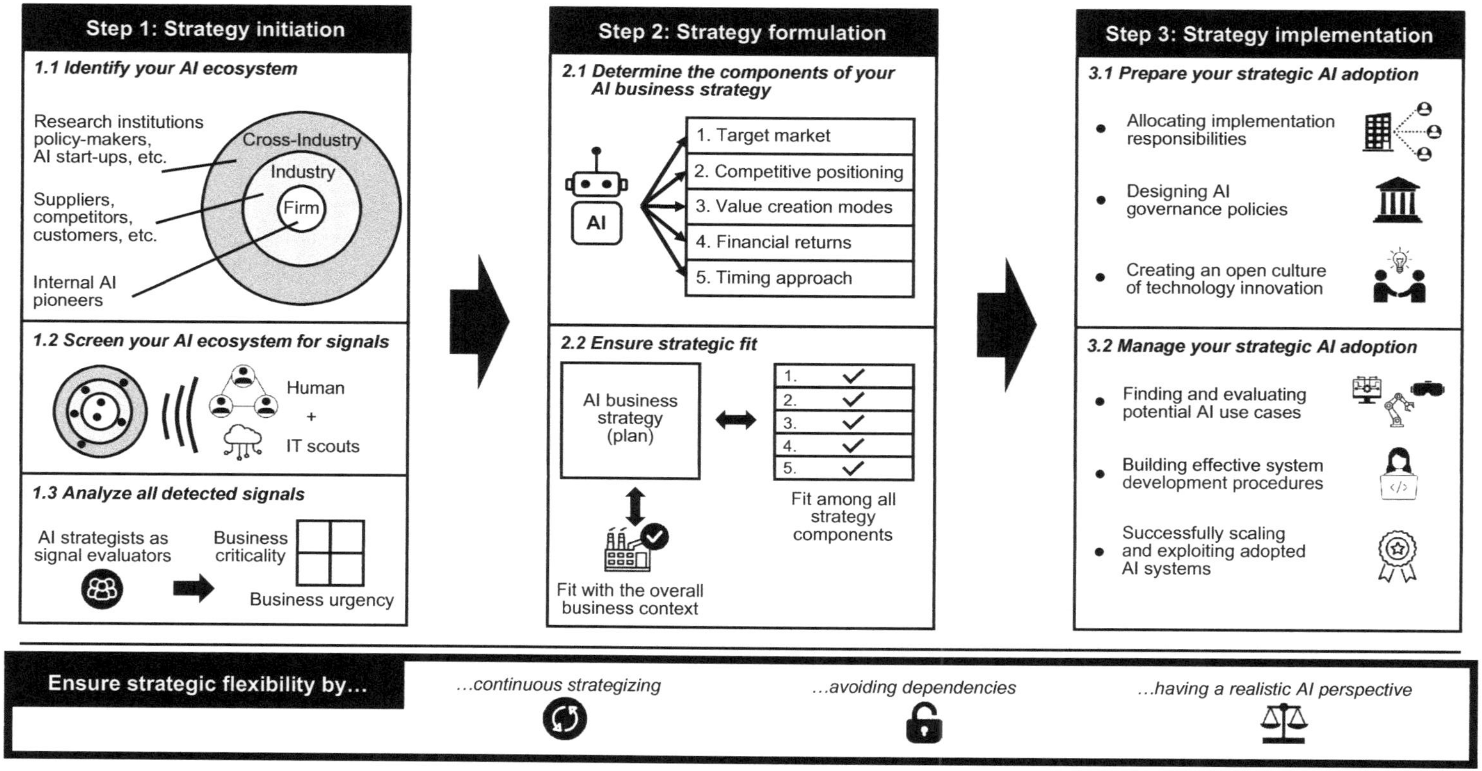

Figure 7.1 The AI Business Strategy Frame© – Ensuring Strategic Flexibility

unanticipated actions, internal AI pioneers could propose promising new use case ideas, or researchers could achieve technological breakthroughs in one of AI's subfields. However, the strategizing process should also be revisited when firms recognize that some decisions for their strategy components are ineffective and need reformulation. The same is true if a firm struggles with its actual transformative progress since implementation measures are much less fruitful than expected. Based on that, AI leaders continuously reassess an AI business strategy's initiation, formulation, and implementation phases.

7.1.1 Reassessing strategy initiation

First, continuous strategizing means updating and rescreening AI ecosystems at frequent time intervals. New players may evolve everywhere in an ecosystem, whereas others might lose their importance or entirely disappear in the future. Indeed, AI signals only represent environmental information from a certain point in time, meaning that signals' business impact and urgency can increase or decrease. Whereas a supplier might be open to cooperation opportunities today, they may plan a forward integration in the value chain in the next year, that is, entering the business of its current customer. Big tech companies, like Amazon with its tele-healthcare offerings, have particularly started to diversify their portfolio with the help of AI competencies.

As a result, it becomes crucial that human and technology-based signal scouts screen for monitor ecosystem changes at short intervals. Otherwise, essential signals might get lost or changes remain undetected. Notably, with a growing focus on strategic AI adoption, the signal screening structure requires updates, too. For example, the more a company invests in AI, the more critical the hub-and-spoke approach could become as more scouts emerge from individual subsidiaries, whose signals could, in turn, be centrally bundled by an AI hub.

Furthermore, because urgent signals require urgent evaluations, it is advisable to always have competent internal AI strategists at hand. In reality, some strategists will switch job positions or leave the company. However, technology experts from all management levels, including the lower, middle, and top management, are constantly needed.[3] Multiple strategists are also important because each of them can develop biases regarding signals or their sources. Thus, AI strategists should challenge each other to ensure

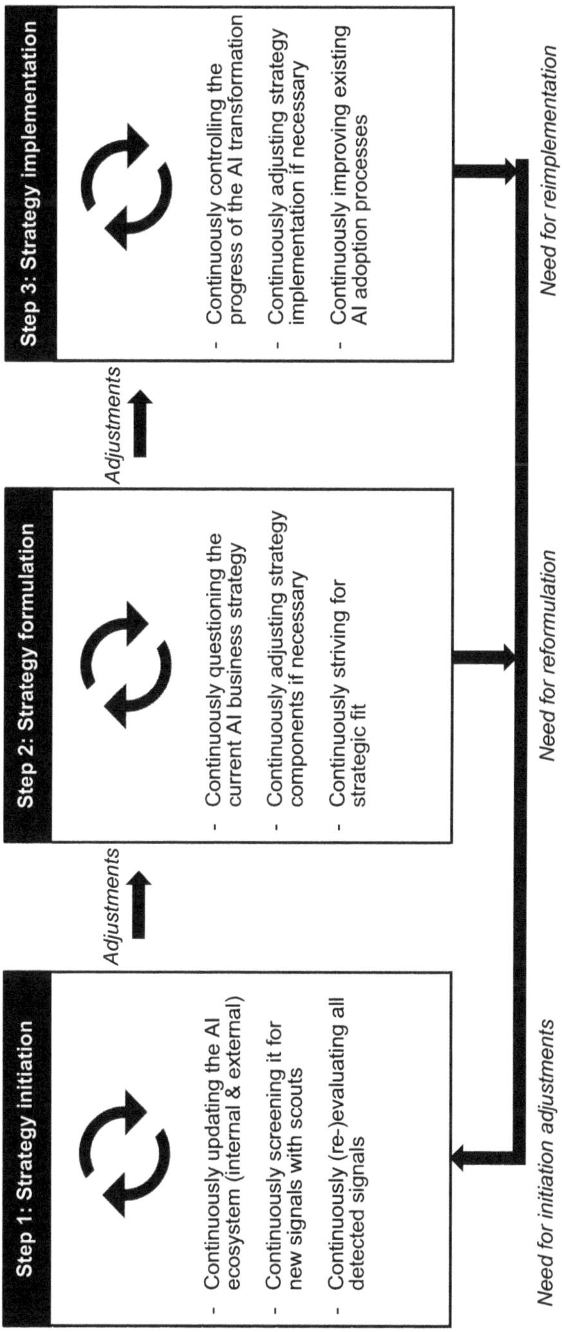

Figure 7.2 What Continuous Strategizing Is About

that different, in the best case, interdisciplinary perspectives are included in the signal evaluation process.

7.1.2 *Reassessing strategy formulation*

Regarding the formulation part, strategists should reassess the components of their AI business strategy whenever doubts arise or new information becomes available. When existing AI signals change their message or new signals emerge, each component could be addressed differently than before. That implies one might have to change the decisions for one or multiple strategy components. For example, one should check whether existing deployment areas remain attractive or whether better opportunities arise. Moreover, firms should strive to further improve and defend their competitive positioning and financial returns with strategic deployment ideas. On top of that, executives must steadily ensure that sufficient AI competencies are accessible and actions can get reprioritized in terms of timing and sequence.

Another crucial aspect is that firms could discover that formulated strategy components are actually ineffective or unaligned. Such a scenario does not necessarily indicate mistakes during the initial formulation round. Instead, environmental change can reduce strategic fit over time. Independent of the precise reasons, an AI business strategy needs reformulation whenever an AI transformation does not support achieving a firm's goals. To quickly overcome existing strategy problems, we recommend that firms have multiple fixed AI business strategy discussions each year, but can also quickly meet in case quick responses are necessary.

7.1.3 *Reassessing strategy implementation*

The reformulation of the components of an AI business strategy typically has significant implications for strategy implementation, too. Existing initiatives may become redundant or require modifications to realign efforts. Responsible implementation roles are to be informed immediately to adapt their actions to the new strategy as soon as possible.[4] Additionally, operational plans across different departments require revision to reflect the updated direction. For instance, if a company shifts from internal development to outsourcing, the procurement department must rapidly identify and evaluate potential service providers. If an incremental development approach is replaced by a more radical one, project priorities and resource allocations must be reassessed.

Nonetheless, even though strategies are well-formulated, their implementation can still be ineffective. That is often the case when existing measures do not yield the desired results, even though the formulated strategy still appears very promising. Perhaps the wrong responsibilities were allocated to the wrong people, leading to misalignments. Maybe the governance framework is incomplete, the quality of the algorithmic training data is very low, internal resistance is bigger than anticipated, or a lack of cross-functional collaboration becomes evident.

To minimize the chance of those issues, strategy implementation can learn a lot from the principles of "Kaizen," the Japanese term for continuous improvement often applied in lean management.[5] One should always strive to make AI adoption processes even more efficient. More stakeholder education or technology promotion might be necessary when employees do not utilize AI systems as planned. If use cases do not meet expectations, technology experts should learn from such events to find better ideas in the following brainstorming rounds. By consistently monitoring and refining existing implementation procedures, substantial inefficiencies are detected and eliminated early on.

7.2 MINIMIZING STRATEGICALLY CRITICAL DEPENDENCIES

The more business-central AI systems become for a firm, the more strategically consequential dependencies can arise. This includes dependencies on both external AI competency providers (from which you access pre-developed systems, knowledge, infrastructure, or workforce) as well as implemented machine learning systems. Such AI dependencies can generally reduce a firm's flexibility to react to environmental changes by evoking provider or system lock-in effects through extraordinarily high switching costs. Following a company's targeted long-term AI transformation, critical dependencies should be avoided or at least strongly mitigated. Otherwise, one could become vulnerable to opportunistic provider behavior or face difficulties to manually control and correct AI systems, as human task knowledge might get lost. Whereas we will go further into the topic below, Table 7.1 summarizes some practical dependency mitigation approaches.

Table 7.1 Examples of How to Mitigate Strategically Critical Dependencies

	Description	*Mitigation recommendations*
Dependencies on external AI competency providers	When external AI competencies become critical for implementing an AI business strategy, vendor lock-in effects can occur, potentially leading to opportunistic provider behavior	• Watch out for multiple comparable competency providers in a technology market • Try to standardize the technology infrastructure and use contracts • Learn strategic AI competencies in-house (at least over time)
Dependencies on internally applied AI systems	When an AI system is deployed within the firm, human experts might lose relevant task knowledge as they concentrate on other things. This could make manual task interventions much more difficult	• Do not stop fostering human task learning and use AI itself to extract algorithmic knowledge • Store all business information in a central (AI-based) knowledge management system • Proactively collect and store potential future training data

7.2.1 *Mitigating dependencies on external AI competency providers*

On the one hand, dependencies regarding the competencies of external AI providers require your attention over the entire transformation. The more critical external data, infrastructure, algorithmic model training, use case knowledge, or other AI competencies are, the bigger the external provider dependencies. The more a firm relies on a specific provider, the higher the risks of potential lock-in burdens, that is, extraordinarily high costs for switching providers or accessing alternative value creation modes. Lock-in effects make firms vulnerable to opportunistic provider behavior due to substantial power asymmetries between all parties involved. For example, providers could heavily raise prices, reduce the quality of services they offer, or try to gain control over their customers without fearing serious retaliation threats.

To counteract provider dependencies, the first measure is to check whether multiple comparable providers are in the market that can be simultaneously approached. When different providers offer similar competencies, a firm has more alternatives, which increases its bargaining power. That is especially true in high levels of technology or consulting standardization. For instance, many firms acquire not only one but multiple large language models from external providers. Standardized application programming interfaces (APIs) are valuable assets in such a scenario. Standardization with APIs, in this context, enables digital systems to easily connect to each other, which strongly reduces migration efforts.[6]

Additionally, it becomes crucial to acquire strategic AI competencies internally over time. The more essential AI capabilities and resources a company directly controls, the less it relies on external support. To do so, we recommend a twofold approach consisting of internal experimentation and external knowledge absorption. Whereas internal AI experimentation creates hands-on experiences, knowledge absorption is about transferring best practices from external experts into the firm. German technology manufacturer Bosch invites internal technology-interested individuals from many different firm departments as well as external AI experts to co-develop machine learning solutions for real-world business challenges.[7]

Nevertheless, please consider that AI competency dependencies are created not only by AI providers but also by partners, suppliers, or customers if they own outstanding technology skills that are important for your business.[8] Hence, contractually preventing potentially evolving opportunistic interests from all parties is always highly relevant. Strong legal expertise in this area can save you from consequential surprises.

7.2.2 Mitigating dependencies on internally applied AI systems

On the other hand, dependencies regarding adopted and exploited AI systems might also arise, independently of whether externally acquired or internally developed. When intelligent machines take over specific business tasks, humans can concentrate on very different things that fit their individual strengths more. However, to some extent, this could lead to the loss of human task knowledge, making supervision and manual intervention efforts in case of system malfunctions or extraordinary task conditions much more difficult.

Indeed, the higher the level of task automation with machine learning, the more system dependencies could be created. Consequently, a firm should not lose too much human task knowledge, especially for critical business activities. Instead, we still recommend supporting humans in learning critical task knowledge to some degree, even though automating machines are obviously superior in certain task portions. This is another reason why effective human-AI collaboration is of outstanding importance.

Whereas state-of-the-art machine learning-based AI systems might outcompete humans for some tasks, employees should learn essential task knowledge from these algorithms if possible. For example, one could use the help of AI systems themselves, like chatbots, to extract task knowledge from other AI systems. Based on that, human experts can extract valuable insights about task processes, influencing factors, and potential error sources by letting powerful generative AI-based chatbots analyze a model's algorithmic decision-making tendencies and task outputs. The gained insights, in turn, could then be discussed and shared internally among task stakeholders to enhance organizational learning and reduce system dependencies.[9] Nonetheless, intellectual property obligations regarding algorithmic knowledge must also be considered.

Ultimately, we recommend that critical task knowledge is centrally stored within the firm so that human experts can access a common information source when they want to look up something. To do so, one can also integrate AI modules into knowledge management systems.[10] Correspondingly, employees can search for relevant technical specifications via direct search interfaces or automatically create precise business reports, bills of materials, process diagrams, etc.

On top of that, we recommend proactively collecting as much potential training data as possible. This strongly facilitates things when new use cases are found that could make using a current machine learning system redundant. As mentioned, the data strategy should always incentivize employees to collect and store potentially needed task data in good shape.

7.3 DEVELOPING A REALISTIC PERSPECTIVE ON AI ADOPTION

A final but equally important aspect of staying strategically flexible is that firms must develop a realistic perspective on AI technologies. Machine learning-based AI is a powerful strategic instrument, not an ultimate business success dogma. The goal should not be to implement AI systems anywhere within an organization; they should only be implemented where a perceivable impact can be created. Hence, it is essential to clearly understand what machine learning can and cannot do to avoid falling into the trap of overhyping its potential. A realistic perspective substantially helps to progress with one's strategic transformation step by step.

Unfortunately, many firms still overestimate the extent and speed of their AI transformation or get blinded by overhyped promises.[11] In fact, many IT vendors use the term AI as a marketing buzzword to attract customers for their products and services. However, promoted applications do not necessarily involve powerful (machine learning) models. One should always be cautious and purposefully evaluate the potential competencies of providers, including the real-world technological sophistication of their promoted AI systems.

Whereas machine learning provides many technological business opportunities, it cannot be exploited for every type of process or product. Approaching unfitting use cases would lead to unnecessary investments, block alternative projects, or even impede a firm's competitiveness. Further, humans often possess more relevant task skills, and not all customers sufficiently value AI features.

The limitations of AI and the strengths of humans indicate that self-learning AI cannot replace all types of jobs.[12] AI will only eliminate jobs for which human skills are unnecessary or are much more expensive. For all other types of jobs, which are the far majority, humans will concentrate on the task portions they are better at. The focus could particularly be on creative, communication-intensive, or context-centered tasks.[13] Integrating different AI agents will also initiate the retraining of employees so that they can effectively collaborate.[14] Furthermore, AI will create new jobs that have much career potential in the future, such as the prompt engineer, AI auditor, or AI strategist.

Finally, we would like to highlight again that AI also has a dark side.[15] For example, besides technological limitations, self-learning algorithms can facilitate hacking or other fraud attempts. For instance, there is a growing wave of deepfake-based phishing attacks, where cybercriminals use AI-generated voices, manipulated images, or false email messages to extract sensitive company information from firms and their employees.[16] With these approaches, a UK-based energy company has lost several hundred thousand USD.[17] Therefore, in addition to perceiving strategic opportunities by systematically integrating AI into business strategies, it is also relevant to consider potential technological threats that could negatively shape a firm's AI journey. In the end, those firms that will appropriately balance both AI's bright and dark sides will remain strategically flexible regarding their multi-faceted AI transformation.

7.4 CHAPTER SUMMARY

- Regarding future environmental change, firms must achieve a certain level of *strategic flexibility* for their AI business strategies. For this, we have emphasized three crucial measures:
  - Companies need to establish a *continuous strategizing process* as new AI signals can suddenly pop up or existing signals alter their relevance. Further, firms might realize that strategy components or implementation procedures are less effective or mutually aligned than anticipated.
  - One must purposefully mitigate critical AI dependencies to avoid lock-in effects. There are *dependencies on external AI competency providers* and *dependencies on internally adopted AI systems.* To handle external dependencies, firms should look for multiple comparable providers, foster standardization, rely on contracts, and try to learn strategic AI competencies in-house over time. To handle system dependencies, firms should promote human task learning, extract algorithmic task knowledge with generative AI tools, and build central knowledge management systems.
  - Last but not least, firms are required to develop a *realistic perspective on strategic AI adoption*. While contemporary AI can evoke competitive and financial advantages, the technology comes with several limitations and threats. Therefore, firms must be aware of what machine learning can and cannot do to achieve their goals.

7.5 HANDS-ON PRACTICE

Since internal and external firm environments change dynamically, creating and applying an AI business strategy requires a continuous strategizing process. Consequently, we have aggregated essential control questions to help you identify whether it is time to revisit specific strategizing steps (Worksheet 14). Once you notice strategy issues, you can use the previously introduced worksheets within the corresponding framework chapter again.

A firm's strategic flexibility gets strongly decreased when it suffers from critical dependencies on AI competency providers or adopted machine learning systems. Thus, your last worksheet will help you identify existing and potentially arising dependency threats (Worksheet 15). It can also help you brainstorm about appropriate mitigation approaches. We have given you two illustrative examples as a starting point for this task.

Strategizing steps		Control questions	Check
Step 1: Strategy initiation	1.1 Identify your AI ecosystem	• Are new signal sources evolving in my AI ecosystem? • Are existing signal sources disappearing from my AI ecosystem? • Are existing signal sources dynamically changing its role?	
	1.2 Screen your AI ecosystem for signals	• Are my technology scouts frequently searching for potential AI signals? • Are my technology scouts regularly exchanging with each other? • Are my IT systems effectively supporting human scouts?	
	1.3 Analyze all detected signals	• Do I still have competent AI strategists from each management level? • Have signals changed their business criticality and urgency? • Are new signals evident that come with a high business criticality and urgency?	
Step 2: Strategy formulation	2.1 Determine the components of your AI business strategy	• Does my AI business strategy consider the latest detected internal signals? • Does my AI business strategy consider the latest detected external signals? • Are all components of my AI business strategy still appropriate?	
	2.2 Ensure strategic fit	• Have I recently checked my AI business strategy for strategic fit? • Is there still a high level of fit among strategy components? • Is there still a high level of fit with the overall business context?	
Step 3: Strategy implementation	3.1 Prepare your strategic AI adoption	• Are all allocated implementation roles doing their jobs effectively? • Is my created AI governance framework still up-to-date? • Have I already realized a strong culture of innovation in my firm?	
	3.2 Manage your strategic AI adoption	• Am I identifying and evaluating AI use cases purposefully? • Am I developing AI systems smoothly and effectively? • Am I realizing a substantial business impact with my adopted AI systems?	

Worksheet 14 When Should You Start the Strategizing Process Again?

My critical AI dependencies		Strategic relevance	Potential mitigation approaches for me	Actors
Dependencies on external AI competency providers	*Example: External technology consultancy*	***Higher:*** *We lack deep knowledge about a specific AI project internally*	*Hire AI experts; transfer knowledge and copy best practices from the consultancy*	*HR, technology scouts, project managers*
	1.			
	2.			
	3.			
	4.			
Dependencies on internally applied AI systems	*Example: Applied supplier selection system*	***Medium:*** *Buyers did not know how suppliers were selected by our AI tool in the past*	*Identify the most important self-learned task output criteria of the AI system with an additional generative AI tool (e.g., chatbot)*	*Procurement teams, system developers, technology promoters*
	1.			
	2.			
	3.			
	4.			

Worksheet 15 Have You Mitigated All Critical AI Dependencies?

NOTES

1 Shik, M., "Jeff Bezos – What's Dangerous Is Not to Evolve", *Fast Company*, March 3, 2010, available at https://www.fastcompany.com/1569357/jeff-bezos-whats-dangerous-not-evolve.
2 Often the word VUCA, which stands for volatility, uncertainty, complexity, and ambiguity, is used to describe the turbulent and dynamic business environments we live in today. sSee Bennet, N. and Lemoine, J., "What VUCA Really Means for You", *Harvard Business Review*, 92/1 (2014).
3 Perhaps, you might also need the help of external consultants, freelancers, trainers, etc.
4 It could also become necessary to reallocate strategy implementation roles from time to time.
5 The concept of Kaizen was originally introduced by Toyota to make its production processes more efficient. One goal of Kaizen is to eliminate any non-value creating or even value destroying activities. This concept is at the core of today's lean management practices. For more information, please refer to Womack, J. P., Jones, D. T., and Roos, D., *The Machine that Changed the World: The Story of Lean Production – Toyota's Secret Weapon in the Global Car Wars that Is Revolutionizing World Industry* (New York: Free Press, 2007).
6 Géron, A., *Hands-on Machine Learning with Scikit-Learn, Keras, and TensorFlow: Concepts, Tools, and Techniques to Build Intelligent Systems* (Sebastopol: O'Reilly Media, 2019).
7 "Bosch Connected Experience 2024", *Bosch*, no date, available at https://bosch-connected-world.com/hackathon/.
8 For instance, your customers and suppliers could consider backward or forward integrations. They could think about entering your precise value chain stage in your selected target market if they have control over your business.
9 An interesting article that explicitly deals with the impact of machine learning on organizational learning is Balasubramanian, N., Ye, Y., and Xu, M., "Substituting Human Decision-Making with Machine Learning: Implications for Organizational Learning", *Academy of Management Review*, 47/3 (2022): pp. 448–465.
10 Jarrahi, M. J., Aksey, D., Eshragi, A., and Smith, P., "Artificial Intelligence and Knowledge Management: A Partnership between Human and AI", *Business Horizons*, 66/1 (2023): pp. 87–99.
11 Some issues regarding unrealistic AI perspectives are given in Acar, O. A., "Is Your AI-First Strategy Causing More Problems than It's Solving?", *Harvard Business Review*, March 18, 2024, available at https://hbr.org/2024/03/is-your-ai-first-strategy-causing-more-problems-than-its-solving.
12 We recommend having a look at "Future of Jobs Report", *World Economic Forum*, May, 2023, available at https://www3.weforum.org/docs/WEF_Future_of_Jobs_2023.pdf.
13 Huang, M.-H., Rust, R., and Maksimovic, V., "The Feeling Economy: Managing in the Next Generation of Artificial Intelligence (AI)", *California Management Review*, 61/4 (2019): pp. 43–65.
14 Further insights are summarized by Brynjolfsson, E. and Mitchell, T. M., "What Can Machine Learning Do? Workforce Implications", *Science*, 358/6370 (2017): pp. 1530–1534.
15 Some more details on the dark sides of AI are given in Grewal, D., Guha, A., Satornino, C. B., and Schweiger, E. B., "Artificial Intelligence: The Light and the Darkness", *Journal of Business Research*, 136 (2021): pp. 229–236.
16 Heiding, F., Schneier, B., and Vishwanath, A., "AI Will Increase the Quantity and Quality of Phishing Scams", *Harvard Business Review*, May 30, 2024, available at https://hbr.org/2024/05/ai-will-increase-the-quantity-and-quality-of-phishing-scams.
17 Damiani, J., "A Voice Deepfake Was Used to Scam A CEO Out of $243,000", *Forbes*, September 3, 2019, available at https://www.forbes.com/sites/jessedamiani/2019/09/03/a-voice-deepfake-was-used-to-scam-a-ceo-out-of-243000/.

OUTLOOK

Dear readers,

At the very end of this book, we would like to congratulate you. By going through all the content and filling out all the provided worksheets, you have comprehensively understood how to initiate, formulate, and implement AI business strategies. You are now equipped with essential knowledge for dealing with AI ecosystems, signal screening structures, and signal evaluations. You can purposefully analyze AI signals to systematically integrate self-learning technologies into each of the five business strategy components. You are also familiar with critical implementation roles, AI governance dimensions, innovative work cultures, and several best practices regarding machine learning operations. On top of that, you are well aware that strategizing must be seen as a continuous process, that you need to mitigate strategically critical dependencies, and that one should consider the limitations of today's technological possibilities.

To make the most out of your newly acquired knowledge, let us give you some final recommendations:

- Practically apply the strategic instrument of machine learning-based AI to differentiate your firm from competitors. You might achieve first-mover advantages, be a fast-second, or reduce competitive pressure. However, remember that the longer your firm waits, the more time your competitors have.

DOI: 10.4324/9781003673170-11

- Share your knowledge within your firm. Even though you are not a strategic decision-maker (yet), you can spark conversations and propose new ideas. In doing so, you can become an internal AI pioneer yourself.
- Relatedly, consider that having strategic knowledge about today's AI systems can separate you from coworkers, fellow students, or researchers. Use your advantage and make yourself noticeable.
- Regularly exchange with other similarly-minded AI strategists, inside and outside your firm, classroom, or lab. Perhaps you can create your own personal AI network of multiple valuable exchange partners.
- Stay informed about new technological developments. AI is a fast-moving and multifaceted field. Breakthroughs and focus shifts could happen everywhere, at any time. Staying curious will be the key to future success.

Last but not least, we want to emphasize that our book is designed to be more than a one-time read. It can be used as an ongoing reference throughout your strategic AI transformation. Whether starting from scratch or refining an existing AI business strategy, let this book be your long-term companion for your AI transformation.

We wish you the best of luck with your AI business strategy!

Thomas Hutzschenreuter and Tim Lämmermann

Index

About the Authors

Dr. Thomas Hutzschenreuter is University Professor and holds the Chair of Strategic and International Management at the Technical University of Munich (TUM). His work focuses on strategizing and technology-enabled competitive and corporate strategies, governance structures, and organizational transformations. Dr. Hutzschenreuter has extensive experience designing (AI-enabled) strategies and governance structures and has worked for leading large and medium-sized enterprises. He has frequently been invited to give keynotes and guest speeches on strategy topics, including AI business strategy and AI business transformation. Dr. Hutzschenreuter has published in leading international journals, such as, the *Strategic Management Journal*, the *Journal of International Business Studies*, the *Journal of Management Studies*, the *Journal of Management, Leadership Quarterly*, and the *Academy of Management Perspectives*, among others. His research received multiple international awards. Dr. Hutzschenreuter was awarded several Best (Executive) Teaching Awards.

Tim Lämmermann is Doctoral Research Associate at the Chair of Strategic and International Management at the Technical University of Munich (TUM). His practitioner-oriented research predominantly lies at the intersection of strategic management and artificial intelligence. He has already published in international, highly reputable management journals, including the *Academy of Management Perspectives* and *MIS Quarterly Executive.* His passion is to transfer academically gained insights into practical impact. For this, he regularly collaborates with technology strategists from globally leading firms and teaches AI strategy topics in university classrooms. Besides his research, Tim Lämmermann is a senior AI strategist at a German management consultancy, where he systematically supports firms in their strategic AI transformation.